NOVELL'S

Internet Plumbing Handbook

NOVELL'S

Internet Plumbing Handbook

PETER RYBACZYK

Novell Press, San Jose

Novell's Internet Plumbing Handbook
Published by
Novell Press
2180 Fortune Drive
San Jose, CA 95131

Library of Congress Catalog Card No.: 97-077540

ISBN: 0-7645-4537-X

Printed in the United States of America

10 9 8 7 6 5 4 3 2 1

1P/RZ/QR/ZY/FC

Distributed in the United States by IDG Books Worldwide, Inc.

Distributed by Macmillan Canada for Canada; by Contemporanea de Ediciones for Venezuela; by Distribuidora Cuspide for Argentina; by CITEC for Brazil; by Ediciones ZETA S.C.R. Ltda. for Peru; by Editorial Limusa SA for Mexico; by Transworld Publishers Limited in the United Kingdom and Europe; by Academic Bookshop for Egypt; by Levant Distributors S.A.R.L. for Lebanon; by Al Jassim for Saudi Arabia; by Simron Pty. Ltd. for South Africa; by Pustak Mahal for India; by The Computer Bookshop for India; by Toppan Company Ltd. for Japan; by Addison Wesley Publishing Company for Korea; by Longman Singapore Publishers Ltd. for Singapore, Malaysia, Thailand, and Indonesia; by Unalis Corporation for Taiwan; by WS Computer Publishing Company, Inc. for the Philippines; by WoodsLane Pty. Ltd. for Australia; by WoodsLane Enterprises Ltd. for New Zealand. Authorized Sales Agent: Anthony Rudkin Associates for the Middle East and North Africa.

For general information on IDG Books Worldwide's books in the U.S., contact our Consumer Customer Service department at 800-762-2974. For reseller information, including discounts and premium sales, contact our Reseller Customer Service department at 800-434-3422.

For information on where to purchase IDG Books Worldwide's books outside the U.S., contact our International Sales department at 415-655-3078 or fax 415-655-3281.

For information on foreign language translations, contact our Foreign & Subsidiary Rights department at 415-655-3018 or fax 415-655-3281.

For sales inquiries and special prices for bulk quantities, contact our Sales department at 415-655-3200 or write to the address above.

For information on using IDG Books Worldwide's books in the classroom or for ordering examination copies, contact our Educational Sales department at 800-434-2086 or fax 817-251-8174.

For authorization to photocopy items for corporate, personal, or educational use, contact the Copyright Clearance Center, 222 Rosewood Drive, Danvers, MA 01923, or fax 508-750-4470.

For general information on Novell Press books in the U.S., including information on discounts and premiums, contact IDG Books at 800-434-3422 or 415-655-3200. For information on where to purchase Novell Press books outside the U.S., contact IDG Books International at 415-655-3021 or fax 415-655-3295.

John Kilcullen, *CEO, IDG Books Worldwide, Inc.*
Steve Berkowitz, *President, IDG Books Worldwide, Inc.*
Brenda McLaughlin, *Senior Vice President & Group Publisher, IDG Books Worldwide, Inc.*

KC Sue, *Publisher, Novell Press, Inc.*

Welcome to Novell Press

Novell Press, the world's leading provider of networking books, is the premier source for the most timely and useful information in the networking industry. Novell Press books cover fundamental networking issues as they emerge — from today's Novell and third-party products to the concepts and strategies that will guide the industry's future. The result is a broad spectrum of titles for the benefit of those involved in networking at any level: end user, department administrator, developer, systems manager, or network architect.

Novell Press books are written by experts with the full participation of Novell's technical, managerial, and marketing staff. The books are exhaustively reviewed by Novell's own technicians and are published only on the basis of final released software, never on prereleased versions.

Novell Press at IDG Books Worldwide is an exciting partnership between two companies at the forefront of the knowledge and communications revolution. The Press is implementing an ambitious publishing program to develop new networking titles centered on the current version of IntranetWare, GroupWise, BorderManager, ManageWise, and networking integration products.

Novell Press books are translated into 14 languages and are available at bookstores around the world.

KC Sue, Publisher, Novell, Inc.

Novell Press

Publisher
KC Sue

Program Manager
Lois Dudley

Projects Specialist
Robin Wheatley

Executive Acquisitions Editor
John Read

Acquisitions Editor
Jim Sumser

Development Editors
Kevin Shafer
Stefan Grunwedel

Technical Editor
Keith Brumbaugh

Copy Editors
Kevin Shafer
Anne Friedman
Nicole Fountain

Project Coordinator
Ritchie Durdin

Graphics and Production Specialists
Jude Levinson
Linda Marousek
Maureen Moore

Illustrator
David Puckett

Proofreader
Christine Sabooni

Indexer
Carol Burbo

Cover Photographer
Jake Wyman/Photonica

About the Author

Peter Rybaczyk started to work as a programmer, and later a network administrator and technical manager for a publishing house, Summit University Press. He first became involved with networks in 1986 and has designed and installed numerous local-area networks (LANs) and wide-area networks (WANs). Since 1990, he's been an internetworking consultant for his privately held firm, PME Enterprises. His clients include law firms, car dealerships, retail and wholesale distributors, health care providers, and Internet Service Providers (ISPs).

In 1992, Rybaczyk started to teach four-day intensive seminars in advanced technology for Learning Tree International. He specializes in seminars on routers, internetworking, data communications and TCP/IP. In the past five years, he's delivered more than 70 seminars to audiences at corporate sites, military bases, and Learning Tree training facilities throughout the United States and in Europe. His corporate technical audiences included those of Xerox, Lucent Technologies, Pacific Bell, IBM, and others.

Rybaczyk is a practicing CNE, holds an Internetworking Professional Certification from Learning Tree International, and is working on becoming a CCIE.

Rybaczyk can be reached by e-mail at `psrsam@ycsi.net`.

I dedicate this book to all those who've made the Internet possible and continue to embody its true spirit; to my best friend, spiritual twin, and life-long companion, my beloved wife, Maria Elizabeth; and to my ever-present guardian angel who saved my life on the Bozeman pass during a snowy winter night.

Preface

The Internet and the Web are now household words. Walk into any bookstore and you'll find its shelves laden with dozens of volumes on the Internet and the World Wide Web. So, you ask the obvious question, "Why do we need another book about the Internet?" The answer lies in the pages that follow.

About This Book

Novell's Internet Plumbing Handbook is a unique book. It's all about the Internet plumbing: a vast infrastructure that supports a myriad of events resulting from a single mouse click in a Web browser. It's about what takes place behind the scenes when you use a search engine, connect to a favorite Web site, or download a file. It's about what happens when you click on "Send" in your favorite e-mail package. It's about all the stuff we generally don't see or think about when we use the Internet.

This book is about the Internet backbones and how they interconnect. It is about the computer networks that comprise the Internet. It's about routers, switches, and the connections (or pipes) between them. It's about routing principles, routing protocols, and router configuration. This book is about *how* the Internet works and *what* makes it work. *Novell's Internet Plumbing Handbook* focuses on what goes on behind the *screens*!

This is not a book on how to install or use a Web browser. It's not a guide on how to communicate via e-mail. It's not a tour of the hottest Web sites or a tutorial to Web navigation. This is a plumbing handbook, pure and simple.

Who Should Read This Book?

How many of us think about the path that water takes to reach our kitchen sink when we turn on the faucet? How often do we trace the tap water to its original source through the maze of pipes, water mains, and treatment plants? When we turn on that faucet, we expect the water to flow. The same holds true for the Internet. When we click, we expect results. So, if you're curious about how all this Internet plumbing hangs together, read on.

As an Internet user, you may be surprised to find out what it takes to visit those favorite Web sites. Chances are, after reading this book, you may even acquire more patience and refrain from calling the Internet "the Interditch" or the Word Wide Web "the World Wide Wait" when the responses to your mouse clicks are not instantaneous.

If you are an Internet provider, you will find many practical tips on how to set up your routers — and what pitfalls to avoid. If you are a LAN/WAN administrator connecting an organization to the Internet, you will benefit from the discussion on routing protocols and router configuration.

How This Book Is Organized

If the inner workings of the Internet intrigue you, and if you are curious about the origins of the Internet and its current architecture, then whatever your level of technical expertise, this book was written with you in mind. You can use the information in this book to broaden your knowledge and enrich your Internet experience. This book is organized into three parts.

Part I — Routing and Internet Basics

Part I, "Routing and Internet Basics" (Chapter 1–3), is intended for all audience levels. It introduces routing, computer communications concepts, and the grandparent of the Internet in a way that's understandable to a novice and entertaining to all, even the network pros.

Part II — TCP/IP Routing: Protocols, Configurations, and Hardware

Part II, "TCP/IP Routing: Protocols, Configurations, and Hardware" (Chapters 4–9), is aimed primarily at network administrators, Internet Service Providers, and technical managers. A beginning reader need not feel excluded. Plenty of understandable examples and illustrations make the complex topics of routing protocols, configurations, and hardware come alive. Technical managers will gain greater appreciation for the issues that their staffs must deal with after reading this part.

Part III — The Internet: Architecture, Routing, and Switching

Part III, "The Internet: Architecture, Routing, and Switching" (Chapters 10–11), is meant for all audiences. Everyone will benefit from tracing the Internet's evolution and exploring the complex technical issues that it continues to face. Emerging routing and switching technologies are explored for the more advanced readers.

End matter

The afterword is my reflection as an Internet user and internetworking professional on the future of the Net that has become so much a part of our social fabric. Many people are making dire predictions about the Internet. This section presents some personal thoughts on the Internet's future.

This book ends with four appendixes, each of which provides valuable resource and reference material. The following is a brief synopsis of the appendixes:

- *Appendix A, "RFC References"* — This appendix lists all of the Requests for Comments (RFCs) referenced in the book. It's a list that includes all of the possible current administrative information about an RFC, including its status and category and Internet Engineering Task Force (IETF) working group (if any) responsible for the area covered by it.
- *Appendix B, "Bibliography"* — This appendix contains references to excellent works on computer networks, TCP/IP, history of the Internet, satellite communications, and other topics that could only be touched on lightly in this book.
- *Appendix C, "Acronym and Abbreviation Guide"* — This appendix is a guide to acronyms and abbreviations. Most (but not all) of them are defined in the book. Several data-communications glossary references are also listed.
- *Appendix D, "Excerpt from NSF 93-52 Solicitation"* — This appendix includes an excerpt of the NSF 93-52 solicitation that, to a large extent, defined the current structure of the Internet.

Acknowledgments

First and foremost, I would like to thank my parents, Anna and Henryk Rybaczyk, for their example of the work ethic, and the vision that they held for their children under the most trying circumstances. I would like to thank my sisters, Elizabeth, Barbara, and Dorothy, and my cousin Wladzia for the many years of encouragement in all aspects of my life, including this project. My deep gratitude to Mother, El Morya, and Saint Germain for your spiritual support over the many years, especially during the writing of this book.

A big thank you to my acquisitions editor, Jim Sumser, of IDG Books Worldwide. I never told you, Jim, that when I made a suggestion to write this book I was actually joking. Since you called my bluff, however, and gave me a contract, I didn't have any choice but to write it.

Many thanks to my development and copy editor, Kevin Shafer, for his excellent editorial suggestions and writing tips. This book would not have happened without your encouragement along the arduous path of writing. Special thanks, Kevin, for allowing me to use my favorite word processor to submit the original manuscript. Thank you to my technical editor, Keith Brumbaugh, for your insightful input, suggestions, and corrections that helped me immensely to refine the manuscript.

Many thanks to my friend, and a fantastic designer, Nancy Badten of Prism Graphics Design for your patience in working with my rough sketches and translating them into wonderful drawings and cartoons for this book. Big thanks to Boyd Badten for helping to scan photos of vendor products.

Special thanks to Dr. Andres Fortino for my first lessons in internetworking, connecting me with Learning Tree International, and offering me the co-authorship of my first book. Thank you to my friend Dr. Karanjit Siyan for helping me learn many details of TCP/IP and offering me the opportunity to contribute a couple chapters to one of his books.

Thank you to my many friends and colleagues over the years — Chris Wilbert, Lloyd Leidermann, Michael Kopczyk, Ron Lichtwardt, Doug Jackman, Peter Aven, James Grover, Peter Duffy, Harold Libster, Clyde Laakso, Ken Haug, Peter McPhee, James Grover, Larry Cummings, Don Kintzing, Karen Ila Coteus, Frank Sarlo, Greg McKay, Dave Zeter, and Will Adams — with whom I shared many experiences and stimulating discussions regarding computer technology and the Internet.

Thank you to my friend and buddy Jack McShae — a devoted Macintosh fan and a fiber-optics expert — for not only believing that this book could be written, but for helping me (free of charge) with writing the fiber-optics portion of Chapter 7. Thanks to Arlene McShae, Susan and Vernon Hamilton, and Robert and Linda Worobec for your friendship and support.

My profound gratitude to Dr. Haruko Ueyda for having the unwavering faith that this writing project would come to completion, even when my own faith was waning. Dr. Ueyda, you are the greatest cheerleader in the world. Thank you to Dr. George and Linda Lopos for your encouragement during this project. My deep gratitude to Dorothy Lee for composing the most exquisite music that has inspired me during this writing project.

Thanks to many friends and colleagues at Learning Tree International, especially Tim Watts and Chuck Markusich for words of encouragement when I shared with you the idea of writing this book. Special thanks to Boles Sykora for writing a course on OSPF and BGP that I love to teach, and to Nancy Harrison for your most remarkable skill and patience in scheduling courses. Thank you to the hundreds of my students whom I consider some of my best teachers.

Thank you to all of you who've given of your time in interviews to allow me to refine my understanding of the many subjects covered in this work. Many thanks to Charles Lee, Rick Wilder, and Tracy B. Smith of MCI for discussing vBNS-related issues and granting permission to reprint the vBNS-related figures. Thanks to Patricia Schaffer of BBN Corporation, Mike Tobin of UUnet, George Kelly of AGIS, and Katie Greene of Concentric Network Corporation for permission to reprint the BBN, UUnet, AGIS, and Concentric VPN network maps.

Thank you to Jeff Ogdan for taking the time to discuss Merit's role in the development of the Internet, and to Jordan Becker for explaining how the NSFnet evolved after ANS took over its operation. Special thanks to Kevin Kosh of CHEN PR for arranging an interview with Jordan and getting me the ANS network maps and permission to reprint them.

Thank you to Andy Schmidt of Ameritech, Laura Geary of Livingstone Enterprises, and DeAnn Strenke of MultiTech for reprint permissions. Thanks to Les Addison of AGIS for your time to discuss the details of AGIS peering and routing policies. Thanks to Robert H'Obbes' Zakon for permission to reference the Internet Timeline.

Thank you to Melissa Morales and Pat Sluz of DEC for permission to reprint a picture of DEC's Gigaswitch/FDDI and for taking the time to discuss the intricacies of the Gigaswitch. Thank you to Sue Jensen and Michael Hakkert of Cisco Systems for permission to reprint drawings of Cisco routers. Many thanks to Tom Downey of Cisco for the most clarifying discussion on

Cisco's tag switching. Special thanks to Clare Whitecross for arranging an interview with Tom Downey.

Thank you to Bev Toms and Cheryl Rasmussen of Ipsilon for permission to reprint a picture of the Ipsilon IP switch. Many thanks to Jeff Baher for taking the time to discuss the technical details of Ipsilon's IP switching. Thank you to Susan S. Adams of Optical Cable Corporation for permission to reprint diagrams relating to Optical's fiber products. Thank you to Randy Sosnowitz of Interface Technology for permission to reprint pictures of your cable products.

Thank you to Steve Vogelsang of FORE Systems for your time to discuss FORE's implementation of MPOA. Thank you to Linda Young and Rich Borden of FORE for supplying and granting permission to reprint a picture of a FORE switch. Thank you to Theresa Parenteau of FitzGerald Communications for supplying and granting permission to reprint a picture of a Bay Networks router.

Thank you to Barbra Burlington of Ascend Communications for supplying the graphics of Ascend's products. Thank you to Jeannette Bitz of Gallaher PR for permission to reprint the Ascend graphics, supplying the GRF IP Switch Architecture Guide, and arranging an interview of Cindy Flam of Ascend Communications. Thank you, Cindy, for your time to discuss the details of Ascend's GRF product line.

Thank you to Lois Dudley at Novell Press for supplying Novell's routing products referenced in this book. Thank you to all of my clients in Livingston, Montana, and my Merise sales rep, Wade Foster, for being most supportive during this writing project.

How can I thank my best friend, spiritual twin, and beloved wife, Maria Elizabeth, who's been with me every step along this project and has endured the symptoms of a "computer widow" on many occasions? My profound gratitude for your patience, understanding, and countless hours spent reviewing the manuscript and suggesting how to make it more readable. Without your constant love and support, this book would still be a dream.

Contents at a Glance

Contents

PART I

Routing and Internet Basics

CHAPTER 1

Routing Demystified

Information on the Internet is exchanged through *packets*. One definition in *Webster's Dictionary* defines a packet as "a short fixed-length section of data that is transmitted as a unit in an electronic communications network." Later chapters in this book define packets in more technical terms. For now, a simple way to relate to a packet is to think of it as a postal package with a *to* and a *from* address on it. You can also think of it as a person traveling to a predetermined destination.

Thousands, millions, trillions of packets flow daily through the various arteries of the Internet. This flow is not random. Packets know their origins and their destinations. They know where they came from and where they are going. However, packets need help in finding the best way to reach their destinations.

Internet *routers* are the devices that direct packets to their destinations through the maze of computer networks they interconnect. The process of finding the optimal way for the packets to reach their destinations is called *routing*. How fast packets are routed through the Internet is one of the factors that determines how fast you get a response to your mouse clicks when you surf the Web. Consider the elements of routing in the context of what most of us can relate to — physical travel.

Physical Travel and Basic Routing Concepts

Physical travel can be stressful and complex. However, understanding the concepts of physical travel puts you miles ahead in understanding just what Internet routing involves. Most of us have traveled in a car, train, bus, boat, or a plane. Most trips require us to use several modes of transportation to get to our destination.

Getting out of a cab at an airport and getting on a plane may sound like a trivial action, but it corresponds to a key routing concept: *a packet changing its encapsulation*. Getting on a crowded bus or waiting for a plane that is delayed may be annoying but it embodies two more concepts in routing: *congestion* and *delays*. Making a decision to take a freeway versus a two-lane scenic highway to reach a destination shows that *multiple paths exist between locations* — another key routing concept.

All these travel experiences are fairly common. Surprisingly, the concepts they embody are the foundation of Internet routing. To explore many of the basic routing concepts in more detail, consider the travel analogy shown in Figure 1.1.

FIGURE 1. *Travel analogy illustrating basic routing concepts*

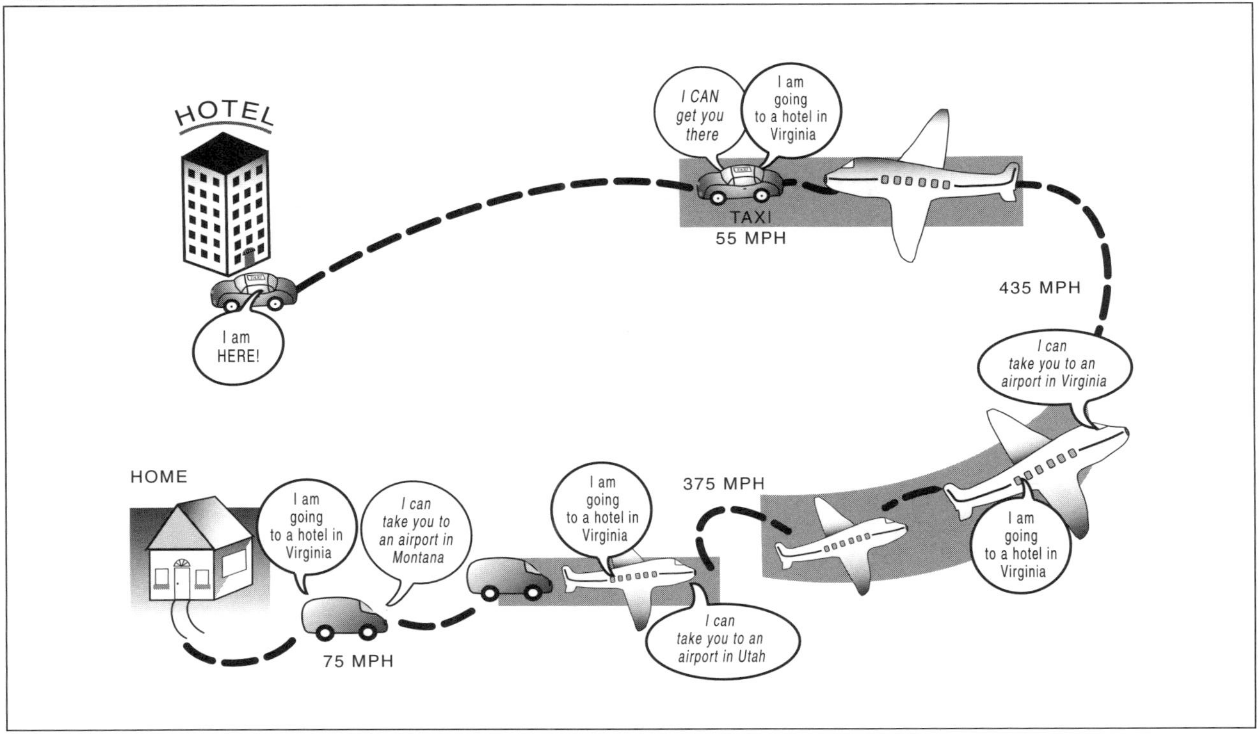

Movement and encapsulation of packets

Physical travel is synonymous with the movement of travelers going from their points of origin to their predetermined destinations. Cyber travel is similar. Compare yourself as a traveler to an Internet packet. The vehicles in which you travel correspond to the packet's *encapsulation*. When an Internet *packet* is encapsulated inside one of the "physical vehicles" operating on the Internet, it becomes a *frame*.

A frame is like your car taking you to the airport, or a plane delivering you to another airport, or a cab getting you from an airport to a hotel. Notice that as you change your travel vehicles, you (the packet) stay the same, but your travel vehicles (frames) change. Figure 1.1 shows examples of physical vehicles acting as frames.

The basic routing concept conveyed here is that packets moving through the Internet are encapsulated in different physical vehicles or frames. A more technical discussion of packets and frames follows in Chapter 3 and Chapter 7.

Congestion and delays

Have you ever been at a crowded airport waiting for your plane to take off? The planes coming and going are the vehicles or the encapsulation of the arriving and departing passengers. The passengers are the packets. The concept of packet encapsulation has already been introduced. However, the facts that planes may arrive and depart late, and that most airports are teaming with people (packets), introduces the routing concepts of *congestion* and *delays*.

Feedback and multiple paths to destination

Have you ever been at an airport ready to leave on a business trip or vacation only to find that your flight has been canceled because of a mechanical problem with the plane? How about if the plane is functioning perfectly well but weather conditions at the destination airport are so bad that it's impossible to land safely? You begin to feel helpless. Your travel plans are disrupted. Your intended travel path is unavailable.

Your airline may try to find an alternate way to get you to your destination. You may be forced to change planes several times instead of taking a direct fight. Most likely, your trip will take longer than originally planned. There's even a possibility you must spend the night at a nearby hotel before alternate flights become available. Eventually, you'll get to where you are going.

Now, put yourself in the position of an Internet packet trying to get to its destination through a maze of networks and routers. The airport is almost a perfect analogy of a router. Routers on the Internet (just like the airports) talk to each other and receive feedback about conditions of other routers (other airports). Routers can also detect if there is a problem with one of their physical interfaces over which packets must be sent to their destinations. So, if a path or a route becomes unavailable, a router attempts to locate an alternate path over which packets can be sent to their intended destinations. It may take longer for these rerouted packets to arrive. They may never arrive. Internet packets are not as fortunate as people. If a path becomes unavailable during their journey, they only have so much time left before they hit the *bit bucket* (they are discarded).

The basic routing concept conveyed here is that *routers receive feedback about conditions on the Internet and also try to maintain an awareness of multiple paths to the same destination.*

Ultimate source and destination addressing

When we travel, we start from a certain location (say, our home) and we proceed to a destination, whatever it may be. Just look at what happens to me when I leave my home in Montana and travel to a major city to teach a seminar on computer routing. First, I get in my car, drive it to the airport, park it, and rush to get on a plane. My car got me to the airport in Montana, but it did not get me to my final destination.

Typically, I have to take at least two or three planes to get anywhere from Montana. If I travel to Virginia, as shown in Figure 1.1, I first fly into Salt Lake City, I change planes in Salt Lake City, and fly into an airport in Virginia. From the airport terminal in Virginia, I take a cab to my hotel. So, what does all this have to do with routing in the Internet? Just about everything.

I am the packet moving from my starting point to my ultimate destination and all of the various vehicles I use encapsulate me along the way. In my mind, I knew all along my point of origin (my home) and my ultimate destination (a hotel in Virginia). My awareness of where I was coming from and where I was going to never changed even as I used my car, several planes, and a cab.

The basic routing concept conveyed here is that *Internet packets have in them the address of their source and ultimate destination.* In technical terms, these addresses are referred to as *logical addresses* and are explored in more detail in Chapter 3. In Figure 1.1 you can't see me (the packet) because I am inside of the frames (my car, planes, and a cab). But you *can* hear me saying that I am going to Virginia, right?

Local source and destination addressing

All the various means of transportation I used to get from my point of origin to my ultimate destination had a limited range of operation. I can't drive my car from Montana to Virginia in a half day, but I can use it to get to the airport. Planes can get me from one airport to another but they don't pick me up in my driveway. The cab is great between the airport and the hotel but generally not between airports hundreds of miles apart.

All these different means of transportation have a predefined range of operation. They are all capable of getting me from one location to another within that range of operation. We consider that range of operation to be *local*. Not one single mode of transportation was adequate to get me to my final destination, given my time constraints. However, when I used them all with my awareness of my ultimate destination, they got me where I was going. It was the last mode of transportation (the last frame) that delivered me to the exact final location.

The physical vehicles from the travel analogy in Figure 1.1 correspond to the Internet physical vehicles or frames. The basic routing concept conveyed here is that *frames have their own addresses, separate from the addresses of packets*. The addresses in frames have local significance and are referred to as the local source and destination addresses. They are valid for only a portion of a packet's journey.

The packet, with its ultimate destination address, relies on these local addresses in the frames to move it along. When a frame arrives at a router, the router extracts the packet from it and discards the remainder of the frame. In technical terms, addresses in the frames are referred to as *hardware* or *Data-Link Layer addresses*, which are discussed in greater detail in Chapter 8.

Varying speeds and carrying capacities of physical vehicles

Additionally, all the transportation vehicles I used in my example to get from my home to my final destination have quite different characteristics. They operate at different speeds and have different carrying capacities. Generally, more people can fit on a jet than in a minivan or a cab. Here, the analogy breaks down somewhat, because on the Internet a single frame carries a single packet. It's not likely that pretending to be an Internet packet, I would get a jet to travel in all by myself. So, switch gears for a moment, and think of a packet as the entire cargo of a plane or a cab. It means that some frames that are operational on the Internet can carry bigger packets than others. This reinforces the basic routing concept conveyed here: *Different Internet frames have different carrying capacity and they move or are transmitted at different speeds.*

Why Would Anyone Want to Route?

If you understand the basic concepts that have been related through this example, you understand the key issues involved in routing. The rest are technical details discussed in later chapters.

If you travel physically or through cyber space, you will route. When you travel physically, the routing experience is rich. You feel yourself getting on and off that plane, getting in a cab, getting in the elevator, and so on. Cyber travel is rich also, but an aspect of it is hidden from you.

You point a Web browser to a desired destination and, within seconds, you are there on your screen. You experience the destination, but you miss the trip. All the different cyber pipes, cyber airports and planes, cyber cabs and elevators that an Internet packet goes through are not part of your experience. But they are all there, and that's what this book is all about: explaining the cyber freeways and back roads, explaining the cyber cops (the routers and switches), and explaining how they handle cyber traffic.

And finally, we explore what happens when the number of cyber travelers or packets grows exponentially. Who must be concerned about that growth and why? Who are the people and companies that are in the forefront of building the cyber freeway junctions where billions of packets converge looking for the right way to go?

What's Needed to Route?

In the travel example, routing involved many elements. There must be something to route — a *message*. A message could be, for example, a reply to a request for information through a Web browser. There must be a translation of that message into packets. There must be a mechanism to encapsulate packets into frames. There must be pipes over which the encapsulated packets will flow. Routers are needed to direct packets, and there must be some rules to govern that whole process. It all boils down to communication. So, let's explore the communication process and how it works in Chapter 2.

CHAPTER 2

The Communication Model

The communication model in this chapter consists of five major components: transmitters, receivers, a message, transmission media, and protocols (or rules). All information exchanges on the Internet can be reduced to this model.

Communication Defined

We communicate all the time, or so we think. What does it really mean to communicate? What's the difference between effective communication and poor communication? How many of us can clearly define what communication is? *Webster's Dictionary* says that communication has several definitions. The one that comes closest to the communication model in this chapter states that communication is "a process by which information is exchanged between individuals through a common system of symbols, signs, or behavior."

By examining the five components of this communication model in the context of this definition. You'll see how the Internet's plumbing (or infrastructure) and the information exchanges on the Internet can be made to fit Webster's definition.

Transmitters and receivers

The "individuals" exchanging information on the Internet are the user computers, server computers, and routers (or packet switches). They can act as *transmitters*, *receivers*, or both. When you send an e-mail message across the Internet, you trigger a chain reaction of information exchanges between many computers and routers. Assume that you are a computer user on a small network interfaced to the Internet through a local Internet service provider (ISP). When you click "Send" in an e-mail program, your computer becomes a transmitter. Your e-mail message is then placed in packets and sent to the mail server on your network (see Figure 2.1).

When the mail server receives the packets carrying your e-mail message, it acts as a receiver. When the mail server passes your e-mail packets on to a router, the mail server takes on the job of being the transmitter and the router becomes the receiver. Unless network traffic is extremely light (fat chance!), Internet computers (such as mail servers and routers) process incoming and outgoing packets simultaneously. Web servers, FTP servers, and user computers also transmit and receive packets simultaneously. Notice that in Figure 2.1, the transmitters and receivers are joined together through a transmission medium and, in all likelihood, are using some rules to exchange the e-mail packets.

FIGURE 2.1 *Exchange of e-mail in the context of a communication model*

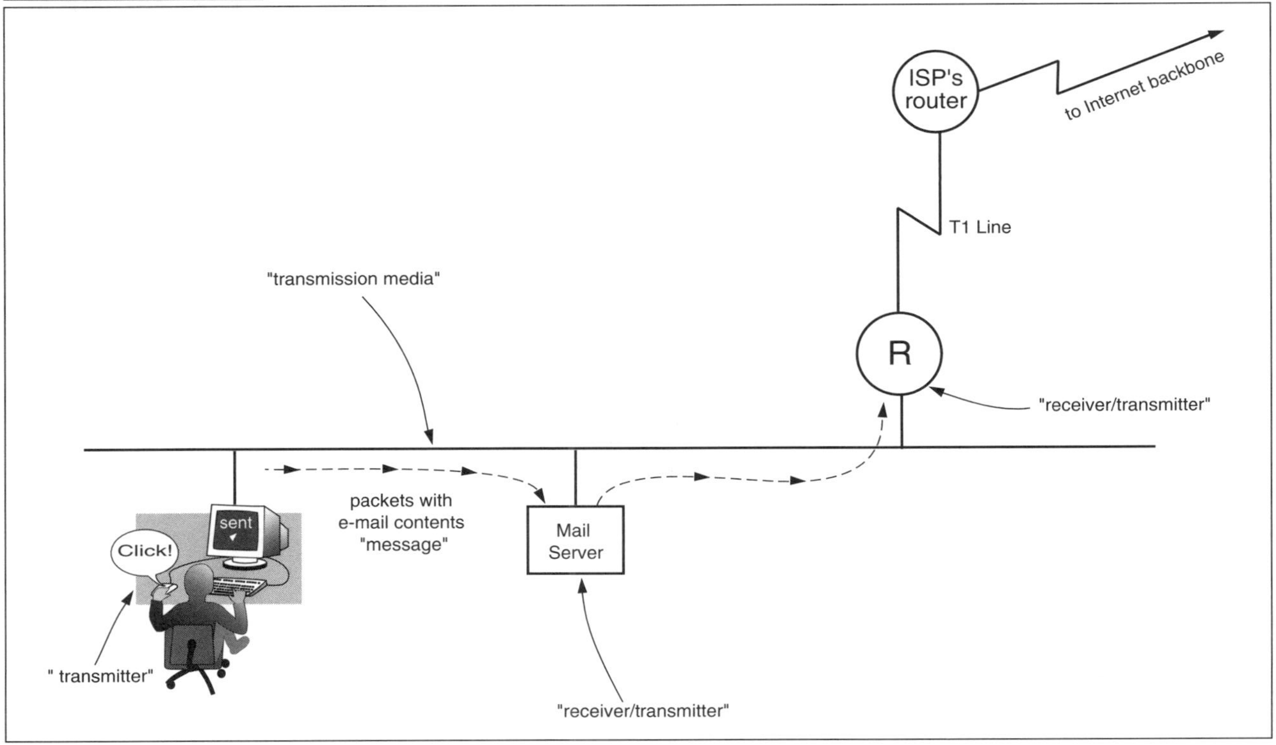

The message

The "information exchanged" from the Webster's definition of communication is the *message* component of the communication model. The message is placed in packets for transport across the Internet. In the example in Figure 2.1, the message is the e-mail contents placed in Internet packets to be forwarded by routers to their ultimate destination.

Internet routers exchange two types of packets.

- *Packets with user data.* These packets contain e-mail message contents, requests from users to access Web sites, information coming from Web sites, file-transfer requests, contents of files being downloaded, and more. These packets carry data that has a direct meaning to you: data that either you see or want someone else to see. These packets originate either on a user computer or on a server.
- *Packets with administrative data.* These packets originate with routers and are meant for routers. The contents of these packets — when received and processed by fellow routers on the Internet — enable routers to create internal routing tables detailing how to reach various Internet locations. These tables are then used by routers to direct packets with user data to their intended destinations. The process of routers exchanging packets among themselves to maintain their internal routing tables is very complex. Chapter 4 is dedicated to a technical discussion of the rules that govern these exchanges between routers (the routing protocols). In the example shown in Figure 2.1, the ISP's router would be exchanging packets with the "administrative data" with other routers on the Internet, so that when it received the packets with e-mail contents from router R, it would know where to direct them next.

The transmission media

The message must travel over a medium. When you turn on the faucet in a kitchen sink, the transmission medium for the water is a series of pipes, called *plumbing*. The *transmission media* (or plumbing) for Internet packets can take on many forms. The Internet pipes can be fiber-optic or copper cables. They can be satellite and terrestrial microwave links. They can be the plain old-fashioned telephone lines that come into your home. Ten years ago, hardly anyone would have envisioned that these plain telephone lines would be used to access the Internet on the scale that's done today. Various types of Internet pipes are discussed in greater detail in Chapter 7.

Protocols: the communication rules

In computer jargon, the "symbols, signs, or behavior" from Webster's definition of communication are the *protocols* (or rules) component of the communication model. Hundreds (if not thousands) of computer protocols exist. This book focuses on the protocols that relate to routers and the transmission media. If you like an alphabet soup, you'll love the acronyms for the protocol names. There's RIP, OSPF, BGP, or DVMRP, to start with. These three-, four- and five-letter alphabet soups are endless.

RIP, OSPF, and BGP are the routing protocols. Routers are very social creatures. They like to talk to each other. Actually, they don't have a choice. They must talk to each other if they are to do their jobs. Routing protocols allow the routers to exchange packets, which helps them create and maintain the routing tables. These routing tables in turn enable routers to forward incoming packets with user data on to the next leg in their journey across the Internet. RIP, OSPF, and BGP are explored in Chapter 4.

Computer networks

For the purposes of this discussion, the definition of a *computer network* shall remain simple. A computer network is a collection of computing devices (transmitters and receivers) that exchange information with one another over a transmission medium using rules or protocols to govern those exchanges. Figure 2.1 is an example of a simple computer network. The protocols are not shown in Figure 2.1. They are imbedded in the transmitters and the receivers on the network. Typically, one device on the network has something to offer to the other devices. Servers have something to offer to the user computers. For a classic on computer networks see Tanenbaum, Appendix B.

Put It All Together — The Internet Is Born

A simple definition of the Internet is that it's a network of networks — thousands of computer networks connected together to create a global super network. And, for computers from one Internet network to communicate with computers on another Internet network, a router is required. Tens of thousands of routers are deployed in the Internet today making it perhaps the most complex communications network in history. How did it all begin?

The early days

The roots of the Internet go back to the founding of the Advanced Research Projects Agency (ARPA) in 1957. ARPA was created hastily during the Eisenhower administration after the Russians surprised the U.S. by launching the first satellite into orbit, the Sputnik. ARPA's initial charter was to ensure that America took the lead in the technological race, and, at the same time, reduce military interservice rivalry by placing the federal research budget under ARPA's control. However, in 1958 when NASA was enacted into law, it began to take on ARPA for the federal research budget. The collision course set by NASA challenged ARPA's reason for being. Determined to survive the NASA challenge, ARPA redefined its mission.

A leaner ARPA defined its mission away from military goals and objectives to long-term, way-out scientific research — especially the development of information technologies — that would draw on the best and brightest personnel from top research labs and universities. ARPA's newly defined mission and goals reinvigorated the scientific community of the late fifties and early sixties. Many scientists and researchers believed that under ARPA's sponsorship, their dreams could become a reality in the not-too-distant future.

In 1966, Bob Taylor, head of ARPA's Information Processing Techniques Office (IPTO), recruited Massachusetts Institute of Technology (MIT) Lincoln Labs computer scientist Larry Roberts to design and implement a computer network based on the revolutionary concepts of that time: packet-switching and distributed networking. The idea of a packet-switched computer network was revolutionary, but it wasn't new. It had been bandied about in many quarters since the early sixties. Now, with ARPA's funds and direction, it was about to manifest physically.

Roberts wasted no time. His years of research at MIT made him uniquely qualified for the job that Taylor envisioned for him. He also had a wide circle of friends whose ideas and creativity were matched only by their professional credentials. By 1968, drawing upon the expertise and ideas of his colleagues from their days at MIT (researchers such as Leonard Kleinrock and Wesley Clark), Roberts put together a request for proposal (RFP) to be sent out to more than 100 companies who might be interested in building an Interface Message Processor (IMP) for the initial four-node ARPA network. This ARPA network was intended to connect four computers at the selected sites into a single time-sharing network.

The IMPs

The idea of an IMP in designing a network was a stroke of genius by Wesley Clark. The IMP was to be a computer — separate from the four to-be-connected mainframe hosts — that would be responsible for all the network functions. The basic idea behind a computer network is to share resources and provide resiliency in communication. However, what if the resources to be shared are very scarce? Do you think that all of the institutions with computing resources in the sixties were eager to share them with others?

The processing power and cost of computers in the sixties was drastically different from what it is today. They were far less capable and much more expensive. If these mainframe computers were to be networked, they would not only be subject to their existing use, but they would now have to deal with all the added functions of the network, as well as being accessed by other network users. So, while there was an excitement about a computer network that ARPA was proposing there was also a natural reluctance on the part of some of the computing resources owners (universities and research labs) to jump in and make their computers available to others over ARPA's network.

At least with the IMPs between the host computers and the network there would be some sort of buffer. The IMPs would handle the network functions. The mainframe hosts connected to the network would interface to a common protocol that the IMPs would share — another big plus for the IMP idea. There was also an administrative advantage to using IMPs. The "network" they would help to create could be thought of as being "separate" from the host computers and would remain under ARPA's control. Don't the IMPs sound a little like the earliest ancestor of today's routers?

In December 1968 one of the responders to Roberts's RFP, the Bolt, Beranek and Newman (BBN) consulting firm from Cambridge, Massachusetts, was selected as the ARPA contractor to design and build the IMPs. The BBN designers contracted to purchase Honeywell's DDP-516 units to be modified and programmed as IMPs. By 1969, the four sites that would become the future home of the IMPs for the initial four-node network had been chosen.

The first ARPANET

The IMPs began to arrive at their chosen sites in stages: first at the University of California at Los Angeles (UCLA) around the Labor Day weekend in 1969, then at Stanford Research Institute (SRI) in October 1969, University of California at Santa Barbara (UCSB) in November 1969, and finally at Utah State in December 1969. Although the first session between two hosts connected through a network using the IMPs took place between UCLA and SRI in October of 1969, it is December 1969 that's generally recognized as the birth of the ARPAnet when the four chosen sites were connected together using 50-kilobit phone lines. The grand experiment began, and it has continued ever since. Figure 2.2 and Figure 2.3 show the early ancestors of today's Internet.

FIGURE 2.2 *Two-node ARPAnet, October 1969*

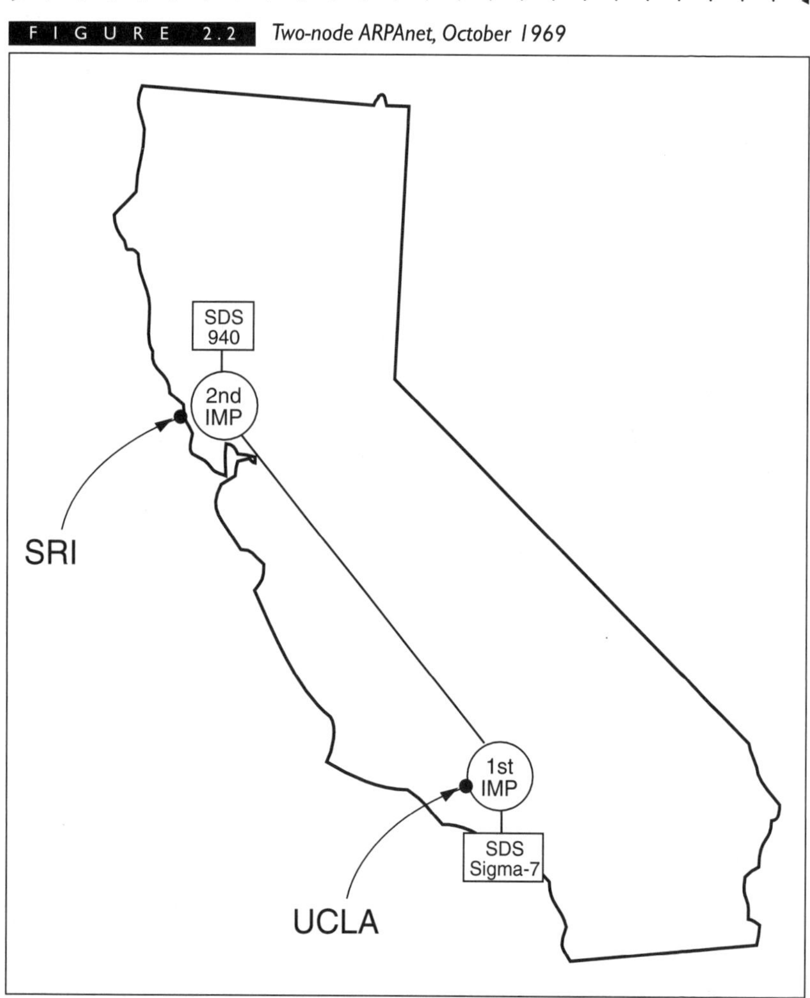

Indeed, the rest is history. You can find it in the various accounts on the history of the Internet and in the memories of the hundreds and thousands of those who contributed to what we almost take for granted today — surfing the Net.

FIGURE 2.3 *Four-node ARPAnet, December 1969*

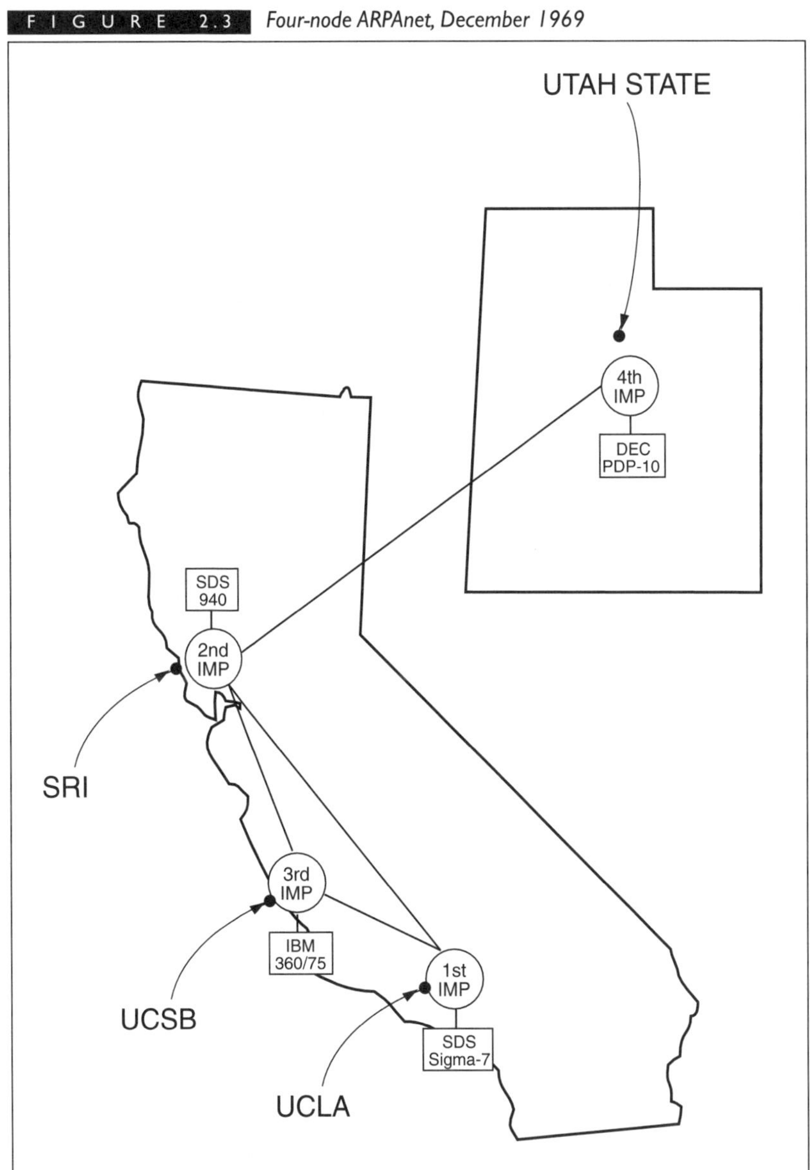

The key players

Many references have been made to a single individual as the father of the Internet. There are individuals who've made outstanding contributions to the initial ARPAnet and beyond, but it's been a collective effort since the beginning. The idea of a computer network was a concept held by many individuals in the early sixties, and there are many fathers of the Internet, just as there were many founding fathers of our nation.

Larry Roberts was no stranger to the idea of a computer network. Before he was recruited for ARPA, he was put in charge of setting up a dial-up connection between computers at Lincoln Labs and at CCA, a time-sharing company in Santa Monica. It wasn't exactly a network, just two computers interfaced with each other, but at least it was something that had to do with the stuff that goes on between computers, rather than what goes on inside of them.

No wonder Bob Taylor was so determined to get Roberts to design and implement the ARPA network. Roberts had initially resisted the ARPA offer!

Another key figure in laying the theoretical foundation for the ARPAnet and who played a major role in its creation was Leonard Kleinrock. After doing his doctoral thesis on data networks at MIT, Kleinrock joined the UCLA faculty in 1963. In 1968, Kleinrock was awarded an ARPA contract to build the Network Measurement Center that would measure and analyze the proposed ARPA network. It was Kleinrock who worked with Roberts on the RFP for the IMP, and it was Kleinrock who assembled a phenomenal team of researchers, graduate students, and engineers to install the first IMP at UCLA. Many of the founding fathers of the Internet were Kleinrock's students at UCLA, including Steve Crocker, Vinton Cerf, Jon Postel, and Robert Khan. The contributions of these individuals to the Internet are enormous. This book could not include enough pages to adequately discuss the contributions of the many founding fathers of the Internet.

The other players

Between 1960 and 1965, independent of Larry Robert's research and experiments at MIT, Paul Baran of RAND corporation was developing the concepts of a distributed network and the breaking up of large messages into small pieces to be sent over such a network. Baran's work proceeded in parallel with the research at MIT, but the researchers were not aware of each other's work. Baran's emphasis was on designing a more robust national telephone network in case of a nuclear scenario. However, his ideas were just too revolutionary for the industry entrenched in circuit-switching concepts. Even though RAND sponsored Paul's research and there was some interest in it at the Pentagon, convincing the telephone company of the feasibility of such a network proved to be an impossible task.

Meanwhile, in England at the National Physical Laboratory, researchers Donald Davis and Roger Scantlebury actually came up with the term "packet network." They were also working independently of Baran at RAND and the researchers at MIT. So, by 1968 when Larry Roberts was sending out the RFP to build the IMPs for the initial ARPA network, at least three groups of researchers had worked independently of each other on the ideas of packet switching and distributed networking.

How things have changed since those days in the sixties, and how they continue to stay the same! The Internet has been built on the packet-switching technology, and the packet-switching concepts that Paul Baran proposed unsuccessfully for many years to AT&T were eventually embraced even by telephone companies. Just think about it. Today, who are some of our major ISPs and backbone operators if not the phone companies?

Yet the evolution of the nature of communication on the Internet continues full circle. Packet switching relies on each packet carrying in it the address of its final destination. The intermediate devices or routers must examine the address in each packet to make a decision where to forward it next. When the volume of packets to be processed by routers increases by larger and larger numbers, the routers begin to choke. More and more computing power must be built into routers to allow them to process more and more packets in less and less time. It appears that we are now going back to some form of supercharged circuit-switching technologies to tackle this problem. The question is, where are we going to be 10 or 15 years from now? Some form of supercharged packet switching? And then super-supercharged circuit switching? See Chapter 11 for a more detailed discussion on the latest Internet routing technologies being developed to address this critical issue.

The unsung heroes

Getting back to the founding fathers of the Internet — doesn't Joseph Licklider deserve recognition for contributing to today's Internet? Licklider joined ARPA in 1962 and by the time he left in 1964, he had transformed its Command and Control Research Office into the IPTO of which he became the first head. His revolutionary ideas about man-computer interactions were published in 1960 in a paper entitled "Man-Computer Symbiosis" and his visions of a computer network had a definite impact on both Bob Taylor and Larry Roberts. In fact, ARPA's Bob Taylor carried on Licklider's vision when he

received the funding for the ARPA network and recruited Larry Roberts to be the point man for its implementation.

How about the engineers and programmers at BBN and Honeywell who designed and built the first IMPs? They certainly played their part in parenting the Internet. How about the research teams at UCLA, SRI, UCSB, and Utah State where the first IMPs were installed? How about those who for almost 30 years have continued to build and maintain "the Net" into what it is today? Thank you to all of you — those mentioned here and those not.

SMART LINKS

For more information on the history of the Internet point your browser to the following Web sites:

- http://www.isoc.org/internet-history/
- http://millenium.cs.ucla.edu/LK/Inet/
- http://unix.sri.com/policy/stp/techin/
- http://beanie.contruct.net/wizards/

Also see Randall, Hafner & Lyon in Appendix B and RFC 1000 in Appendix A.

Examples of Today's Internet Backbones

We've come a long way since those first ARPAnet experiments in 1969. Today's Internet looks nothing like its distant ancestor, yet those early beginnings were indispensable to the Internet's evolution.

The main pipes through which information flows in today's Internet are referred to as the *backbones*. Some backbones operate at speeds of up to 622 megabits per second (Mbps), with still higher speeds in the planning stages. That's more than 10,000 times the speed of the initial ARPAnet lines of 50 kilobits per second (Kbps)!

Major Internet backbones are operated by companies such as Sprint, MCI, UUnet Technologies, and BBN Corporation. These backbones come together and interconnect at Internet exchanges, which are the nerve centers of today's Internet. Various Internet exchanges are discussed in more detail in Chapter 10. See Figure 2.4, Figure 2.5, and Figure 2.6 for examples of today's backbones.

FIGURE 2.4 *BBN's U.S. backbone (courtesy of BBN Corporation)*

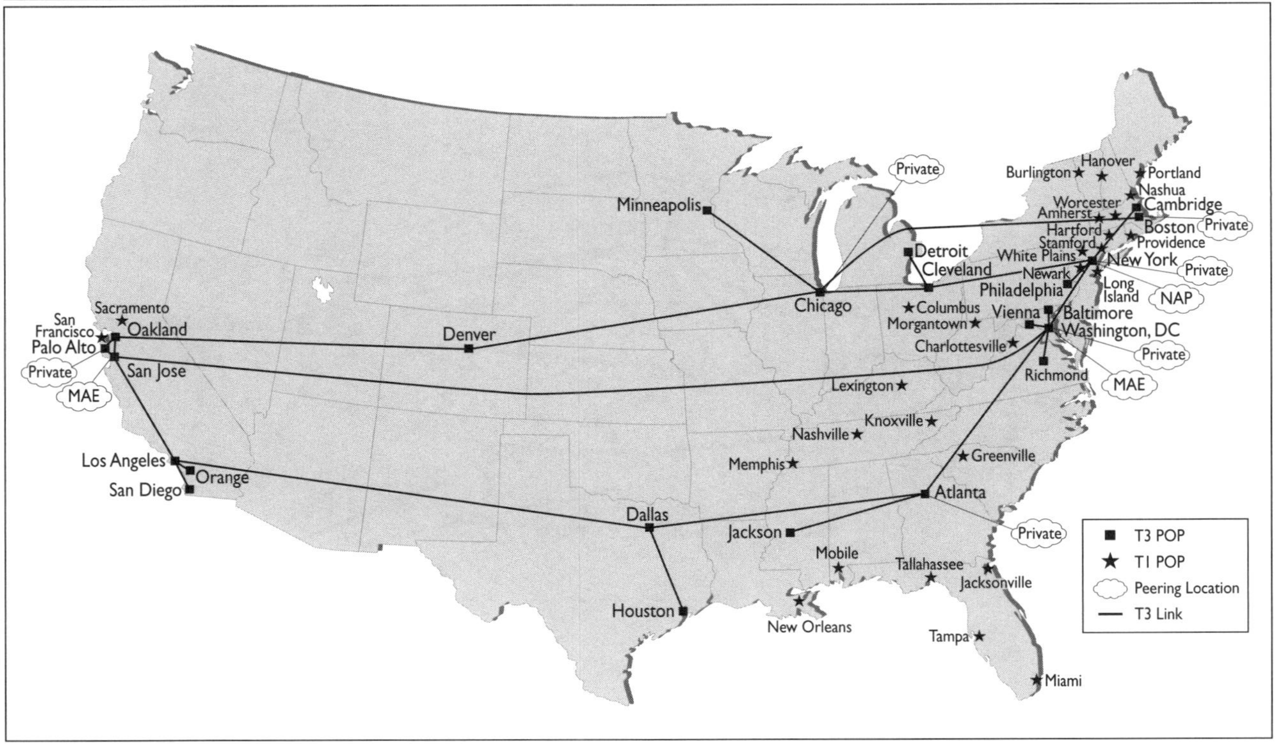

FIGURE 2.5 *UUnet's planned U.S. backbone (courtesy of UUnet Technologies)*

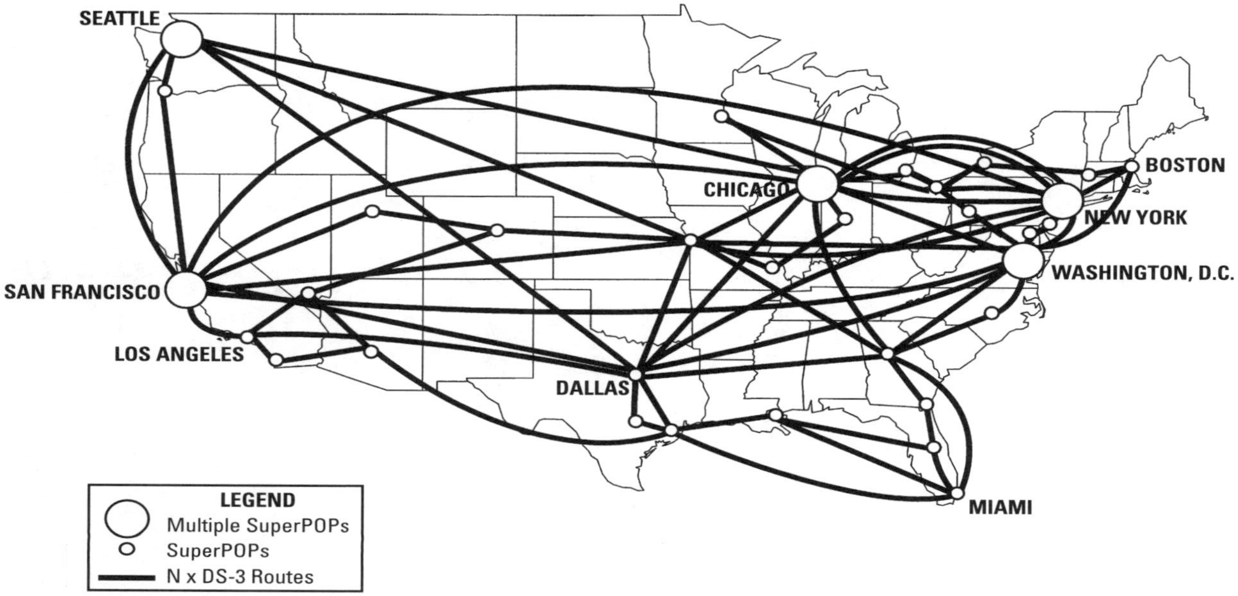

FIGURE 2.6 *UUnet's planned world-wide backbone (courtesy of UUnet Technologies)*

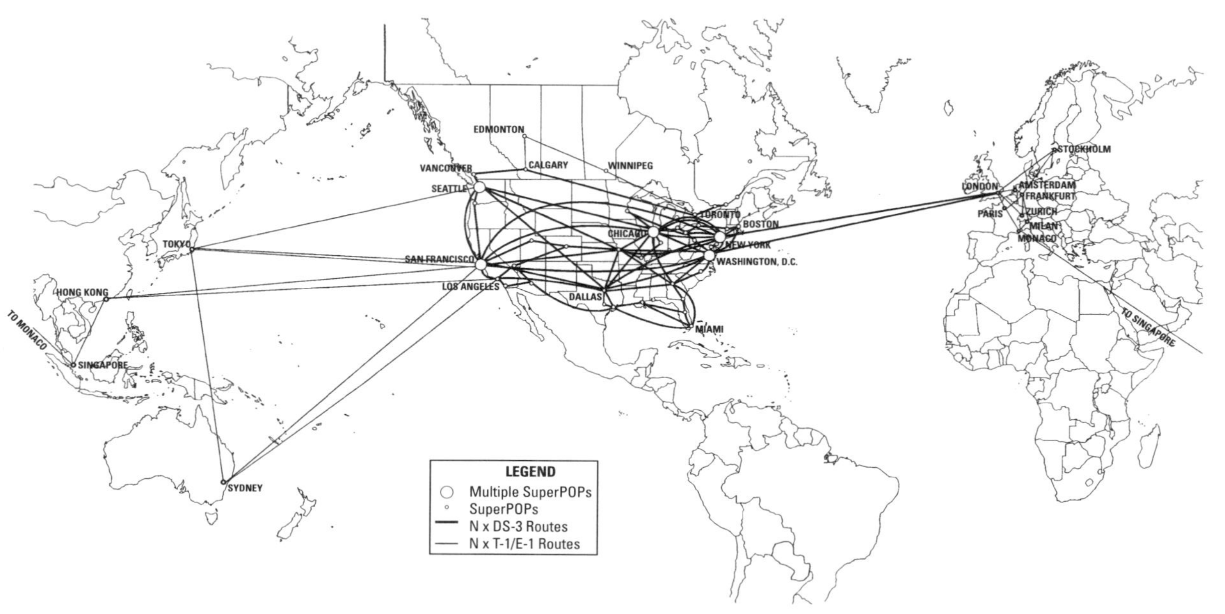

Where Do Routers Come In?

Routers can be referred to as the glue that allows computers on thousands of Internet networks to talk to each other. Routers have not always been called routers. First we had the IMPs. When ARPAnet switched from Network Control Protocol (NCP) to Transmission Control Protocol/Internet Protocol (TCP/IP) on January 1, 1983, routers were referred to as *IP gateways*. Routers are also referred to as *packet switches* or *intermediate systems*. The new name for routers that seems to be emerging is *layer 3 switches*. Whatever the name, the basic function of the devices referred to as routers remains the same: *interconnect networks and forward packets onto the next leg of their journey based on the packets' addresses and the contents of the routing tables*. Routers, like the Internet, have been evolving and, no doubt, will continue to evolve. It wasn't all that long ago when the major router vendor, Cisco, did not even exist. (Cisco was founded in late 1984.) There are hundreds of router vendors out there. Just use one of the search engines on the Net and search for a "router."

Do We Need a Hierarchical Routing Structure on the Internet?

Today's Internet is no longer a single network like the ARPAnet was when it first came online in 1969. Today's Internet is an interconnection of tens of thousands of networks, with millions of computers attached to them. When a very large group of people is working together toward a common goal, it's natural to break it up into smaller teams and establish a mechanism for the teams to communicate with one another. Not everybody in every team needs to know what everybody else in every other team is doing. Individual members of each team don't even have to know what other teams are doing at all. The representatives from each team, however, must maintain some form of contact if the common goal is to be pursued effectively. It's even possible that some of the teams with similar projects will band together into coalitions, with the coalitions maintaining contact through coalition representatives. The process can go on *ad infinitum*. The need for some kind of a hierarchical structure in this scenario stems from the fact that too many lines of communication between individual team members might bog down the effectiveness of the effort pursued by the imaginary large group of people.

Analogies of course only go so far. The Internet is not unlike a very large group of people. In fact, it's a very large group of computer networks. To facilitate an effective flow of information between the computers and those networks, some form of hierarchical routing structure is needed. Consequently, not all routers on the Internet are created equal.

As the analysis of the routing protocols proceeds in later chapters, you will discover that some routers are more important than others. Some routers are called *edge routers*, some are called *backbone routers*, some are called *border routers*. Those are positions that routers hold in the Internet routing hierarchy. Despite the apparent flatness on the Internet, which allows anyone who is connected to send a message to anyone else who is connected, there is a definite hierarchy in the way that messages flow through it. The Internet may create the perception of flatness in communication — anyone can talk to anyone else — but this flatness in the ability to communicate is undergirded by a very strict hierarchical structure in the way in which the messages are routed across the Internet. As the Internet continues to grow and evolve, there will be no end to the new techniques that come along, techniques that will only increase the hierarchical nature of routing on the Internet.

CHAPTER 3

Layered Computer Architecture

When people communicate, they do so at many levels. When computers communicate, they must follow many rules to make their communications successful. The basic communication model described in Chapter 2 identified the rules governing communication between computers as protocols.

Computers are complex creations. The many functions that computers perform and the specifications required to perform these functions, are often lumped together and referred to as a *computer architecture*. Since there are many companies manufacturing computer equipment, there are many computer architectures. However, just as people can be very different from one another and yet share many common characteristics, computer architectures are different from one another but with certain things in common.

Since the earliest days of computer networking (starting with the ARPAnet), the challenge has been to allow computers with varying architectures to communicate with one another. Today's Internet is a perfect example of that challenge met successfully. Just about every type of a computer under the sun (mainframes, minicomputers, desktops, laptops) can connect to the Internet and communicate effectively. What makes this possible is a set of common, open communication protocols that are implemented in the varying computing architectures. This set of common, open communication protocols is the TCP/IP protocol suite.

The OSI Reference Model

The OSI Reference Model breaks down the process of communication between a computer architecture into layers, seven to be exact. Each layer is responsible for a set of communication functions implemented in the form of protocols. For two computing devices to communicate effectively, the communication protocols at each layer must be implemented correctly on each device. Additionally, the protocol layers do not operate in isolation. They must interface with one another and work together in harmony for a computing device to operate properly and be able to communicate with other devices.

The layers of the OSI model that we focus on in this book are the bottom three: the Physical Layer, the Data-Link Layer, and the Network Layer. The Network Layer receives the emphasis of this discussion since this is where the routing decisions are made. Because entire volumes have been written on the subject of the OSI Reference Model, this discussion does not repeat what's already out there. For a detailed discussion of the OSI layers see Tanenbaum, Appendix B. This chapter explores the OSI Reference Model to the extent necessary to facilitate the understanding of routers and the Internet.

The OSI Reference Model is a guide. It is a gauge against which implementations of communication protocols from varying computer architectures can be compared. The communication protocols from the TCP/IP protocol suite can be "mapped" to the layers of the OSI Reference Model. For example, it's common to say that the Internet Protocol (IP) operates at Layer 3, or the Network Layer, and Transmission Control Protocol (TCP) operates at Layer 4, or the Transport Layer. The OSI Reference Model is not to be confused with the OSI protocols. The OSI protocols — just like the TCP/IP protocols — are specific communication protocols with functions corresponding to the various layers of the OSI Reference Model.

Chapter 2 defined the message component of a communication model used in this book as the packets with user or administrative data that routers exchange. Packets are the vehicles of communication at the Network Layer of the OSI Reference Model. Communication protocols that operate at the Network Layer govern the creation and behavior of packets. See Figure 3.1 for a graphical (perhaps humorous) representation of the OSI Reference Model.

In Figure 3.1, a couple of computer users are trying to communicate across the Internet. Both users are sitting in front of their workstations, which in the OSI jargon are considered to be the *end systems*. On the Internet, one user's end system can be separated from another user's end system by any number of routers. In the OSI jargon a router is an *intermediate system* (IS). The functionality of an end system spans all seven layers of the OSI Reference Model. This means that an end system implements the communication protocols corresponding to all the layers of the model. The functionality of a router as shown in Figure 3.1 extends to the level of the Network Layer (Layer 3).

User data originates in a user application on an end system. Think of the user applications as being "on top" (or above) the highest layer of the OSI Reference Model (which, incidentally, is called the Applications Layer because it directly supports user applications). Follow the flow of data between the two users as indicated by the dotted line with the arrows. First, data originating at the sending end system descends through all the protocol layers to the Physical Layer. Then, the data ascends to the Network Layer in an intermediate system or a router, before it descends back to the Physical Layer in the same intermediate system. Then the data ascends through all the protocol layers at the receiving end system to be ultimately received by the end user's application. Why all this hoopla? Blame it on packet switching! Packets with user data need help from the intermediate systems (routers) to deliver the data to their destinations. Typically, there are many intermediate systems that user data will cross going through the Internet, not just one as shown in Figure 3.1.

FIGURE 3.1 *Graphical representation of the OSI Reference Model*

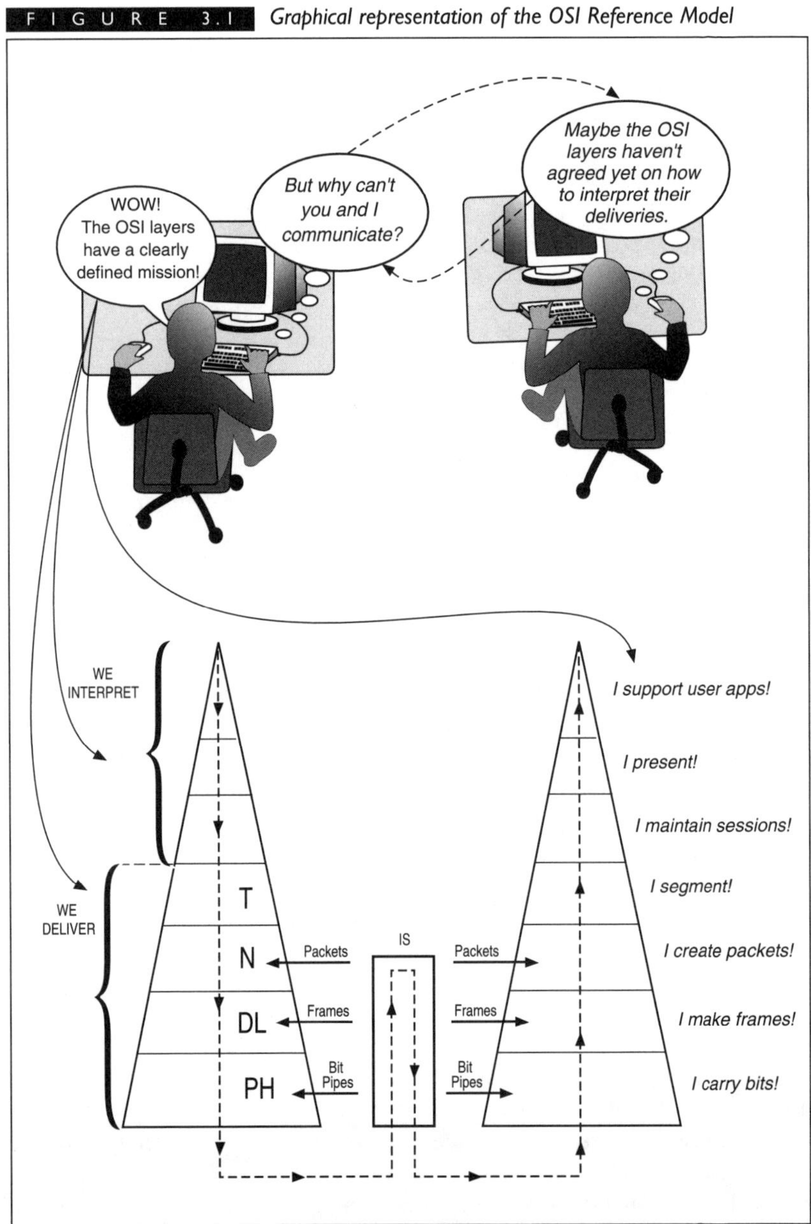

Each OSI layer is responsible for many communication functions. Figure 3.1 shows the OSI layers proclaiming one of the functions that they perform. It's part of their mission statement. Additionally, the bottom four layers are collectively referred to as the ***internetworking layers***, while the top three layers are referred to as the ***interoperability layers***. The primary responsibility of the internetworking layers (router functionality is covered by these layers) is to deliver data from one end system to another. But it's not enough simply to deliver the user data from one end system to another through a series of routers. Data must be meaningfully interpreted. The meaningful interpretation of the data is the responsibility of the top three layers of the OSI Reference Model.

It's just like writing a book. If you write a book that no one can understand, you've done something. You've delivered a message. The question is, so what? You might as well have written the book in a language that's spoken on Jupiter that no one on planet Earth understands. It's not enough for data to be delivered between the end systems. Data must be correctly interpreted at each end system for effective communication to take place. The interpretation part is the responsibility of the higher layers of the OSI Reference Model, which are not discussed in this book. There is enough going on at the internetworking layer (the Internet plumbing layers) to keep you busy for the remainder of this chapter and beyond.

It does happen on occasion (wish it was really only occasional) that users are not able to communicate across the Internet. Has it ever happened to you? If you are determined to blame someone when you find yourself in that predicament, just refer to Figure 3.1. Look at how many communication layers there are and how many interfaces between the layers there are. Then multiply this by the number of routers between you and the end system you are trying to reach. Add good fortune with finding the OSI layer responsible for your misfortune. This process is called ***troubleshooting***. Dealing with one layer is enough for now.

The Network Layer

Functions at the Network Layer were discussed lightly in the travel analogy in Chapter 1. These functions are implemented through communication protocols operating at the Network Layer. The four categories of protocols operating at the network layer are as follows:

- Routable protocols
- Routing protocols

- Feedback/flow-control protocols
- Address resolution protocols

Representatives of these protocols are discussed in the context of Internet routing in the remaining sections of this chapter and in Chapter 4.

Routable protocols

For routing to take place, a routable protocol is needed at the network layer of a protocol stack. IP has emerged as the most popular routable protocol on the Internet. It is also gaining popularity in private networks because it is supported in all major operating systems (such as UNIX, NetWare, and Windows NT). However, IP is not the only routable protocol around. Others include NetWare's Internet Packet Exchange (IPX), Appletalk's Datagram Delivery Protocol (DDP), and Banyan's VINES Internet Protocol (VIP), to name just a few.

At a minimum, every routable protocol must support the following three functions:

- package user data and the overhead from the higher-layer protocols into packets
- supply each packet with the logical addresses of its origin and destination
- identify the packet contents

These functions and others are discussed in the context of IP.

IP packaging

IP receives the user data and the overhead from the higher-layer protocols and packages it all into packets by prepending it with a *header*. The IP header (which, from the perspective of the user data becomes the "extra baggage") is the Network Layer overhead. The IP header contains in it all of the information needed to support the remaining IP functions. The IP packaging process is shown in Figure 3.2

FIGURE 3.2 *IP packages user data and the overhead from higher-layer protocols into packets*

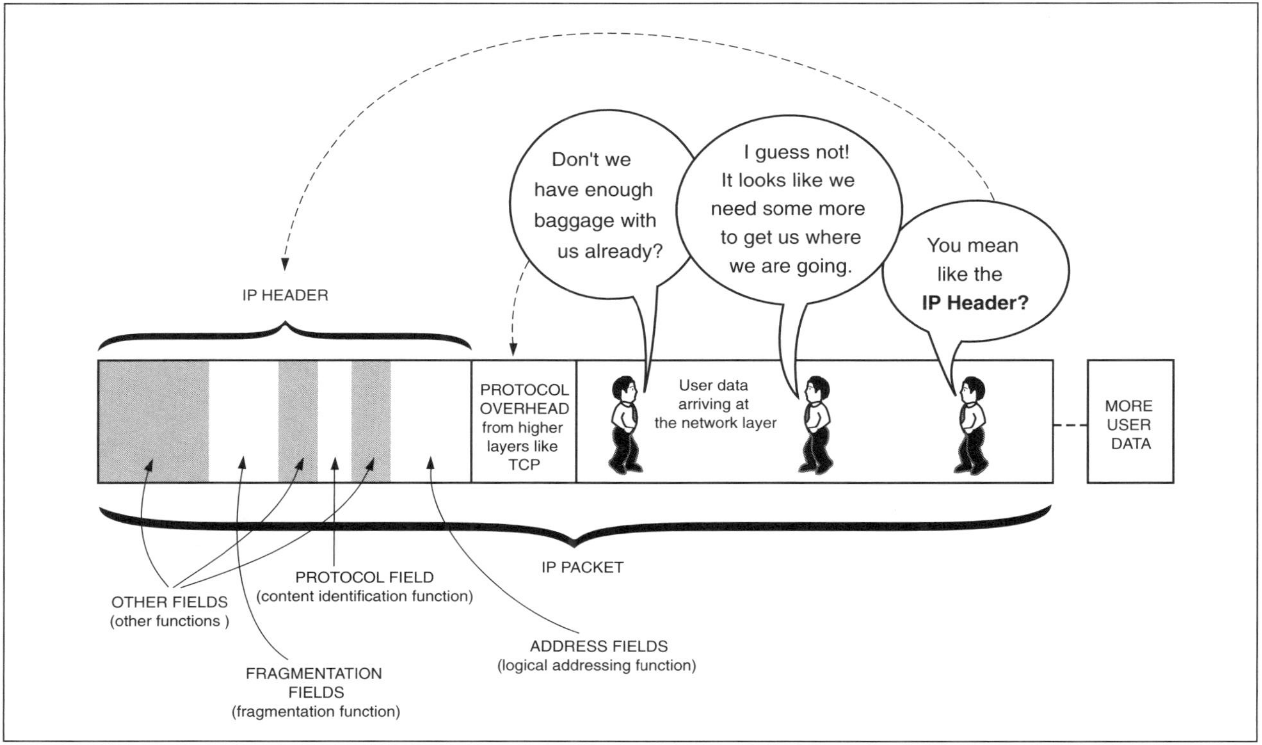

IP addressing

IPv4 addresses are most commonly represented with a dotted-decimal notation. A binary address space of 32 bits is divided into four groups of 8 bits each. Each group of 8 bits is then converted to a decimal number. When the decimal numbers are joined together with dots, you have a familiar representation such as 192.168.33.1. These logical addresses are assigned to the physical interfaces on computers and routers participating in IP networks. The source and destination addresses in an IP packet header represent, respectively, the IP addresses assigned to the Network Interface Cards (NICs) on the computers originating and receiving an IP packet. Figure 3.2 shows the location of the IP addresses in the IP header.

The 32-bit IP address space is divided into two parts: the *network portion* and the *host portion*. IP addresses are also assigned to address classes as a function of the size of their network portion. Table 3.1 summarizes the IP addressing scheme and shows the possible number of networks and hosts in each class.

IP packet content identification

The *protocol* field in the IP header supports the function of identifying the IP packet contents. The value in the *protocol* field allows IP to determine what to do with the packet contents when a packet arrives at its final destination.

In the example shown in Figure 3.2, the IP packet contains the overhead (header) from the higher layer Transport Layer protocol TCP, followed by user data from any TCP/IP application (such as TELNET, FTP, or the Word Wide Web). However, when we look at the IP packet from the perspective of the user data, the TCP header precedes the IP header (the user data was already "saddled" with the TCP header before IP got hold of both of them for packaging into packets).

When the TCP header separates the IP header from the user data as shown in Figure 3.2, the *protocol* field in the IP header identifies TCP as the packet content. From IP's perspective, it's TCP that's inside of the packet. IP is not directly aware of the kind of user data that's inside of the packet that it created. Think of IP as the creator and carrier of a package (packet) without fully knowing what's inside of it. IP is isolated from the real packet contents (user data) by another layer of packaging (the TCP header).

TABLE 3.1 *Summary of Ipv4 Address Formatsand Values*

CLASS	NUMBER OF BITS RESERVED: VALUE OF THE RESERVED BITS IN BINARY	NUMBER OF BITS IN NET ID – NUMBER OF RESERVED BITS = NUMBER OF BITS AVAILABLE FOR NET ID ADDRESSES	MAXIMUM NUMBER OF NET IDS	VALUES OF THE FIRST OCTET IN DECIMAL	NUMBER OF BITS IN HOST ID	MAXIMUM NUMBER OF HOSTS PER NET ID	DEFAULT SUBNET MASK
A	1:0	8 – 1 = 7	$2^7 - 2 = 126$	1 – 126	24	$2^{24} - 2 = 16{,}777{,}214$	255.0.0.0
B	2:10	16 – 2 = 14	$2^{14} - 1 = 16{,}383$	128 – 191	16	$2^{16} - 2 = 65{,}536$	255.255.0.0
C	3:110	24 – 3 = 21	$2^{21} - 1 = 2{,}097{,}151$	192 – 223	8	$2^8 - 2 = 254$	255.255.255.0
D	4:1110	Reserved for multicast addresses					
E	4:1111	Reserved for future use					

When the IP packet from Figure 3.2 arrives at its final destination, IP passes it for further processing to the destination's TCP, rather than to the destination's application. IP passes the packet contents to the destination's TCP because the *protocol* field will identify TCP as the packet occupant. It will be up to TCP to identify the application that needs to receive the user data. TCP uses the *port* field in the TCP header to identify the applications. At the TCP level (Transport Layer), the *port* field performs a similar function to what the *protocol* field performs at the IP level (Network Layer).

Protocols such as Open Shortest Path First (OSPF) and Internet Control Message Protocol (ICMP) use IP directly without any overhead from the Transport Layer. When IP encapsulates the OSPF or ICMP messages directly, the value of the *protocol* field in the IP header identifies OSPF or ICMP as the packet occupants. RFC 1700 (see RFC 1700, Appendix A) lists the well-known assigned numbers in the Internet protocols, including the values of the IP *protocol* field.

IPv4, which at this time is the predominantly used version of IP on the Internet, supports additional functions: fragmentation, type of service, error checking of the header, and the preventing of packets caught in a routing loop from forever circulating on the Internet.

Fragmentation is a function that supports the breakup of a large IP packet into smaller fragments, which are then placed into the smaller Data-Link Layer frames. For reference, the maximum size of an IP packet is 65,535 octets, whereas the payload portion of "Ethernet" frames varies from 1,492 to 1,500 octets. "Ethernet" in this context is used in reference to Ethernet_II, 802.3/2 and Ethernet_SNAP frames. Frames on the WAN links can be even smaller.

Initial fragmentation of large IP packets that can't fit into the Data-Link Layer frames is performed by a host where the packets originate. Fragmentation can also be performed by routers that the packets cross as they make their way to their destinations. A router performs fragmentation if it receives a packet that it can't fit into just one Data-Link Layer frame on one of its outgoing interfaces.

When a large IP packet is fragmented, each fragment becomes a smaller packet with its own IP header. The information in the headers of the smaller packets (or fragments) indicates that all of the fragments are part of the larger packet. Four fields inside the IP header are required to support fragmentation, and years of experience with the Internet have convinced TCP/IP developers that the direct support for the fragmentation function in the IP header carries a price tag in terms of performance and implementation.

The proposed new version of IP, IPv6 still supports fragmentation, but it does so through a fragmentation extension header rather than the use of fields in the base header. IPv6 routers can also reject (drop) oversized packets and use ICMP to notify the packet's origin of that decision. *Oversized packets* are packets that a router can't fit into the underlying Data-Link Layer frames on its outgoing interfaces.

For more details on remaining IPv4 functions see RFC 791 (RFC 791 in Appendix A). Also see Commer, Appendix B for an excellent reference on TCP/IP.

Routing protocols

Routing protocols are the largest group of protocols operating at the Network Layer in the TCP/IP suite. They are also the most complex communication protocols. A vast portion of Chapter 4 is dedicated to a very technical discussion of just three representatives from this group; Routing Information Protocol (RIP), OSPF, and Border Gateway Protocol (BGP).

Feedback/flow-control protocols

The feedback and rudimentary flow-control protocol that operates at the network layer in the TCP/IP protocol suite is the ICPM. It is specified in RFC 792 (see RFC 792, Appendix A) and it's discussed here in the context of an overall routing equation.

Imagine yourself as a router on the Internet that's getting overwhelmed by the number of IP packets you receive for forwarding to their destinations. What do you do? Well, of course, you send an ICMP message to the originators of the packets telling them to "slow down." That's an ICMP *source quench message type*.

How about if you are the last router in the communication chain between two end systems? You are responsible for the final leg of an IP packet's journey — from you to the receiving end system. However, you discover that the end system identified by the destination address in the IP packet header does not exist. What do you do? Well, of course, you send an ICMP message to the source of the packet telling it that the packet it originated could not be delivered. That's an ICMP *destination unreachable message type*.

The popular TCP/IP PING utility is also an implementation of a couple ICMP message types, the *echo request* and *echo reply*. How about if a packet got lost in the Internet and it has been circulating in a routing loop for a while? IP packets have a Time to Live (TTL) field inside of them that is decremented by one by each router that a packet crosses. When the value of TTL decreases to 0, packets are discarded. Suppose that you as a router receive a packet with a TTL of 1. What do you do? After decrementing the TTL to 0, you send the packet to the bit bucket and send an ICMP message to the originator of the packet telling it that the TTL value in the packet reached 0 before the packet could be delivered to its final destination. That's ICMP *time exceeded message type*.

There are many other ICMP message types. These representative ones illustrate that feedback is useful and appreciated in communication between computers, just like it is useful in communication between humans. Feedback helps the overall effectiveness of a communication process.

Address resolution protocols

For any network to function properly, the devices that are participating in the exchange of information on that network must have unique addresses both at the Network Layer and at the Data-Link Layer. It's no different than a group of people at a party. Suppose that the women and all the men have the same names. You come in and, spotting a couple you know, you greet them by their first names. Of course, you don't realize that all the other couples in the room have the same first names. What will the reaction be? Probably quite a few other faces are going to look at you, resulting in some confusion. It's the same thing on computer networks. Duplicate addresses cause confusion and problems.

Unique addresses, however, are not a sufficient condition for a network to function properly. An IP packet header does not carry in it the Data-Link Layer hardware address of its destination. In only carries the IP address of the destination. It's like going to a party to meet someone, but you only know this person's last name. The party protocol requires that you know the person's full name before you can fully communicate. What will you do? Somehow you must match the last name you have to the person's first name.

Now, put yourself in a position of router R in Figure 3.3. This router receives an IP packet destined for station 192.168.33.3 on network 192.168.33.0. Effectively the router knows the station's last name. The rules of communication on a computer network require the router to encapsulate the packet into a Data-Link Layer frame for transmission to the final destination. However, the Data-Link Layer frame requires the hardware address of the destination. What's the router to do? It must somehow figure out the hardware address of the destination. This process is called *address resolution* or *mapping*.

FIGURE 3.3 *ARP example*

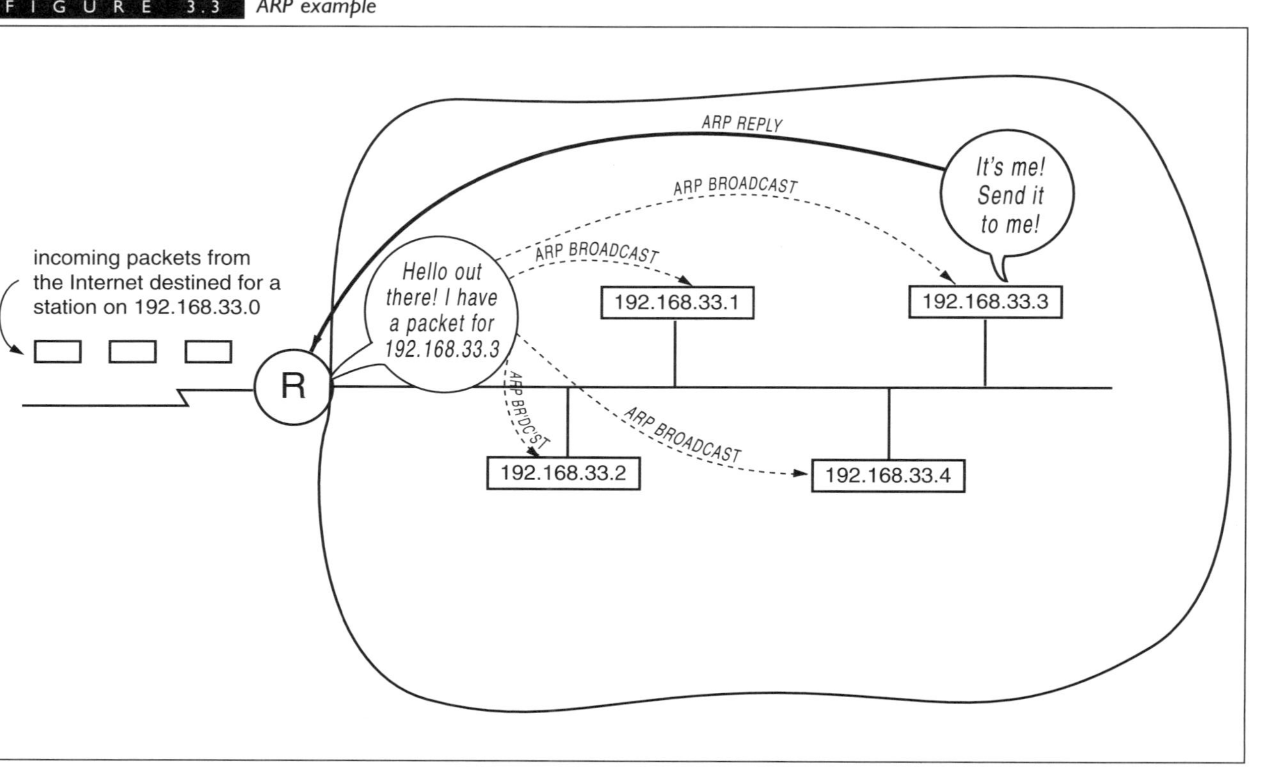

In the TCP/IP protocol suite, the mapping between the IP addresses and the Data-Link Layer hardware addresses is the responsibility of the Address Resolution Protocol (ARP). ARP does assume a broadcast-capable Data-Link Layer technology, but most of the local-area network (LAN) technologies are broadcast-capable.

Continuing with the party example, the last name of the person you must meet is a little strange — it's an IP address of 192.168.33.3 — but that does not bother you at all. You come in to the party and you decide to create a little commotion. You yell (that's ***broadcasting***) so that everyone can hear you, "Hello out there, I need to speak to a person with a last name of 192.168.33.3." The person with this strange name responds "It's me." Now, the two of you can communicate.

That, in essence is how ARP works. Figure 3.3 depicts a router sending out an ARP broadcast. An ARP broadcast is a Data-Link Layer broadcast frame that has in its payload the destination IP address from the packet the router has just received. All the stations on that network must respond to the hardware broadcast by examining the broadcast frame's payload or content. Upon that examination, only one station realizes that the frame's payload includes its IP address. This station now responds to the router with an *ARP reply*. The ARP reply is a Data-Link Layer unicast frame that includes the destination station's hardware address, which is what the router was after in the first place. When router R receives the ARP reply (indicated by a solid arrow in Figure 3.3), it can then forward to that station the packet it has received for it from someplace on the Internet. And if that packet happens to be a request by you for access to a Web server installed on that station, there is hope now that your request will be fulfilled.

Are We Ready to Route Yet?

When the categories of protocols are implemented in a computer network environment, routing is possible. However, we have not yet explored in any detail the most complex category of protocols operating at the Network Layer: the routing protocols themselves. That's Chapter 4.

PART II

TCP/IP Routing: Protocols, Configurations, and Hardware

CHAPTER 4

TCP/IP Routers: The Workhorses of the Internet

Internet routers facilitate your cyber trips through the cyber space. Routers move your packets along to enable them to reach the most remote locations of the Internet. Without the Internet routers, the size of the Internet would be limited to being a single network. Routers enable the Internet to grow and expand. Today, the Internet is a collection of tens of thousands of computer networks with no end in sight to its growth.

However, when you look at a powered-down router, it's no more then an expensive chunk of metal. What makes routers tick is the implementation of the routing protocols they support. The intricacies of the routing protocols enable us to understand what takes place behind the scenes of cyber travel.

Routing Protocols: The Social Creatures

The primary function of Internet routers is to direct IP packets with user data to their correct destinations. To do this, routers exchange *administrative packets* with routing information. As the Internet grows, and the number of routers and networks in the Internet increases, the volume of the administrative packets exchanged by Internet routers continues to increase. As this discussion examines some of the most popular routing protocols, you may be perplexed by their complexity. This complexity stems from a singular objective on the part of the protocol designers and implementers: to make routing protocols as efficient and as scalable as possible.

Routing protocol efficiency is related to the usage of network bandwidth and the usage of central processing unit (CPU) cycles in a router. A *bandwidth-efficient routing protocol* minimizes the administrative exchanges between routers while still allowing them to maintain an accurate awareness of how to get to any location in an internetwork. A *CPU-efficient routing protocol* will not place undue demands upon the processing power of a router to maintain its tables and make forwarding decisions. An ideal routing protocol will be both bandwidth-efficient and CPU-efficient. However, ideal routing protocols don't exist in a real world of Internet routing.

A *scalable routing protocol* will be efficient in any size internetwork, big or small. Considering the phenomenal growth rate of the Internet, the challenge of developing scalable routing protocols is a serious one.

Routing protocols are divided into two broad groups:

- Interior Gateway Protocols (IGPs)
- Exterior Gateway Protocols (EGPs)

The IGPs are routing protocols intended to route within organizational internetworks. Example organizations include a university, a government research lab, a commercial corporation, or an ISP. Protocols such as RIP, OSPF, or Cisco's Interior Gateway Routing Protocol (IGRP) are examples of IGPs. They allow routers within an organization to be aware of the structure of the organizational internetwork (how to reach any destination within that internetwork). When many organizations come together to form a larger internetwork (such as the Internet), there is no need for all routers from one organization to know about every router and network in other organizations. In fact, for many organizations, it would be a serious security threat if the details of their internal internetworks were shared with everybody else on the outside.

Also, consider the impact on the size of the routing tables if every organization connected to the Internet shared the details of their internal networks with every other organization. The Internet routers would choke very quickly from the information overload in their routing tables.

The question that must be answered is this: How do organizations running IGPs internally communicate with one other and how do their routers maintain manageable-sized routing tables? The answer is through EGPs and through the use of default routes. EGPs introduce hierarchy into Internet routing. The most commonly used EGP in the Internet is Border Gateway Protocol (BGP) version 4, discussed in the section, "BGP: The Long-Distance Runner," later in this chapter.

RIP: The Broadcaster

RIP's legacy endures. With its origins dating back to the networking research done at Xerox's Palo Alto Research Center (PARC) in the seventies (when the Internet did not exist and the ARPAnet was still in its infancy), this ubiquitous routing protocol is not quite ready to *Rest In Peace*.

Xerox's Palo Alto Research Center was founded in the heart of Silicon Valley in 1970 and charged to be the architect of Information Age. For more information, point your Web browser to `http://www.parc.xerox.com/AboutPARC.html`.

The PARC-developed RIP was formally defined in the *Internet Transport Protocols* publication in 1981 as part of the Xerox Network Service (XNS) protocol suite. The IP RIP, the IPX RIP, the Appletalk's Routing Table Maintenance Protocol (RTMP), and several other routing protocols are the direct decedents of the Xerox RIP — each with its own minor modifications to make the protocols incompatible with one another.

The IP RIP was popularized in 1982 when it was implemented as a UNIX daemon *routed* (pronounced "route dee") and, along with the other protocols from the TCP/IP suite, was incorporated into the Berkeley Software Distribution (BSD) 4.2 release of UNIX. Beginning with the BSD 4.2 release in 1982, UNIX and TCP/IP became inexorably linked. When ARPAnet began a formal transition to the TCP/IP suite from the aging Network Control Protocol (NCP) on January 1, 1983, RIP's fate as the Internet's most popular routing protocol was sealed. However, it was six years before the IP RIP was formally specified and approved as an Internet standard in 1988 as RFC 1058 (see RFC 1058, Appendix A).

The internetworking environment of the early 1980s was a far cry from the Internet of today. RIP is easy to configure and works well for small networks with simple topologies. However, RIP lacks scalability and cannot be considered a viable routing protocol for today's Internet. RFC 1923 (see RFC 1923, Appendix A) has declared the RIPv1 standard, RFC 1058, as a historical document and recommends that RIPv1 "only be used in simple topologies, with simple reachability. It may be used by any site which uses fixed subnetting internally, and either uses a default route to deal with external traffic or is not connected to the global Internet or to other organizations."

The problems of RIPv1 are well known and documented. The slow convergence caused by the *count to infinity* problem, lack of security, the maximum hop count of 15, the use of broadcasting, lack of support for variable-length subnetting, and very poor support for Classless Interdomain Routing (CIDR), or *supernetting*. Despite of all these shortcomings, the appeal of this simple distance-vector algorithm has led to the development of RIPv2 specified initially in RFC 1388 (see RFC 1388, Appendix A). Within less than two years RFC 1388 was obsoleted by the current RIPv2 standard specified in RFC 1723 (see RFC 1723, Appendix A). Work is also in progress on RIPng (RIP new generation) proposed in RFC 2080 (see RFC 2080, Appendix A). RIPng will operate with the new proposed version of IP, IPv6.

Consider the basics of RIP operation, since the protocol (despite all its shortcomings) is still supported (almost by default) by all router vendors. Understanding the basics of RIP operations and its shortcomings also facilitates a better understanding of the more complex protocols that explored later.

RIP routers communicate with each other by using broadcasting. Imagine yourself addressing a group of people. When you are talking to the entire group, you are *broadcasting*. When you divide the group into smaller subgroups and you are addressing only one of the subgroups, you are *multicasting*. When you single out a specific individual in a group and you are addressing only that individual you are *unicasting*.

Translate this analogy into network terms. When a RIP router sends out an update, the RIP process creates an IP packet with a destination broadcast address of 255.255.255.255. If the underlying Data-Link Layer technology supports hardware broadcasting, this broadcast IP packet carrying RIP updates is translated into a hardware-level broadcast (a Data-Link Layer frame with a hardware destination address of all 1s, which is equivalent to a broadcast).

NOTE

RIP updates are not actually encapsulated directly inside of IP. RIP interacts first with the connectionless Transport Layer protocol, UDP, which passes the RIP update and its own header for packaging to IP. In contrast to RIP, OSPF updates are carried directly inside of IP packets without the overhead of a transport protocol.

When a hardware broadcast resulting from a RIP update goes out on a network, the NICs in all the computers and routers on that network must respond to it and pass the broadcast frame to their device drivers, which link the NICs to the operating system software. This means that the operating system on all devices (not just the RIP routers) must get involved in determining whether the broadcast frame is really meant for them.

The advantage of broadcasting is that a RIP router can send one broadcast packet and all the other RIP routers attached to the same network will receive it. Herein also lies the disadvantage of broadcasting. RIP routers are not the only devices on the network. Some other devices on the network could care less about what the RIP routers have to say to one another. Devices that do not need to act on the RIP broadcast packets are interrupted unnecessarily.

One way to minimize the interruptions to other network devices from the RIP broadcast traffic is to use static routes and the RIP *neighbor* configuration command. However, these techniques require a greater level of knowledge and involvement on the part of network administrators to configure a RIP routing environment. Static routing also requires manual reconfiguration in cases of router failures.

Static routing has its advantages, however. As discussed in Chapter 2, routers are responsible for transmitting two types of packets: packets with user data, and administrative packets with routing information (which enables them to create and maintain their internal tables). Transmission of any information between devices on a computer network translates into the use of network bandwidth. When the volume of administrative packets between routers resulting from dynamic routing continues to increase, there is less and less available network bandwidth for packets with user data. From the user point of view, this translates into much-dreaded delays in the network. Static routing eliminates the administrative packets between routers. However, it's the network administrator who effectively becomes the traffic director, rather than the routers.

To explore how RIP routers dynamically create and maintain their routing tables, consider Figure 4.1. In a network where there are multiple paths from source to destination, RIP routing tables depend on the order in which the routers were powered up.

NOTE

All IP addresses used in this book are from the three blocks of IP addresses reserved for private networks by Internet Assigned Numbers Authority (IANA) as specified in RFC 1918 (see RFC 1918, Appendix A). This is intended to avoid the use of addresses in the book as examples that may actually be in use on the Internet.

In the example in Figure 4.1, assume that networks 192.168.33.0, 192.168.34.0, 192.168.35.0, and 192.168.36.0 are Ethernet, and the networks 192.168.40.0, 192.168.6.0, and 192.168.41.0 are point-to-point T1 links. A user on network 192.168.33.0 has at least four possible ways (routes) to get to the server on network 192.168.36.0. However, only one of these routes will be used, even though all the routers participate in the dynamic RIP exchanges.

When router RA is powered up after it has been properly configured with the RIP process and the IP addresses on its interfaces, it becomes aware of the two networks (192.168.33.0 and 192.168.34.0) to which it is physically connected. Router RA's table looks like this:

```
Destination         Next hop            Cost
192.168.33.0        Direct              0
192.168.34.0        Direct              0
```

Next, router RB is powered up. Its table looks like this:

```
Destination         Next hop            Cost
192.168.34.0        Direct              0
192.168.35.0        Direct              0
```

FIGURE 4.1 *Example of RIP routing environment*

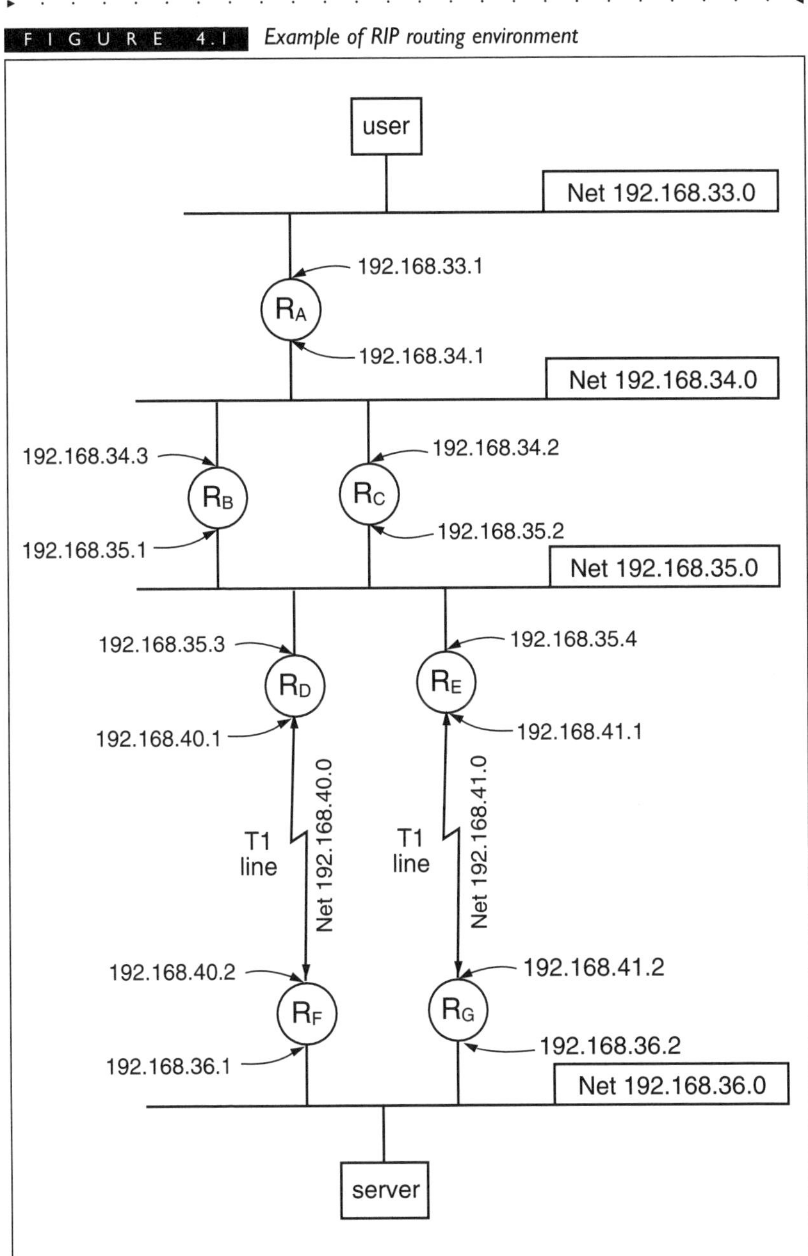

Now, when RB broadcasts its table on all its interfaces (on networks 192.168.34.0 and 192.168.35.0), router RA receives it and starts comparing it with the entries it has in its own table. Router RA ignores the entry for reaching network 192.168.34.0 because it is already directly connected to it. However, RA does not have anything in its table about reaching network 192.168.35.0. So, after the update from RB is processed by RA, RA's table looks like this:

```
Destination         Next hop           Cost
192.168.33.0        Direct             0
192.168.34.0        Direct             0
192.168.35.0        192.168.34.3       1
```

The next hop in the new table entry in RA's table is the IP address of RB's interface. If router RC comes online right now, it will have the same table as the initial RB's table. When RC broadcasts its table on all the interfaces and RA receives it, RA ignores all the entries in it because it is already directly connected to network 192.168.34.0 and it can reach network 192.168.35.0 through router RB at the same cost as through router RC. When a route advertisement in RIP comes in at a cost equal to an existing route, it is ignored. The effect is that router RA will not forward any user packets to router RC unless router RB goes down.

This process could be carried on for the remaining routers on the T1 links. Assuming the power-up sequence of RA, RB, RC, RD, RF, RE, RG, the final routing table for RA looks like this:

```
Destination         Next hop           Cost
192.168.33.0        Direct             0
192.168.34.0        Direct             0
192.168.35.0        192.168.34.3       1
192.168.36.0        192.168.34.3       3
192.168.40.0        192.168.34.3       2
192.168.41.0        192.168.34.3       2
```

What can be detected here is that, even though a second way out exists for router RA through 192.168.34.2 to reach all of the other networks, it will not be used because it is of equal cost as something already in the table.

This is one of the shortcomings of RIP. When multiple paths of equal cost from source to destination exist (in RIP, this translates into the destination being the same number of hops, or routers away from the source), RIP routers install and maintain only one path. The other paths are ignored. This effectively means that in Figure 4.1 even though there are two parallel paths, only one will be used to carry user traffic from the user on network 192.168.33.0 to the server on network 192.168.36.0.

RIP routers transmit their entire routing tables. It does not matter whether the table has changed or not. Every 30 seconds, the contents of the table are placed into IP broadcast packets and broadcast onto the networks to which the routers are connected.

RIP broadcasts can be compared to what takes place at some airports. Some airports offer "moving sidewalks" to help weary travelers with walking between distant terminal locations when changing planes. Every few seconds, a voice says, "This moving sidewalk is for your traveling convenience only; please stand to the right in a single file so that others may pass you on the left." This voice comes out with regularity, regardless of whether anyone is on the moving sidewalk, whether those who are on the sidewalk are standing on the left or the right, or whether some aspiring gymnast is using the sidewalk's rail to walk on his or her eyebrows. So, in a sense, it is very inefficient use of the available bandwidth (the air waves). At the same time, however, even though it may be annoying to some people, it certainly is one way to solve a problem and to keep everybody in line about how to use a moving sidewalk.

It would require a considerable more amount of intelligence to constantly monitor the sidewalk and make a decision whether someone was using it improperly, which would necessitate the repetition of the message.

As the number of networks and routers in an internetwork continues to grow, the size of a routing table in a RIP router increases. Transmitting the entire routing table every 30 seconds places increasing pressure upon the available network bandwidth.

The details of router configuration are discussed in Chapter 5. Suffice it to say that every interface on the router belongs to a different network.

OSPF: The Concerned Neighbor

The OSPF routing protocol was developed by an Internet Engineering Task Force (IETF) in the late 1980s in response to the shortcomings of RIP and a need for a more scalable and efficient routing protocol.

OSPF routers use multicasting instead of broadcasting to exchange routing information with one another. In contrast to RIP, OSPF routers do not transmit routing tables between themselves. Instead they use 5 different message types to exchange information that enables them to derive their routing tables.

All 5 OSPF messages are carried in IP packets with a protocol field of 89 in the IP header.

The five message types that OSPF routers exchange are

1. Hello
2. Database descriptions
3. Link-state requests
4. Link-state updates
5. Link-state acknowledgments

The OSPF message that carries information from which the OSPF routing tables are derived is the link-state update message (type 4). The contents of this message type are referred to as link-state advertisements (LSAs) and are discussed in detail in a later section. The five different LSAs must not be confused with the five OSPF message types. The LSAs create a link-state database from which OSPF routers derive their routing tables through the use of the Diijakstra algorithm.

Comparing RIP to OSPF is like comparing a twin-engine turbo prop to a Boeing 747. Both are planes, both get off the ground and are capable of flying and of landing. However, when it comes to the propulsion mechanics, speed, flying altitude, flying range, and passenger-carrying capacity, they are radically different. Both RIP and OSPF route packets with user data by directing them to their destination through an internetwork. OSPF and RIP differ radically in their approaches to how routers maintain a sense of direction in an internetwork.

OSPF is called the "concerned neighbor" because an OSPF router, at the very first stage of its operation, multicasts "hello" messages on all its interfaces to all other OSPF routers on the network (see Figure 4.2).

If router RD in Figure 4.2 is multicasting hello packets and router RE is also multicasting hello packets, the two routers figure out that they are neighbors. Being a neighbor in OSPF parlance means that two routers are directly connected to the same physical network and can talk to each other without having to go through another router. In the example in Figure 4.2 if all the routers are multicasting hello packets, there will be many neighbor pairs in that internetwork. From Router RD's point of view, it will acquire routers RB, RC, RE, and RF as its neighbors. Router RC will acquire RA, RB, RD, and RE as its neighbors. As an exercise, you should write down all the neighbors of each router.

FIGURE 4.2 *Example of two OSPF routers multicasting "hello" packets*

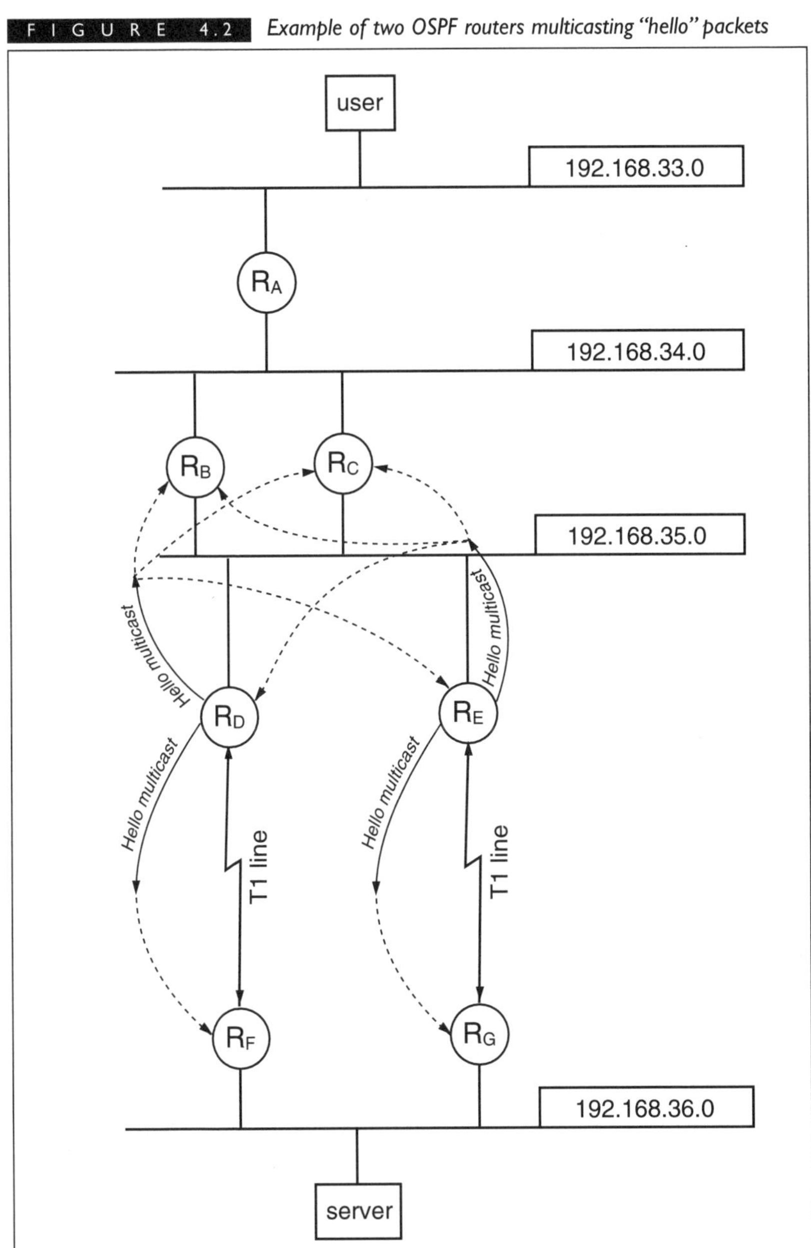

When an OSPF router figures out that it has neighbors, it attempts to establish a relationship with them. There are seven levels (or stages) of a relationship between OSPF routers. The relationships range from a *down state* to a *fully adjacent state*. In a down state, two neighbor routers can't talk to each other at all; in a fully adjacent state, they can exchange all five types of OSPF messages. Depending on a position and configuration of an OSPF router in an OSPF internetwork, it will be generating one or more of the five LSAs and multicasting them in a link-state update message to its neighbors in the internetwork. When all the OSPF routers in an internetwork participate in exchanging LSAs, each one of them ends up with the same database of *links* or a *topological map* of the network.

Just think about it. If you were given the names of all of the different streets in a city with the coordinates of their beginning and ending points, and also with some characteristics about them (how wide they are, if they are paved, and so on), you would be able to create for yourself a map of that city. It would take effort. However, now armed with a map, you can help anyone who passes by asking for directions.

Now put yourself into the position of an OSPF router. When it has gathered all the information about the internetwork from the LSAs, it can derive from that database a routing table that it then uses to direct packets carrying user data to their destinations.

However, just as conditions change in a big city (streets get blocked by construction, accidents, or even strolling ducks), so it is with routers and network cables. Power outages can shut down routers, accidentally pulled or cut cables can disconnect routers from a network and other routers, on-the-fly misconfigurations by network administrators can result in changes to the network. When these kind of events occur, routers affected by them experience changes in their link-state databases.

Each router's link-state database must be kept up-to-date to be reliable. One of the fundamental principles in OSPF is that all routers in an OSPF internetwork must have the same link-state database. Otherwise, their view of the internetwork will be inconsistent, which can lead to routing problems. It would be just like two people in the same city, but with a different version of the city map: one current and one from several years ago. You might be in for a real trip if you asked each of them for directions to the same location.

Consequently, when an OSPF router has a relationship with a neighbor, and it does not hear anything from that neighbor for a period of time (defined as a *dead interval*), this router must conclude that there is a problem with the neighbor and declare the link over which this neighbor was reachable as no longer being "up." This scenario is also referred to as a *link transition*. The information about a link transition must be communicated and communicated fast to all the other OSPF routers in the internetwork through the link-state update message. All routers, in turn, update their link-state databases and recalculate their routing tables. The process of all of the OSPF routers in an internetwork reaching a state where they have the same link-state database is referred to as *convergence*. For an OSPF network to be effective in routing packets with user data, convergence after link transitions must be fast. In a typical OSPF network, convergence is on an order of milliseconds. OSPF areas which are discussed in the following section are a feature of OSPF that helps speed up convergence.

OSPF areas

OSPF has another feature that adds to its complexity but which also makes it a more robust and a scalable protocol. When a group of networks and routers running OSPF gets to be too big, it can be divided into *OSPF areas*, which allow OSPF networks to be organized into a hierarchical structure.

This is similar to taking a large group of people and breaking it into smaller groups. One of the groups would be a little more special than others because it would have the responsibility of interfacing with all of the remaining groups. In OSPF, responsibility falls on the *backbone area*, or area 0.0.0.0. Other OSPF areas in an OSPF internetwork do not interact directly with one another. They interact only with the backbone area (or area 0, for short). See Figure 4.3 for a graphical representation of the concept of OSPF areas.

Having areas reduces the size of the link-state database or the topological map that OSPF routers must maintain, because the requirement of having the same link-state database applies only to routers in the same area. Having a smaller database also means that a router takes less time to derive a routing table from it.

The communication between any area and the backbone area is done through routers known as Area Border Routers (ABRs). These routers have at least one interface in the backbone area and another in area(s) they are connecting to the backbone. ABRs maintain a link-state database for each area to which they are attached. OSPF areas are identified by area IDs, which have the same dotted decimal notation as IP addresses. However, area IDs are not to be confused with the IP addresses of networks and router interfaces. In practice, OSPF areas are often abbreviated to a single number (such as 1, 2, or 3, which would be equivalent to 0.0.0.1 or 0.0.0.2 or 0.0.0.3).

FIGURE 4.3 *Concept of OSPF areas*

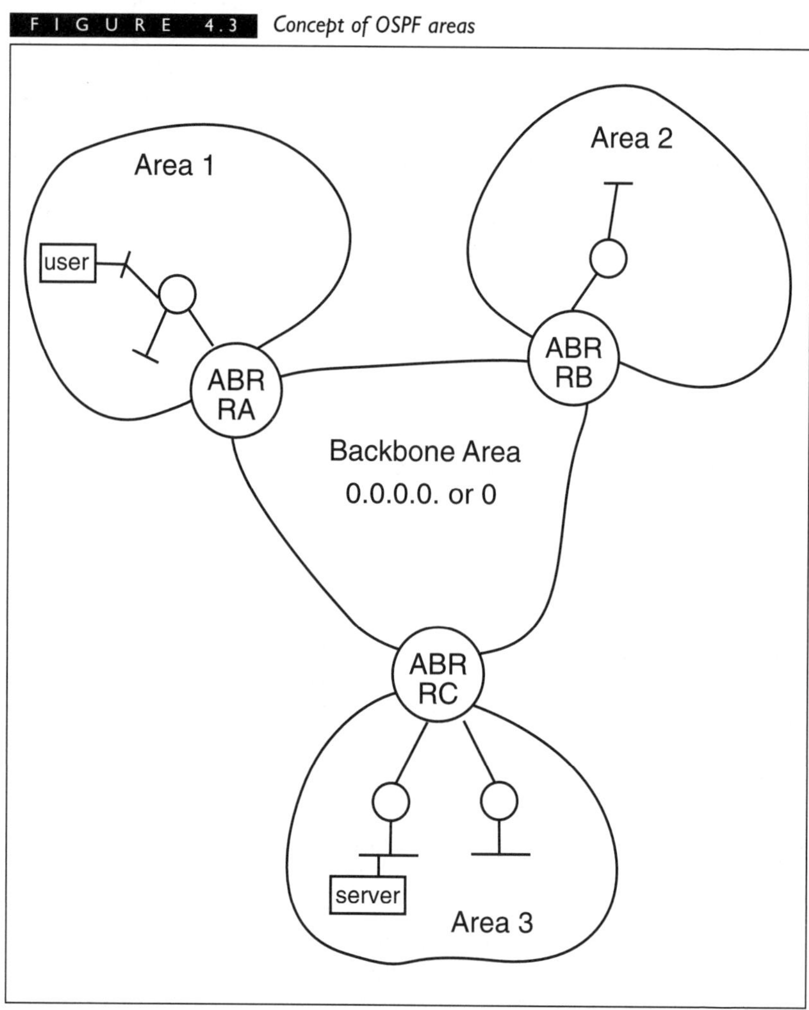

If a user in area 1 wants to get something from a server in area 3, the traffic from that user flows toward the ABR RA, from RA to RC over the backbone, and from RC to a server in area 3. Even if area 1 and 3 had a physical connection between them, the traffic between areas would flow across the backbone.

Designated routers

OSFP has additional intelligence to reduce the level of administrative traffic between routers. When multiple OSPF routers are attached to the same multiple-access broadcast network as shown in Figure 4.2 with routers RB, RC, RD, and RE all interfaced to network 192.168.35.0, OSPF takes into account that establishing full adjacencies and exchanging LSAs between all pairs of neighbors places a great deal of pressure on the network bandwidth.

Consequently, OSPF routers elect a representative from among themselves to maintain full adjacency with the other routers on that network. This representative is known as a *designated router* (DR). To allow for redundancies, a backup DR is also elected at the same time. Having a DR on a multi-access broadcast network reduces the number of communication lines or full adjacencies between routers. This results in less OSPF multicast traffic on the network. Figure 4.4 and Figure 4.5 show examples of the number of adjacencies before and after DR and a backup DR (BDR) election. In Figure 4.5 router RB was elected as DR, and router RD as the BDR.

Multiple-access broadcast networks are considered to be networks that use data-link layer technologies such as Ethernet, Token Ring, or Fiber Distributed Data Interface (FDDI). Even though OSPF routers are multicasting their messages (as opposed to broadcasting), in a situation such as that shown in Figure 4.2, just gaining access to the transmission media to multicast their messages effectively denies access to the media to all of the other devices attached to the network (such as user workstations). User workstations are not shown in Figure 4.2, but they would very likely be there in any real-world scenario.

By reducing the number of adjacencies without compromising the ability of the routers to maintain the same link-state database, OSPF routers make fewer transmissions, thus making the network more available for the most important traffic (packets with user data).

In the example with four routers in Figure 4.4 and Figure 4.5, the number of adjacencies following the DR/BDR election has been reduced only from six to five. However, as the number of routers connected to the same multiple-access broadcast network increases, the level of reduction in the number of adjacencies becomes significant. The formulas that can be used to calculate the number of adjacencies are $N*(N-1)/2$ without a DR/BDR election and $(N-1)+(N-2)$ following a DR/BDR election, where N represents the number of routers. With 10 routers, the numbers are 45 and 17, respectively, or a reduction of more than 50 percent in the number of adjacencies.

FIGURE 4.4 *Possible full adjacencies in an OSPF network before a DR/BDR election*

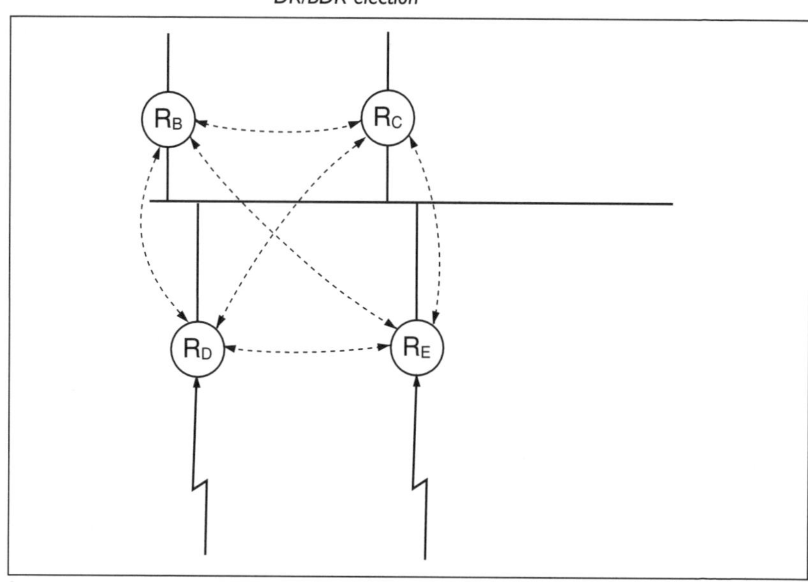

FIGURE 4.5 *Adjacencies in an OSPF network following a DR/BDR election*

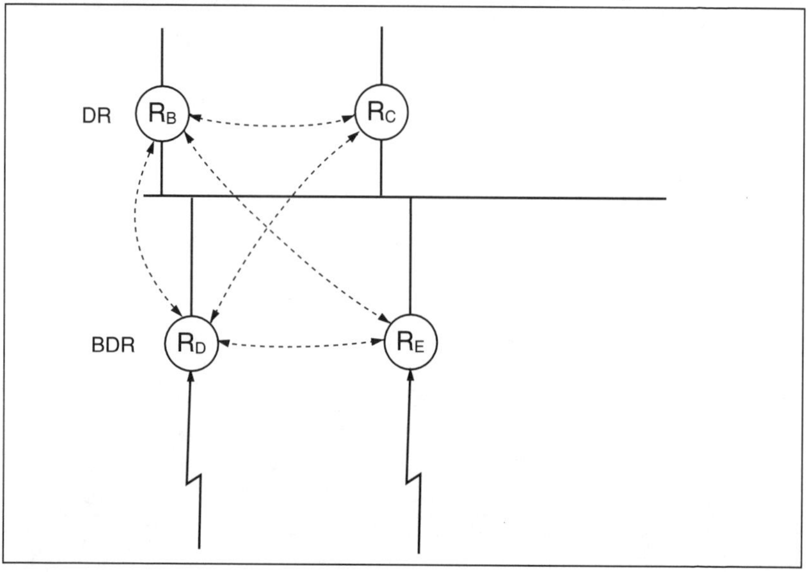

The election of a designated router and a backup designated router is simple in theory. The hello messages that routers exchange to first find and then to maintain contact with their neighbors have a priority field. The value that the priority field can assume is from 0 to 255. The priority value for an OSPF router can be set during router configuration. On a multiple-access broadcast network, the router with the highest priority is elected as a DR and a BDR becomes the router with the next-highest priority value. If there is a tie in the value of the priority field between contending routers, the router ID (IP address of one of its interfaces or a software loopback address) is used as a tiebreaker. Don't you wish it were that simple? Electing a DR and keeping it as a DR may be a bit more tricky in practice.

What happens when a designated router has been elected and another router with a higher priority value comes online? There is no automatic DR re-election. If you want the new router to become the DR, you will likely have to power off the current DR and the current BDR. Powering off routers may be permissible in an experimental lab environment, but not necessarily an easy task in a production environment.

Consider another scenario. Suppose you decided which router should be a DR and are able to force its election through the assignment of a high-priority value and a correct power-up sequence. What happens now if this router temporarily goes down and comes back up even without you as a network administrator being aware of it? The brief interval that the DR is off-line may be sufficient for the BDR to become the DR and for a new BDR to be elected. Meanwhile, if you don't check the router status, you may not even notice that the router you selected for the DR has lost its chosen status, and another router (which may be less powerful or already very busy) becomes the DR, degrading the overall network performance.

DRs and BDRs are the only routers that maintain full adjacencies with all the other routers on the same multiple-access broadcast network. *Full adjacency* means that routers not only exchange hello packets, but also link-state updates, link-state requests, link-state acknowledgments, and database-description packets. OSPF uses three sub protocols (hello, exchange, and flooding) to exchange the five OSPF packet types.

Sub protocols

The sub protocols within OSPF operate at the various stages of the relationship that OSPF routers establish with each other. It starts with the *hello sub protocol* when the routers are discovering each other. The *exchange sub protocol* kicks in when two routers are sufficiently acquainted that they want to exchange some information. Finally, the *flooding sub protocol* is used when two routers establish a full adjacency, which implies that they can exchange all five types of OSPF messages.

Hello sub protocol

The hello sub protocol in OSPF facilitates the election of DRs and BDRs and enables OSPF routers to keep track of their neighbors. The hello messages are multicast by all OSPF every hello interval, which is a very short period of time (typically in seconds). The OSPF hello message carries in it the router-priority field used in DR/BDR election, the value of the hello and dead intervals, and the router IDs of all the router's neighbors.

If, for some reason, a response does not come back from a neighbor within the dead interval, a router must proclaim its link to a neighbor as inactive and multicast an link-state update message to its other fully adjacent neighbors using the flooding sub protocol. The lack of response from a neighbor would be the lack of hello messages generated by that neighbor. The dead interval typically is some multiple of the hello interval. It's not uncommon for the dead interval to be four times the hello interval.

Exchange sub protocol

After the routers have established a certain level of neighbor relationship (known as *two-way*) using the hello sub protocol, the next step is for them to start synchronizing their link-state databases. That's where the exchange sub protocol kicks in. Using the exchange sub protocol, two OSPF routers exchange portions of the link-state records in their databases. The OSPF message type containing those partial link-state record descriptions is the database description type (or type 2). The idea behind routers exchanging partial descriptions of their link state records is to exchange just enough information to determine if any of the link-state records that a fledgling neighbor has may be of interest to the other. Link-state records from a neighbor of interest to a router are those that are different from (or simply nonexistent in) a router's own database.

When one router has determined that it has interest in the other router's link-state records, it requests them through an OSPF message type 3 (the link-state request). The complete link-state records are returned through the OSPF message type 4 (the link-state update). Doesn't it remind you of two people meeting, each striking up an initial conversation and figuring out what their interests are?

Out of the three sub protocols (flooding sub protocol is discussed next), the exchange sub protocol seems to be the most complicated, yet used the least. It is used for the initial synchronization of the link-state databases when routers are on their way to establishing a full adjacency. In stable OSPF network, the predominant OSPF-generated traffic would be from the hello message with occasional flooding of "aged" link state records using the flooding sub protocol.

Flooding sub protocol

The flooding sub protocol maintains accurate (synchronized) link-state databases between routers after the routers have established full adjacencies. The flooding sub protocol uses two OSPF message types: type 4 (the link-state update) and type 5 (the link-state acknowledgment). The flooding sub protocol is used by routers in three situations:

- *To notify their neighbors about link transitions*. This takes place almost immediately after a router becomes aware of a problem on one of its interfaces. The problem may be the absence of hello packets from a neighbor or a more physical problem such as a loss of signal because of a hardware malfunction or a power-related problem.
- *To send out periodic link-state updates, every "update" interval*. A typical value of the update interval is 30 minutes.
- *To send out link-state updates about aged link-state records*. All records in the link-state database have an *age counter*. When the age counter in a link-state record reaches a maximum value allowed (1 hour recommended by RFC 1583 [see RFC 1583, Appendix A]), that link-state record is no longer used in route computations and is slated for removal from the link-state database. However, this removal must be synchronized with other routers. Consequently, aged link-state records will be flooded so that they can be removed from link-state databases in other routers.

When link-state updates are propagated to neighbor routers, they are acknowledged using the OSPF message type 5 (link-state acknowledgment).

OSPF link-state database (the topological network map)

As mentioned in the previous sections, the OSPF link-state database consists of link-state records. OSPF defines five different types of link-state records that are advertised (flooded) by routers in the OSPF link-state update messages:

- Router links
- Network links
- Summary Network links
- Summary Autonomous System Boundary Router (ASBR) links
- External links

These advertised link-state records are generically referred to as link-state advertisements (LSAs), which are defined by a link ID, the advertising router, and a sequence number. The different link types are summarized in Table 4.1, which is based on an analysis of the link-state database in Cisco routers. In practice it is customary to refer to link-state records as *links*.

TABLE 4.1 *Link-state advertisement summary*

LINK STATE TYPE	ORIGINATOR	LINK-ID (HIGH-LEVEL VIEW) LINK-STATE ID (DETAIL VIEW)	LINK ID (DETAIL VIEW)	LINK DATA
Router links	Any router	Router ID of the originator (could be an IP address assigned to a physical interface or a loopback IP address)	Function of link's network type: point-to-point neighbor ID stub: interface IP of DR transit: network/ subnetwork Virtual link: neighbor ID	Stub: net mask. Other nets: Router's interface IP address
Network links	DR	Interface IP address of DR		Netmask + RIDs of attached routers
Summary Network links	ABR	Summary net number		Net mask: TOS: metric TOS: metric
Summary ASBR links	ABR	Router ID of ASBR		Net mask: TOS: metric TOS: metric
External links	ASBR	External net number: 0.0.0.0 for default, CIDR prefix for all others		Net Mask: Metric type: TOS: Metric: Forward Address: External route tag:

In the Cisco Internetworking Operating System (IOS), the commands for viewing the OSPF database are summarized in Table 4.2. These commands are used in the examples of link-state records presented in the next subsections.

TABLE 4.2 *Cisco IOS commands*

COMMAND	DESCRIPTION
show ip ospf database	Presents a high-level view of the database, which is an abbreviated view of all the links present in the database.
show ip ospf database router	Shows the detail view of the router links. *x.x.x.x*, where *x.x.x.x* is a router's ID
show ip ospf database network	Shows the detail view of the network links.
show ip ospf database summary	Shows the detail view of the summary links created through OSPF summarization. (OSPF summarization is discussed later in this chapter.)
show ip ospf database summary -ASBR	Shows the detail view of summary-ASBR links.
show ip ospf database external	Shows the detail view of external network links.

Router links

Router links are advertised by all OSPF routers. They are flooded only within areas to which router interfaces are attached. The link ID for these LSAs is the advertising router's ID. The router ID can be either an IP address of one of its physical interfaces, or a software loopback address (if it has been defined). Using a software-defined router ID makes the link-state database more stable, resulting in fewer recomputations of the routing table. If a physical interface used as the router ID goes down, a router must generate new LSAs for all the router links with the new router ID. A loopback interface (which is software-defined) does not go down, unless there is a drastic problem with the entire router. Using loopback interfaces for router IDs consequently introduces more stability into an OSPF network. The disadvantage of loopback interfaces is that you do have to allocate IP addresses to them on subnets that can't be used for anything else.

If a router has many interfaces, it generates a router-link LSA for each one. Every LSA must have a link ID. The router links are probably the most confusing of the five link types. When a router's link-state database is displayed in a detail view using *show ip ospf database router*, the link ID from the high-level view becomes the link-state ID. The link ID in the detail format display assumes a new meaning as a function of the network type to which the router is interfaced. The four network types are

- Point-to-point
- Stub
- Virtual link
- Transit or multi-access

The detailed link ID varies as a function of the network to which the router is interfaced. The link data also varies (see Table 4.1). A detail view of a router link-state record is obtained via the *show ip ospf database router* command, as shown here:

```
OSPF Router with ID (192.168.16.2) (Process ID 77)
       Router Link States (Area 0.0.0.0)
  LS age: 395
  Options: (No TOS-capability)
  LS Type: Router Links
  Link State ID: 192.168.16.2 (originating
  router's Router ID)
  Advertising Router: 192.168.16.2
  LS Seq Number: 8000000E
  Checksum: 0xB011
  Length: 36
  Area Border Router
  Number of links: 1
   Link connected to: Transit Network
   (Link ID) Designated router Address:
    192.168.16.1
   (Link Data) Router's Interface address:
   192.168.16.2
  Number of TOS metrics: 0
   TOS 0 metric: 10
```

A corresponding high-level view of this link-state record would be as follows:

```
        Router Link States (Area 0.0.0.0)
Link ID          ADV Router       Age    Seq#
192.168.16.2     192.168.16.2     395    0x8000000E
Checksum         Link count
0xB011           1
```

This record is one of several router link-state records that would be seen on routers A, B, C, and D in Figure 5.2 in Chapter 5, following the election of router B as DR for area 0. You should try to describe what the other router link-state records would look like based on the information supplied in Table 4.1. One item to note about router link-state advertisements is that a single OSPF link-state update message can carry multiple router LSAs. That's not the case for the other LSAs. It's one LSA per one OSPF link-state update message.

Network links

Network links are originated by designated routers. They are flooded only within an area where a router has been elected as a DR. The link ID for these links is the IP address of the router's physical interface to the broadcast network. The link data includes the network mask of the network to which the DR is interfaced, and a list of routers with which the DR has established full adjacencies. An example of a detailed network link state record via the *show ip ospf database network* command is as follows:

```
        OSPF Router with ID (192.168.16.1)
        (Process ID 88)
         Net Link States (Area 0.0.0.0)
   Routing Bit Set on this LSA
   LS age: 285
   Options: (No TOS-capability)
   LS Type: Network Links
   Link State ID: 192.168.16.1 (address of
   Designated Router)
   Advertising Router: 192.168.16.1
   LS Seq Number: 8000000D
   Checksum: 0x7326
```

```
Length: 36
Network Mask: /24
 Attached Router: 192.168.16.1
 Attached Router: 192.168.16.2
 Attached Router: 192.168.16.3
 Attached Router: 192.168.16.4
```

The corresponding high-level view of this record would be as follows:

```
      Net Link States (Area 0.0.0.0)
Link ID         ADV Router     Age   Seq#
192.168.16.1  192.168.16.1   285   0x8000000D
Checksum
0x7326
```

Note in this link-state record that the advertising router is the DR, that the advertising router's ID happens to be the IP address of the interface to the network for which it has been selected as a DR, and that there are three other routers that are interfaced to the same network (with their router IDs being 192.168.16.2, 192.168.16.3, and 192.168.16.4).

Summary links

Summary links are advertised by ABRs. They represent networks in other OSPF areas, but within the same autonomous system (AS). Summary links are a result of the OSPF summarization feature. OSPF summarization allows networks internal to an OSPF area to be lumped together into a single advertisement. ABRs inject the summary routes into the OSPF backbone area, and from the backbone, the summary routes are injected into other OSPF areas by other ABRs. The link ID is the summary network and the link data is the summary mask. The following is a detail view of two summary records obtained via the *show ip ospf database summary* command:

```
      OSPF Router with ID (192.168.16.1)
      (Process ID 88)
        Summary Net Link States (Area 0.0.0.0)
  LS age: 1294
  Options: (No TOS-capability)
  LS Type: Summary Links(Network)
```

```
Link State ID: 192.168.64.0 (summary Network
Number)
Advertising Router: 192.168.16.2
LS Seq Number: 80000003
Checksum: 0xDBA6
Length: 28
Network Mask: /19  TOS: 0     Metric: 10

LS age: 317
Options: (No TOS-capability)
LS Type: Summary Links(Network)
Link State ID: 192.168.96.0 (summary Network
Number)
Advertising Router: 192.168.16.3
LS Seq Number: 80000001
Checksum: 0xF5CA
Length: 28
Network Mask: /19  TOS: 0     Metric: 10
```

The corresponding high-level view of these link-state summary records would be

```
Link ID         ADV Router      Age     Seq#
192.168.64.0    192.168.16.2    1294    0x80000003
192.168.96.0    192.168.16.3    317     0x80000001

Checksum
0xDBA6
0xF5CA
```

Summary ASBR links

The OSPF ABRs are also the originators of summary ASBR links. The link ID is the router ID of an ASBR, which is an IP address assigned either to a loop-back or a physical interface. These links allow other routers within the autonomous system to know who the ASBR is. Knowing the ASBR allows routers to get traffic out of the autonomous system.

The following is a detail view of a summary record obtained via the *show ip ospf database summary-ASBR* command:

```
OSPF Router with ID (192.168.16.1) (Process ID 88)
     Summary ASB Link States (Area 0.0.0.0)
  LS age: 922
  Options: (No TOS-capability)
  LS Type: Summary Links(AS Border Router)
  Link State ID: 192.168.16.4 (Router ID of AS
  Border Router)
  Advertising Router: 192.168.16.1
  LS Seq Number: 80000003
  Checksum: 0xDBA6
  Length: 28
  Network Mask: 0.0.0.0  TOS: 0     Metric: 10
```

The corresponding high-level view of this link-state record would be

```
Link ID         ADV Router      Age     Seq#
192.168.16.4    192.168.16.1    1294    0x80000003
Checksum
0xDBA6
```

External links

The originators of external links are the ASBRs (discussed in the "BGP: The Long-Distance Runner" section later in this chapter). These links represent reachable networks external to the autonomous system which the ASBR is connecting to the rest of the Internet. The OSPF internetworks discussed so far would be within the autonomous system. These links must be well-managed in the Internet through router configurations. Otherwise, these links could be very numerous, since there are presently more than 40,000 networks on the Internet.

The following is a detail view of an external link state record obtained via the *show ip ospf database external* command:

```
OSPF Router with ID (192.168.16.1)
(Process ID 88)
```

```
        AS External Link States
  Routing Bit Set on this LSA
  LS age: 407
  Options: (No TOS-capability)
  LS Type: AS External Link
  Link State ID: 172.16.22.0 (External Network
  Number)
  Advertising Router: 192.168.16.4
  LS Seq Number: 80000003
  Checksum: 0x5095
  Length: 36
  Network Mask: /23
   Metric Type: 2 (Larger than any link state path)
    TOS: 0
    Metric: 100
    Forward Address: 0.0.0.0
    External Route Tag: 20
```

The corresponding high-level view of this link-state record would be

```
      AS External Link States
Link ID        ADV Router       Age    Seq#
172.16.22.0    192.168.16.4     407    0x80000003

Checksum    Tag
0x5095      20
```

The key things to note about these two views of an external link state record are that the link ID stays the same in both views and that it represents a reachable external network from outside of the autonomous system. The advertising router in this example is an ASBR. The display commands were executed on a different router, as indicated by a different IP address in the OSPF process section.

This section does not present a very detailed analysis of the individual link-state records, but rather shows their structure and contents. You should pursue further understanding through hands-on experience and possibly some protocol analysis.

Variable Length Subnetting

OSPF allows for variable *subnet masks*. Subnetting was initially developed to make better use of the IP address space. Subnetting allows class A, B, or C network address to be divided into smaller networks. Variable length subnetting takes this process even further.

Consider the following example. Suppose you have a single class C address such as 192.168.33.0, and you must connect four remote sites interconnected for redundancy via point-to-point serial links, as shown in Figure 4.6.

Each site requires up to 25 IP addresses, and the serial interfaces on the point-to-point links must be assigned their own IP addresses. These requirements imply that you will need a total of 8 subnets (4 subnets with a minimum of 25 valid host addresses for the 4 sites, and 4 subnets with a minimum of 2 valid host addresses for the point-to-point serial interfaces). Can you meet these requirements given a single Class C address and using the traditional subnetting as recommended in RFC 950 (see RFC 950, Appendix A)? The answer is no.

FIGURE 4.6 *Internetwork for subnetting examples*

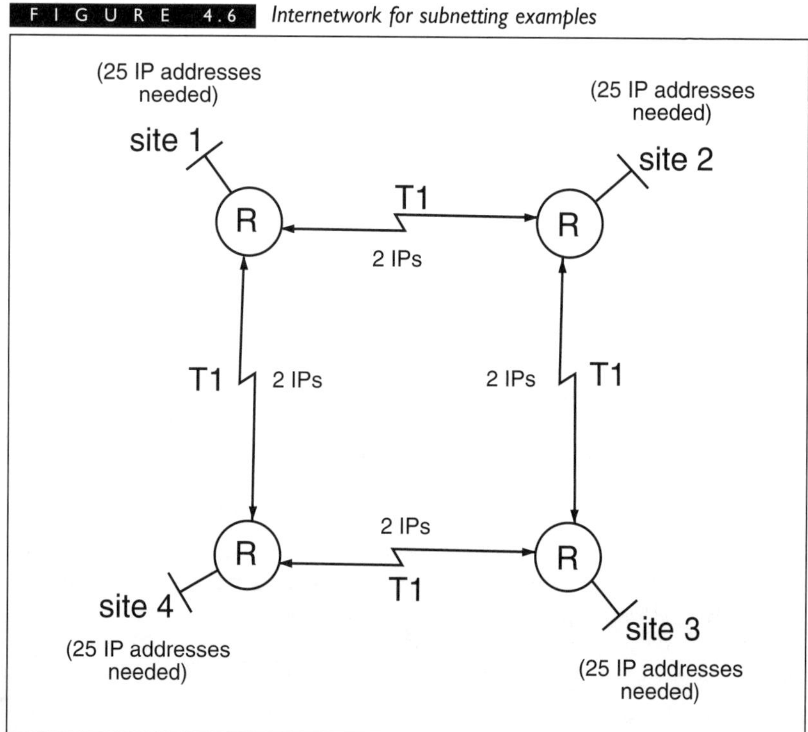

Using the traditional subnetting scheme, the closest you get to meeting these requirements is by having 6 subnets with 30 hosts each, or 14 subnets with 14 hosts each, using a subnet mask of 255.255.255.224 and 255.255.255.240, respectively. Neither subnet mask will work. The mask of 255.255.255.224 does not provide enough subnets and the mask of 255.255.255.240 does not provide enough hosts on each subnet. Figure 4.7 shows a Class C address space with subnet masks of 255.255.255.224 and 255.255.255.240. The circles represent the entire available address space. Subnetting divides the circles into smaller subnets. The numbers in the circles represent the last byte (the fourth byte) of any class C address subnetted with the masks shown in Figure 4.7.

RFC 950 does not recommend the use of subnets with all 0s and all 1s and most implementations abide by those recommendations. The big shortcoming of the traditional subnetting is that once a subnet mask is applied to an address, the *entire* address space is divided into subnets of the same size, as demonstrated in Figure 4.7.

With variable-length subnetting, however, your requirements can be met. Variable-length subnetting enables you to apply multiple different masks to the same single IP network number. Consider the mechanics of a Variable-Length Subnet Mask (VLSM) in the context of the established requirements.

Applying a subnet mask of 255.255.255.224 to the 192.168.33.0 network, you first allocate as many subnets as you need to accommodate the 4 sites with up to 25 hosts. This means 4 subnets of 30 hosts each. Assuming that subnet 0 is not supported (even though some routers will support it now), the valid four subnets numbers, the valid host addresses for each subnet, and the broadcast address for each subnet are as follows (see Figure 4.8):

```
Subnet number   Valid host range
192.168.33.32   192.168.33.33-192.168.33.62
192.168.33.64   192.168.33.65-192.168.33.94
192.168.33.96   192.168.33.97-192.168.33.126
192.168.33.128  192.168.33.129-192.168.33.158

Broadcast
192.168.33.63
192.168.33.95
192.168.33.127
192.168.33.159
```

FIGURE 4.7A *Class C address subnetted for 8 subnets with a single mask*

.224 not used
.0 not used
.32 30 hosts
.64 30 hosts
.96 30 hosts
.128 30 hosts
.160 30 hosts
.192 30 hosts

IP net = 192.168.33.0
Mask(s) = 255.255.224.0

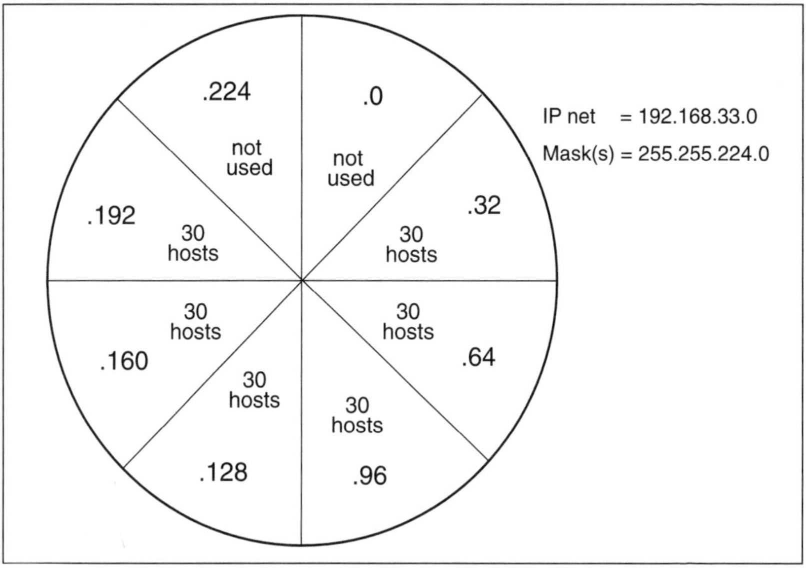

FIGURE 4.7B *Class C address subnetted for 16 subnets with a single mask*

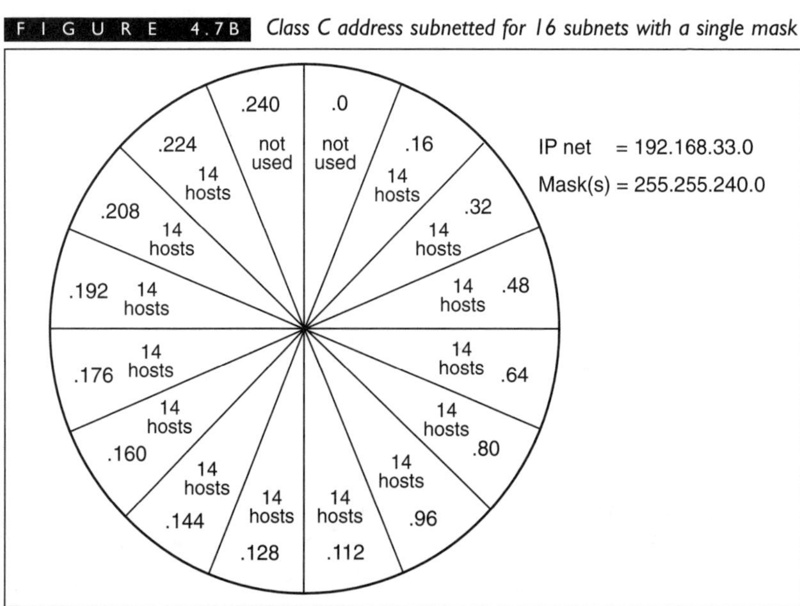

FIGURE 4.8 *Variable length mask subnetting example*

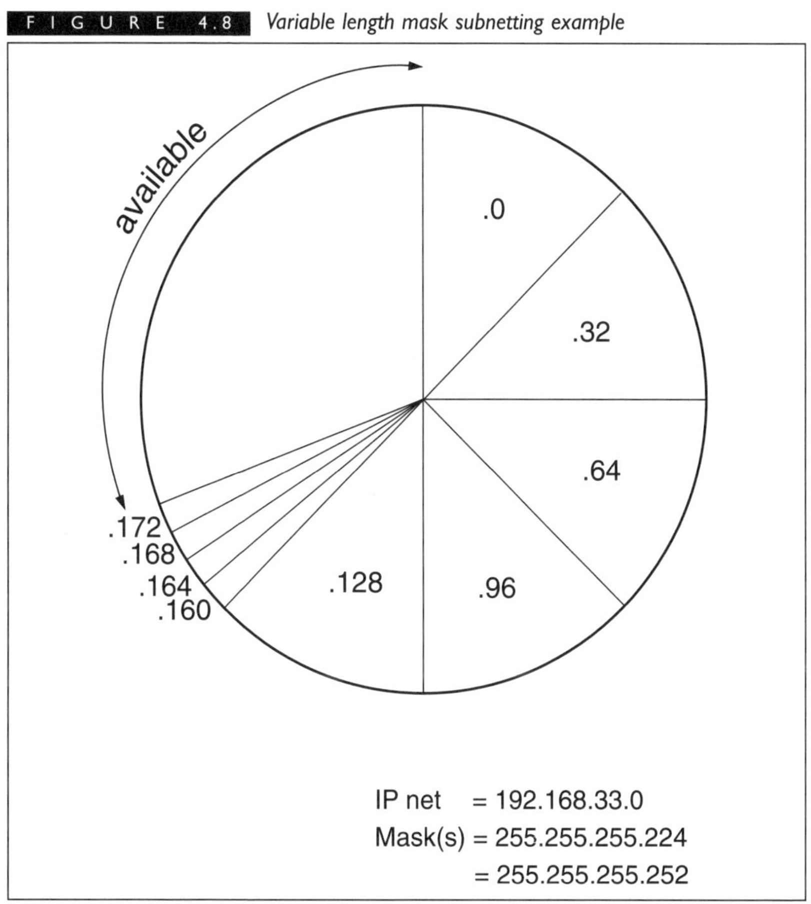

The remainder of the address space beginning with 192.168.33.160 is available for further division. Because you need only two IP addresses for the serial links, you can apply a longer subnet mask of 255.255.255.252. Applying this mask to the remaining address space, you can allocate four more subnets that will give you two hosts on each. Again, the valid subnet numbers, valid host addresses, and broadcast addresses for each subnet are as follows (see Figure 4.8):

```
Subnet            Valid host range
192.168.33.160    192.168.33.161-192.168.33.162
192.168.33.164    192.168.33.165-192.168.33.166
```

```
192.168.33.168    192.168.33.169-192.168.33.170
192.168.33.172    192.168.33.173-192.168.33.174

Broadcast
192.168.33.163
192.168.33.167
192.168.33.171
192.168.33.175
```

So, your requirements to have 4 subnets that can support up to 25 hosts and 4 subnets that can support 2 hosts have been met, with some address space left over for expansion. Variable length subnetting definitely has its advantages, but it also requires care in allocating the address space.

To take this example even further, if you had to add a couple more serial links and two more sites with up to 10 hosts, there is plenty of address space left to allow for this. The serial links would continue to use the mask of 255.255.255.252 and could use the subnets of 192.168.33.176 and 192.168.33.180, as shown here:

```
Subnet            Valid host range
192.168.33.176    192.168.33.177-192.168.33.178
192.168.33.180    192.168.33.181-192.168.33.182

Broadcast
192.168.33.179
192.168.33.183
```

The two additional sites with up to 10 hosts could be masked with 255.255.255.240 giving valid subnet numbers, hosts, and broadcasts as follows:

```
Subnet            Valid host range
192.168.33.184    192.168.33.185-192.168.33.198
192.168.33.200    192.168.33.201-192.168.33.214

Broadcast
192.168.33.199
192.168.33.215
```

There would still be some address space left over. Additionally, the subnet 0 as shown in this example could be broken into smaller subnets, thus creating a smaller subnet 0 and releasing some additional address space.

A note of caution regarding variable length subnetting is in order. When deploying VLSM in an internetwork, it's important to know how many different sized subnets (determined by the mask length) are needed. It is then vital to ensure that these subnets are not allocated from the same portion of the available address space. Otherwise, overlapping can occur between VLSM-subnetted networks.

In the preceding VLSM-subnetting example, overlapping would occur if subnet number 192.168.33.32 was used with a mask of 255.255.255.224 (27 bits) and subnet number 192.168.33.48 was used with another mask. The IP address of 192.168.33.48 is a host address on subnet 192.168.33.32 when 192.168.33.32 is used with the mask of 255.255.255.224. Consequently, it cannot be used as a subnet number. If, however, 192.168.33.32 was used with a longer mask of 255.255.255.240, then 192.168.33.48 would be a valid subnet that could be used with several different sized masks, depending on how many host addresses were needed on it.

The bottom line of VLSM is subnetting: Be careful, and preferably represent your subnet assignments graphically (as shown in Figure 4.8) before committing them to router configuration files. It can save you hours of troubleshooting time.

Summarization

OSPF *summarization* is a technique that allows ABRs to advertise fewer routes on behalf of areas which they connect to the OSPF backbone area. The requirement, however, for OSPF summarization is that network numbers to be summarized must be somewhat sequential or contiguous. It is like working with a group of people whose last names differ by a one or two letters at the ends of their names.

Imagine yourself in a classroom where you are an instructor. Every student in your classroom has a last name with the same number of characters in it. Quite a coincidence already, but it does not stop here. Your students' last names are almost identical. They differ only by the very last character (see Figure 4.9).

There are other classrooms in the building. They experience similar coincidences. In every classroom, student names are the same length and the first part of their names is the same. The length of the common part of the names varies from classroom to classroom. Because the students tend to have very long names, in some classrooms the common part of the names is 23 characters; in others 22 or 21. However, even with very similar names in each classroom, no two students throughout the building have the same name.

FIGURE 4.9 *OSPF summarization analogy*

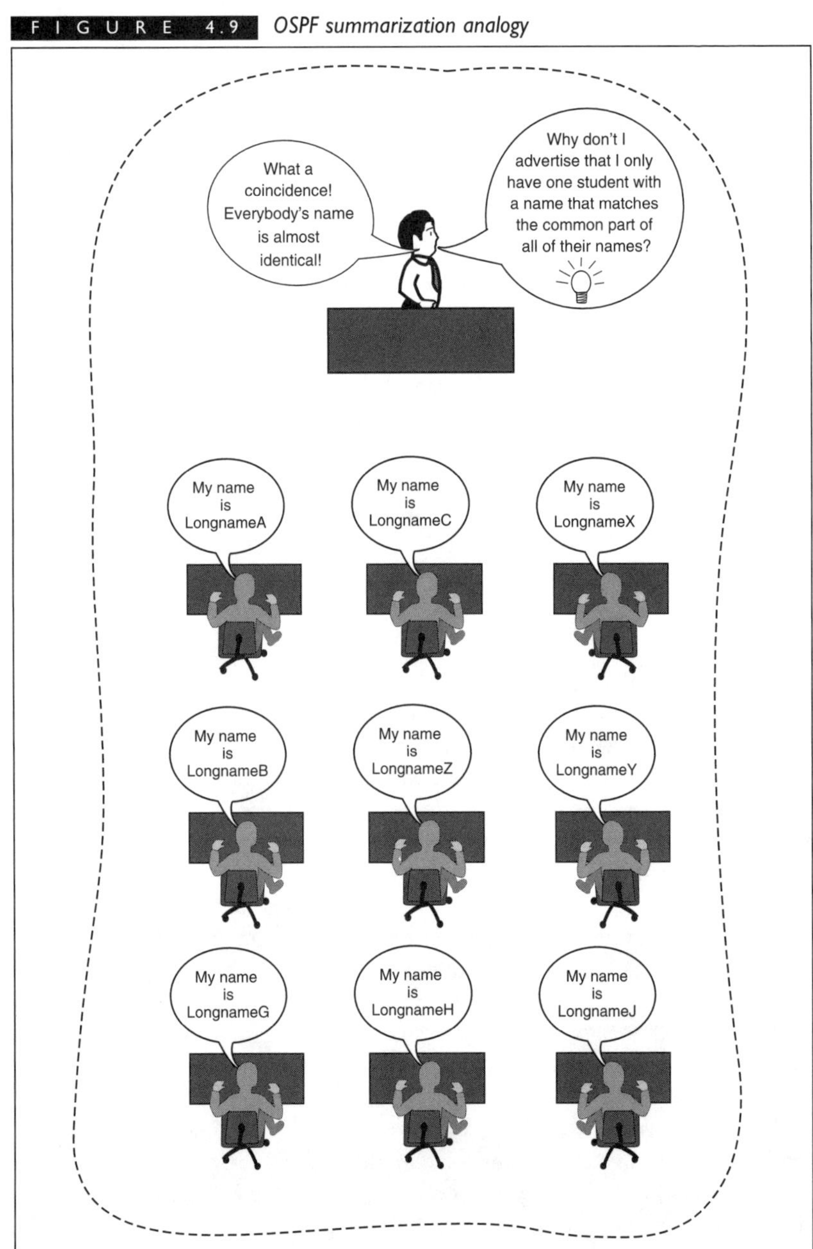

One of your responsibilities as an instructor is to communicate with all the other instructors in the other classrooms and let them know who your students are. This way each instructor will know about all the students in all the other classrooms. The instructors can then pass on this information to the students in their classrooms. Sounds like a lot of names to pass around and keep track of. Effectively, everyone in the whole building would know about everybody else. But at least students could communicate between classrooms. Additionally, one instructor in the building has been designated to receive messages that come in from the outside and pass them on to the right classrooms.

Noticing the pattern in the students' names in your classroom, you come up with a very clever idea. Rather than communicating all names individually, you write only one abbreviated name that's common to all the names in your classroom. The thought process behind the idea is simple. If a message arrives for a student whose name matches the common pattern this message should be delivered to your classroom. You will take the responsibility for getting it to the right person in the classroom. The effect of this clever idea is that you don't have to write down (advertise) many different names for all the other instructors, and all the other instructors have less information to sift through.

Analogies only go so far, but they can stimulate the imagination. The classrooms in our imaginary building are OSPF areas. The instructors are the ABRs. Students are networks connected by other routers internal to each area. The ABRs, rather than advertising every single network that's inside the areas they connect to the OSPF backbone, group the networks so that the entire group becomes a single routing table entry in other ABRs.

For example, assume that in Figure 4.2 all of the routers with the exception of RA belong to a single OSPF area 1. Imagine that router RA has an additional interface over which it connects to an OSPF backbone area 0. The Ethernet networks in area 1 are 192.168.33.0, 192.168.34.0, 192.168.35.0, 192.168.36.0, and the point-to-point T1 nets are 192.168.40.0 and 192.196.41.0. Notice that at least the first two octets of all of the network numbers in area 1 are identical. How about the other octets? To determine the common part in all the network numbers requires that the decimal notation be converted to binary. Converting all the network numbers to binary gives the following bit pattern. For the purposes of easier reading of the bit patterns, a blank space appears between each group of eight bits.

```
11000000 10101000 00100001 00000000 = 192.168.33.0
11000000 10101000 00100010 00000000 = 192.168.34.0
11000000 10101000 00100011 00000000 = 192.168.35.0
```

```
11000000 10101000 00100100 00000000 = 192.168.36.0
11000000 10101000 00101000 00000000 = 192.168.40.0
11000000 10101000 00101001 00000000 = 192.168.41.0
```

If you look at these bit patterns, what emerges is that the common part all the networks have is 20 bits long. After the first 20 bits, the bit patterns differ from one network number to another. Converting the first 20 bits to a dotted decimal notation gives us 192.168.32.0. The length of the summarization mask will be 20, which is the number of bits common to all of the networks. A summarization mask of 20 bits translates into 255.255.240.0 in the dotted decimal notation.

What this all means is that instead of advertising six different networks onto the OSPF backbone, the ABR (or router RA in Figure 4.2) can be configured to advertise just one, 192.168.32.0 with a mask of 255.255.240.0. In fact, going back to the bit patterns, you may notice that if you added a few more networks with similar numbers, they would be covered by the existing summarization. The precise range of networks that would be covered by a single summarization statement in RA's configuration with the calculated summary network and mask is from 192.168.32.0 to 192.168.47.0.

Summarization only works when network numbers are somewhat contiguous. There could be a real confusion on the internetwork if two different ABRs issued the same summary advertisements. In this example, notice that several networks are covered by the summarization that have not been assigned yet. If these networks were to be assigned in another area and advertised with the same summarization mask, there could be some real problems with delivering the packets with user data to their destinations. You should have the summarization mask as specific as possible so that it does not include too many networks that have not been assigned.

Going back to the example, instead of having one summarization advertisement, you could have two: one for the Ethernet networks, and one for the point-to-point serial links. For the Ethernet networks, the common part is 21 bits, which when converted to decimal still gives a network number of 192.168.32.0, but a mask of 255.255.248.0 summarizing the range from 192.168.32.0 to 192.168.39.0. The remaining two networks have 23 bits in common. Converting those 23 common bits to decimal gives a network number of 192.168.40.0 and a summarization mask of 255.255.254.0 with a range of network from 192.168.40.0 to 192.168.41.0. There can be no ambiguity here. Only two networks are in the range, and both of them have been assigned. Having two summary statements to cover the networks results in an extra routing table entry in other ABRs connected to the backbone, but it makes the summarization less ambiguous.

OSPF virtual links

OSPF supports a feature known as *virtual links*. The characteristics of OSPF are that all the OSPF areas must be connected to the backbone area 0, and the backbone area must be physically contiguous. If, for reasons of topology or politics, an OSPF area has no direct connectivity to the backbone area, then a virtual link can be established from that area to the backbone via an intermediate OSPF area. This intermediate OSPF area becomes known as a *transit area*.

Virtual links can also be used in scenarios where the backbone area is not contiguous or two backbone areas from different OSPF internetworks have to be joined together. The additional advantage of virtual links is that they can be used for backup connectivity. The chief disadvantage of virtual links is that their stability depends on the stability of the areas through which they are established. When those transit areas are under someone else's administration, there is a greater potential for misconfigurations and routing instability.

Virtual links are set up between any two ABRs that share connectivity to an area other than the backbone area. A virtual link is treated by OSPF as an unnumbered, point-to-point link. In practice, virtual links are not recommended unless absolutely necessary.

OSPF implementation tips

It is possible to configure and maintain an OSPF network without fully understanding every aspect of OSPF that has been discussed so far. However, some practical considerations a network administrator must be aware of include the following:

- Make use of areas to break up a large OSPF internetwork into smaller parts.
- If possible, avoid the same router from being a designated router in multiple OSPF areas. Since it's not routers (but rather router interfaces) that are assigned to OSPF areas, it is possible for a router with multiple interfaces to be in multiple areas.
- Avoid using an ABR as a designated router since an ABR will already be maintaining at least two copies of the link-state database: one for the backbone area and one for the other area which it is connecting to the backbone. An ABR with a copy of a link-state database for each area will be doing much more processing than a router with all its

interfaces in just one area. Making an ABR a designated router on top of it could bog it down so much with the administrative traffic and activities that it would have little resources left to do what routers are supposed to do first and foremost: forward packets with user data.

- When configuring an ABR, summarize the networks within an area for advertising them onto the backbone and into other areas. Summarization reduces the pressure on the network bandwidth (fewer LSAs to advertise), routers' CPUs (fewer LSAs to process), and the size of routing tables (fewer entries), resulting in better overall performance.

All the features of OSPF that make it a complex protocol serve the same basic purpose: making the protocol more efficient. This includes the election of a DR, five different packet types, five different link types, three different subprotocols, seven stages of establishing a relationship, breakdown into areas, support for type of service, route summarization, or interaction with other protocols such as BGP through a process of redistribution. In contrast to its internal complexities, configuring OSPF is almost simple (see Chapter 5 for more details).

BGP: The Long-Distance Runner

BGP is a routing protocol that enables packets with user data to travel between the most remote locations of the Internet. That's why it is called the *long-distance runner*. However, to discuss remote locations on the Internet, it might be helpful to define what the Internet is in the first place. Chapter 2 provided a very simple definition of the Internet as a network of networks. This chapter changes that simple Internet definition from a network of networks to a more sophisticated definition: *an internetwork of autonomous systems*. BGP was designed to exchange routing information between autonomous systems.

Autonomous systems

A clear definition of an *autonomous system* (AS) is still evolving, even as the Internet itself is evolving. However, a few stabs at defining an AS have been made. The classic definition of an AS (referenced in RFC 1771 — see RFC 1771, Appendix A and in a few other RFCs) is *a set of routers under a single technical administration using an interior gateway protocol and common metric to route packets within the AS, and using exterior gateway protocol to route packets to other autonomous systems.*

The Internet has changed, however, since this classic definition was proposed. The new definition of an AS is shifting more and more in the direction of being a group of routers and networks that have a *uniform routing policy,* and that share similar network addresses for the purpose of address aggregation.

As the old structure of the Internet (centered for many years around the National Science Foundation backbone) gave way to the new structure of multiple interconnected commercial backbones, the Internet is bound to contain autonomous systems to which either one of the definitions can be applied.

According to the classic definition, only a single IGP (such as RIP, OSPF, or IGRP) is used inside an AS. This may have been the case in the earlier days of the Internet when RIP was the only IGP around. However, the coexistence and use of multiple IGPs in a set of routers under the same single technical administration is no longer a disqualifying criteria from being a single autonomous system. The existence of multiple IGPs in a single AS occurs even during a migration stage from a protocol such as RIP to OSPF. Ironically enough, a single technical administration is no longer a sufficient enough reason to become an AS. So, what is the single criteria qualifying a group of routers and networks to become an AS? It boils down to a routing policy discussed in the context of different categories of autonomous systems.

RFC 1772 (see RFC 1772, Appendix A) makes a reference to the Internet topology as "an arbitrary interconnection of transit, multihomed and stub autonomous systems." A very common example of an AS in today's Internet is a group of networks and routers operated by a major ISP. Figure 4.10 shows an example of autonomous systems.

Figure 4.10 shows that not all autonomous systems are the same. Consequently, they may have different routing policies. The three categories of autonomous systems represented in Figure 4.10 are

- Transit
- Multihomed
- Stub

Transit AS

A transit AS allows traffic originating in other autonomous systems to flow through it. A transit AS has connections to at least two other autonomous systems. In Figure 4.10, the transit autonomous systems are AS2, AS3, and AS4. If a user5 from AS5 wants to access a Web server in AS2, the traffic originating from that user5 crosses AS4 and AS3 to get to a server in AS2. If user6 in AS6 wants to access a server in AS5, the traffic originating from user6 crosses AS2, AS3, and AS4. Since the three autonomous systems (AS2, AS3, and AS4) allow traffic originating outside of them to cross or "transit" through their internal networks, they are called transit autonomous systems. Being a transit AS is definitely a policy decision. Not every AS with multiple interfaces to other autonomous systems wants to be a transit AS.

A *multihomed AS* has more than one connection to other autonomous systems, but, because of its configuration, its router does not allow traffic originating in other autonomous systems to flow through it. Traffic originating in other autonomous systems will be allowed to access the resources within a multihomed AS, but not to transit through it. In the example in Figure 4.10, AS1 is a multihomed AS. It is interfaced to at least three other autonomous systems, but it does not allow traffic to pass through it.

An example of a multihomed AS may be a corporation that provides vital financial services to users from around the world 7 days a week, 24 hours a day. To minimize any potential downtime, this corporation decides to use not just one but three different ISPs to provide access to its sites. However, there is no desire on the part of our fictitious financial services provider to allow its routers to be burdened by any "transit" traffic between the three ISPs.

Multihomed AS

If the connection between AS2 and AS3, and the connection between AS3 and AS4 in Figure 4.10 were to fail, there would still be physical connectivity between all the autonomous systems. However, since AS1's policy does not allow any transit traffic, users in AS2 would not be able to access servers in AS3 or AS4 and vice versa. So, the difference between a multihomed AS and a transit AS is a matter of policy relating to network traffic. Routing policies are implemented through appropriate configuration of BGP routers connecting the autonomous systems.

Stub AS

A *stub AS* has a single connection to another AS. With only one connection to another AS, traffic cannot pass through a stub AS. It's literally a stub. It is possible (given the historical evolution of the Internet) that some stub autonomous systems do not even need to be separate autonomous systems, but rather could be part of the parent AS to which they connect. For the two stubs, AS5 and AS6, shown in Figure 4.10, the test would be whether the routing policies within the stubs match those of their parents (AS4 and AS2) to which the stubs are connected. For example, the policy of the transit AS (AS4) might be to allow all traffic to pass through it, whereas the policy of the stub AS (AS5) might be to reject traffic originating in certain autonomous systems. The difference in these policies might be sufficient to warrant the status quo.

FIGURE 4.10 *Representation of autonomous systems*

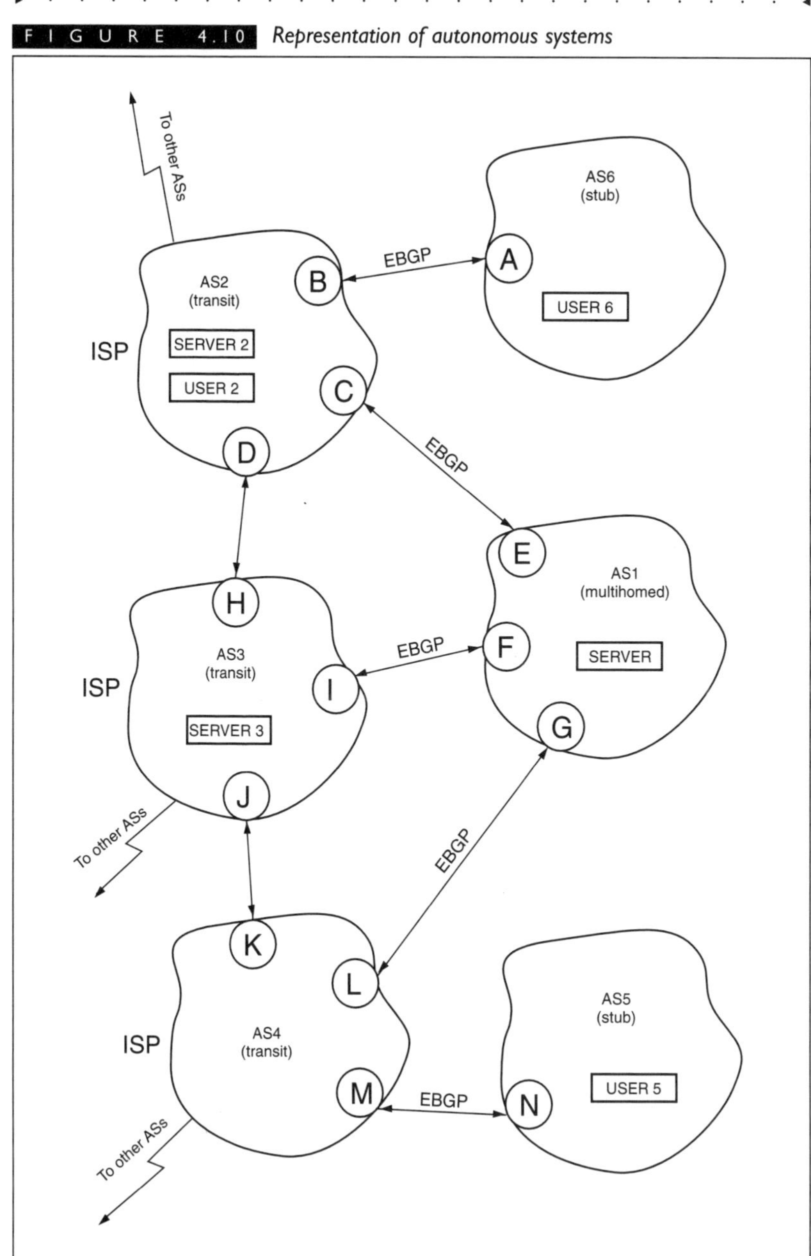

Also, combining multiple autonomous systems into a single one is a non-trivial implementation issue. Many stub autonomous systems could be out there in the Internet, as part of the routine for major organizations of connecting to the Internet before the emergence of ISPs was to get their own autonomous system numbers. Any AS that is a part of the Internet is assigned an AS number, which must be registered with the Internetwork Network Information Center (InterNIC). The AS numbers are between 1 and 65,535 (a 2-byte binary). Autonomous system numbers are used during the BGP process router configuration. See Chapter 5 for more details on router configuration.

In an autonomous system, one or more routers that have been configured to run BGP become *BGP speakers*. Think of BGP speakers as *spokesrouters* that speak on behalf of all the other routers and networks in the AS. These representative routers know about all networks on the inside. They also receive routing updates about networks in other autonomous systems. Their job is to pass on to their peers the routing updates about their internal networks and those they receive from other autonomous systems.

Any two BGP-configured routers that exchange routing updates are known as *BGP peers*. A BGP router acquires its peers or neighbors via the reliable transport protocol TCP using a well-known TCP port, 179. You might be wondering how this acquisition takes place. As part of the BGP configuration, the IP addresses and autonomous system numbers of all the peer BGP routers the configured router will talk to must be specified in a *neighbor* configuration command. The rest is the mechanics of TCP/IP.

After a TCP connection is established between any two potential BGP peers, they use four types of messages to communicate with each other: open, update, keepalive, and notification. The *update message* is used to convey routing information and is the most interesting (as well as complex in structure) of the four message types.

BGP's robustness in making complex routing decisions is derived from its ability to use the phenomenal amount of information that can be contained in its update message. The *open message* and *keepalive message* are used to set up and maintain a BGP session; the *notification message* provides feedback about error conditions between BGP peers.

BGP peers can be either internal or external. *Internal BGP peers* are those that establish BGP sessions within an autonomous system. *External BGP peers* establish BGP sessions between the autonomous systems. External BGP peers are also referred to as ASBRs.

The BGP version 4 protocol incorporates advanced features required for routing in the modern Internet. These include route aggregation (or CIDR), enforcement of different routing policies between autonomous systems, improved scalability through the use of route reflectors and confederations, and interaction with IGPs through redistribution and synchronization.

A precursor to BGP was the Exterior Gateway Protocol (EGP), now relegated to a historical status. EGP, which is specified in RFC 905 (see RFC 905, Appendix A), was developed in the early 1980s when the structure and use of the aging ARPAnet and the fledgling Internet were radically different from what they are today. Although EGP may still be in use, it is recommended that routing exchanges between autonomous systems in today's Internet be done via BGP version 4. Most router vendors still support earlier BGP implementations (BGP-2 specified in RFC 1163 and BGP-3 specified in RFC 1267).

NOTE

All references to BGP in the remainder of this chapter are used in reference to BGP version 4, unless otherwise specified.

Route aggregation

Route aggregation in BGP is conceptually similar to summarization in OSPF. The BGP route aggregation command conveys to the BGP process the aggregate address and the mask, just like the OSPF summarization command includes a summary network number and mask. The big difference is that it is taking place at the level of the autonomous systems, rather than at the level of OSPF areas.

Route aggregation is the result of BGP's support for CIDR. With CIDR, the concept of IP address classes is eliminated. Instead of creating IP subnets by moving the mask to the right of the globally assigned net ID, CIDR allows the creation of supernets by moving the mask to the left. Basically, just like with the OSPF summarization of contiguous addresses, CIDR allows for finding the common part of a group of addresses and advertising them as a single address in the form of a prefix followed by its length. In CIDR representation, the networks used as an example in the OSPF summarization section would be represented as 192.168.32.0/20. Both BGP and OSPF support CIDR.

The "classless" part of CIDR stems from the fact that the network numbers represented in CIDR notation have a different meaning than if used by themselves. For example, an address such as 192.0.0.0 is a valid single class C address. However, when used in the CIDR representation of 192.0.0.0/10, it represents 16,384 class C addresses in the range from 192.0.0.0 to 192.63.255.0. CIDR notation of 192.0.0.0/11 represents 8,192 class C addresses in the range from 192.0.0.0 to 192.31.255.0. Hence, CIDR notation effectively represents segments of IP address space, eliminating the concept of individual network addresses belonging to a particular class.

The BGP process running on a router must be specifically told to perform route aggregation through configuration commands. The bottom line behind route aggregation in BGP is to reduce the number of networks (routes) from within autonomous systems that BGP speakers advertise to their external peers. The concept of route aggregation may be fairly straightforward, but the details of its implementation and its configuration options make it anything but simple. After BGP has been told to perform route aggregation, it must also be told which routes are to be aggregated. The process of telling BGP about routes internal to an AS (and not only for the purpose of route aggregation) generally is referred to as *injecting routes into BGP*. One specific technique of injecting routes into BGP is called *redistribution*.

Route redistribution

Route redistribution into BGP can be either static or dynamic. *Static redistribution* involves telling the BGP process about the routes (networks) to be advertised by BGP, specifying a static route in the router's IP table, and then using a *redistribute static* configuration command in the BGP process configuration section. See Chapter 5 for more configuration details.

Dynamic redistribution involves telling the BGP process to accept routes from an IGP such as RIP, IGRP, or OSPF running on the same router. In terms of configuration, dynamic redistribution involves a modification to the router's IGP configuration section by telling that IGP process to redistribute its routes into BGP. Redistribution, if not implemented carefully, can be very tricky and potentially result in routing loops.

Figure 4.11 shows a routing environment where static, dynamic, and mutual route redistribution between OSPF and BGP can take place. The example in Figure 4.11 is used to explain the principles of redistribution.

The most typical flow of redistribution (reachable networks) is from an IGP into BGP. In Figure 4.11, the ASBRs C, E, and H will be running both the BGP and the OSPF process. Routers D, F, and G will be running OSPF only. The BGP process running on each ASBR learns about the reachable networks in the portions of AS4 serviced by OSPF by static redistribution, dynamic redistribution, or via a *network* command available under the Cisco IOS. All three techniques can be used in the environment shown in Figure 4.11.

FIGURE 4.11 *BGP and OSPF routing environment inside an autonomous system*

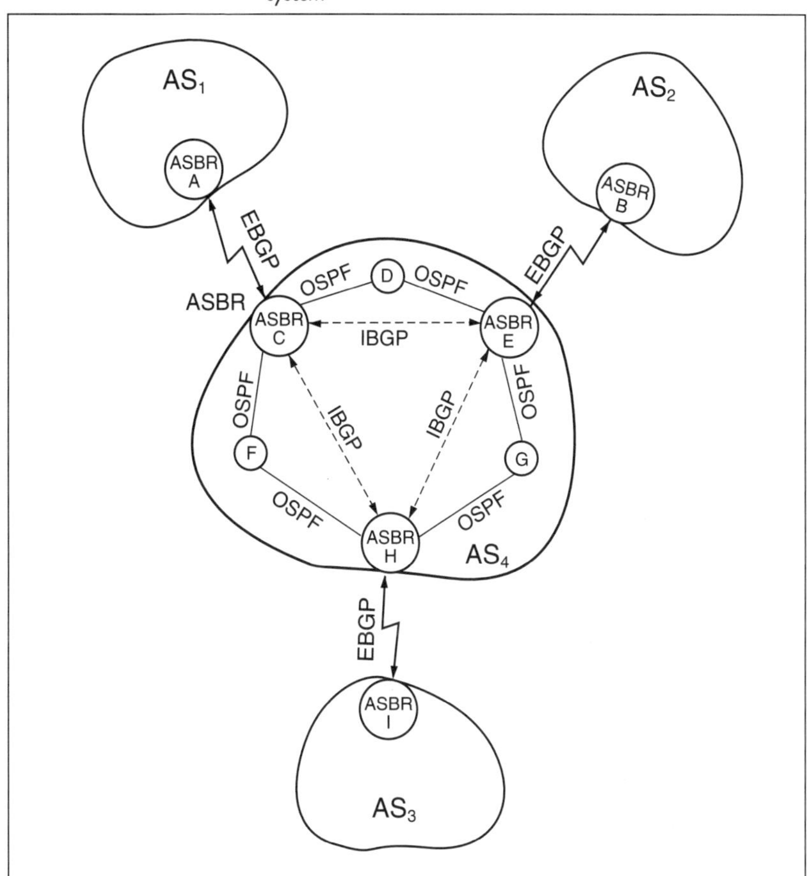

Let's start with dynamic redistribution. In the OSPF configuration sections of each ASBR a r*edistribute* command must be used. What is accomplished by dynamic redistribution is to notify the rest of the Internet outside of AS4 about all the individual OSPF-routed networks inside AS4. It may be nice to do so, however, if there are many OSPF-routed networks in AS4, the rest of the Internet may not be all that interested in knowing about every single one of them. This is where route aggregation (discussed in the previous section) kicks in. The criteria for route aggregation have now been met. The ASBRs have been told to perform it, and they've been notified about the individual networks to be aggregated via dynamic redistribution from OSPF to BGP.

Now, try to imagine what happens if there is a certain level of network instability inside the OSPF-routed portion of AS4, with the OSPF routes being redistributed into BGP dynamically. Any change in the OSPF internal routes results in BGP routing updates. When these routing updates are propagated between many autonomous systems, the level of BGP-generated routing traffic can become significant. This may have a direct impact on how fast packets carrying your data get to their destinations (poor response from the Net). A name for this scenario is *route flapping*, which references unstable routes that can cause massive amounts of network traffic to communicate the route changes.

One way to avoid route flapping is to use static redistribution. Static redistribution configuration details are discussed in Chapter 5. The effect of static redistribution, however, would be to make the entire environment shown in Figure 4.11 more stable.

Redistribution is not a one-way street. It is also possible to redistribute routes learned by BGP from other autonomous systems into an IGP. When IGP-learned routes are redistributed into BGP, and the BGP routes are redistributed into an IGP, you have *mutual redistribution*. Care must be taken when implementing mutual redistribution that routing loops do not occur. Routes that have been learned by an IGP from BGP in the first place must not be redistributed back into BGP. How this is done depends on the vendor implementation but typically some form of filter lists and route maps are involved.

To avoid redistributing massive amounts of BGP updates into an IGP, it is also a fairly common implementation procedure for BGP to redistribute a default static route into an IGP. With a default static route redistributed by BGP into an IGP, the IGP routers internal to an AS direct any packet destined for networks not present in their routing tables to the originator of the default route. The originator of a default route typically is an ASBR with external peering connections to other autonomous systems. You may have guessed by now that redistribution implies that routers involved in it must be configured for BGP and one of the IGPs with which BGP is performing redistribution.

With route redistribution between routing protocols, the potential exists for a significant loss of routing information, depending on how redistribution is implemented. Static route redistribution into BGP, and even dynamic route redistribution from IGPs into BGP, is unavoidable if the networks internal to an autonomous system are to be reachable from the outside. However, when an autonomous system is used for transit (with the topology as shown in

Figure 4.11), there is a potential for route redistribution from BGP into OSPF, and subsequently from OSPF into BGP. This is not a very efficient process, and subject to a significant loss of routing information (definitely something to be avoided).

Consider translating something from one language into another. Then retranslate your translation from the second language back into the original. You might be surprised at how different the re-translation is from the original message.

If you compare the routing information carried in the BGP update message to that propagated through the RIP or OSPF updates, you find that the structure of the update messages in the different protocols is drastically different. All these routing protocols also have a different concept of the route cost or metric. In RIP, the *cost metric* represents the number of hops or routers that must be crossed to reach a destination. In OSPF, the cost metric is an arbitrary number that a network administrator can assign to a router interface that's a function of interface speed, availability, desirability of use, and so on. The BGP *metric* is a rather complex decision-making algorithm that has to do with a number of autonomous systems and their attributes contained in the BGP update message.

A technique used for routers within a transit AS to avoid multiple route redistribution is to establish internal BGP peers using Internal Border Gateway Protocol (IBGP). The BGP that's used between routers in different autonomous systems is External Border Gateway Protocol (EBGP). The dotted lines between the ASBRs in AS4 in Figure 4.11 show that all three of them have been set up as internal BGP neighbors. Because AS4 acts as like a transit AS, setting up internal BGP neighbors inside of it will avoid the need for redistribution of the externally learned BGP routes into OSPF and then redistribution of the OSPF routes back into BGP to pass them on to AS4's peers in the neighboring autonomous systems.

Collectively IBGP and EBGP are referred to as BGP, but there are differences between them. Internal BGP peers do not need to share the same data-link layer — they don't need to be part of the same physical subnetwork — whereas external BGP peers are generally physical neighbors, with some exceptions. By establishing internal BGP peers inside an autonomous system, the BGP routing updates that are coming into an AS4 from the neighboring autonomous systems (AS1, AS2, AS3 in Figure 4.11) pass through the AS4 without being altered. IBGP preserves the BGP path attributes which are discussed later in this section.

BGP "mesh"

For BGP routers to communicate with each other they must be configured as neighbors. In Cisco routers, this is done through a *neighbor id remote-as nn* where *neighbor* and *remote-as* are key words, and *id* represents the router ID (an IP address assigned to one of its interfaces or a loopback address) and *nn* represents an AS number. Both EBGP and IBGP support *neighbor* commands.

BGP is not exempt from scalability problems. Since BGP relies on setting up peering relationships with other BGP routers, and since one of the requirements is that internal BGP speakers be fully meshed, the number of BGP sessions can become significant in a large AS. In contrast to RIP and OSPF, BGP uses the reliable transport protocol TCP to set up and maintain sessions with its neighbors. A couple of techniques that have been proposed and implemented as BGP extensions are route reflectors and confederations.

Route reflectors

Route reflection is a technique that has been proposed as an alternative to a "full mesh" IBGP. Route Reflection is described in RFC 1966 (see RFC 1966, Appendix A), classified in the experimental category. Maintaining a full mesh between internal BGP speakers implies that for every *N* speakers there will be *N**(*N*–1)/2 connections. As an example, for 25 BGP routers in an AS, this would result in 25*(25–1)/2, or 300 TCP sessions. For four BGP speakers as shown in Figure 4.12, the number of internal BGP sessions is six.

A large number of TCP connections resulting from BGP peering sessions puts a significant pressure on the network bandwidth and the routers' processing power. The idea behind route reflection is to minimize that pressure by reducing the number of internal BGP peerings. Conceptually, it's similar to electing a designated router in OSPF. However, because route reflection is an experimental technique, not every BGP implementation supports it. Figure 4.13 shows the internal BGP peering sessions following the implementation of route reflection. Compare this to the peering sessions without route reflection shown in Figure 4.12.

The number of IBGP connections has been reduced to three. Consider a scenario of what happens with and without route reflection. When any one of the routers in Figure 4.12 receives an update via EBGP from another AS, it propagates this update to all its peers. The receiving routers will not continue to advertise the update because it is assumed that all the BGP peers are fully meshed.

FIGURE 4.12 *BGP mesh without route reflection*

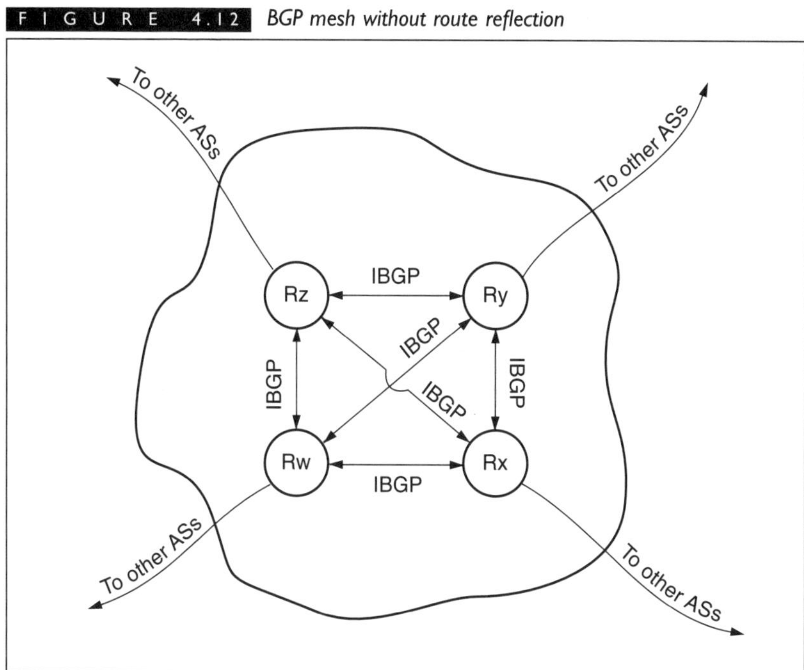

With route reflection as shown in Figure 4.13, assume that Rz (which is configured as the route reflector) receives an external BGP update. It propagates it to all its peers. So far, nothing has changed. However, if any one of the other routers configured as route reflector clients receives an update, it will only propagate it to the route reflector Rz. This is where the change comes in. Rz will now reflect (or re-advertise) the route to the remaining two peers with whom it is meshed. So, there has not been a reduction in the amount of update traffic, but there has been a reduction in the number of BGP sessions that must be maintained between routers in an AS.

A group of routers configured for route reflection is considered a *cluster*. When there are multiple clusters in an AS, the route reflectors from each cluster must be fully meshed. Routers not configured for route reflection must also be meshed with the route reflectors.

FIGURE 4.13 *BGP mesh with route reflection*

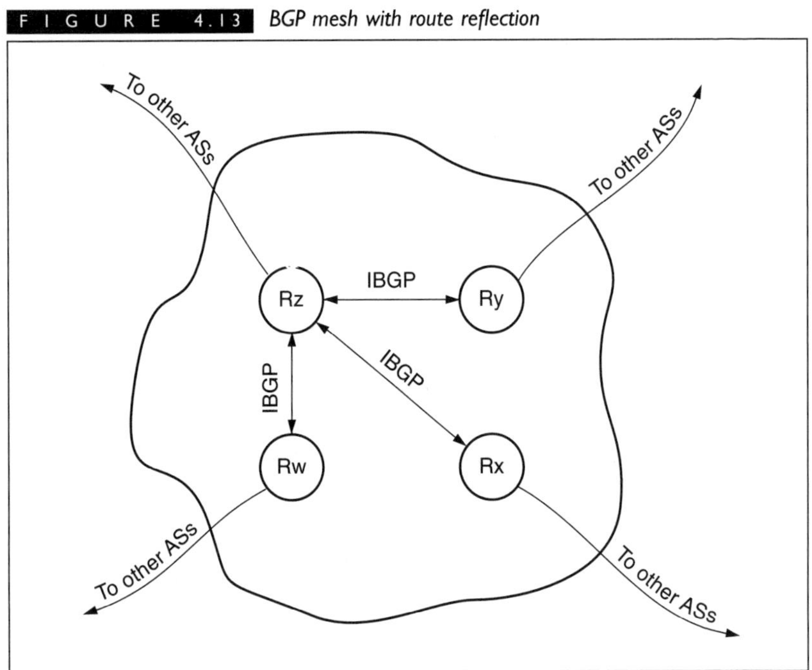

It becomes easy to imagine that a route reflector receiving an update from a client, non-client peer, or an external peer will have to handle it differently. An update received from an external peer must be passed to all client peers and non-client peers. An update coming from a non-client peer must be passed to all client peers. Any other non-client peers will be meshed with the non-client originating this update. Finally, an update received from a client peer must be passed (reflected) to all the other client peers, as well as all the non-client peers.

For additional details regarding route reflection see RFC 1966, Appendix A.

Confederations

BGP *confederations* are another attempt at reducing the internal BGP mesh in an AS containing a large number of BGP speakers. Given a large AS with a large number of BGP speakers, the idea behind a BGP confederation is to make that AS appear as a single AS to all the other autonomous systems with which it has external peering BGP connections. However, inside the AS, the BGP speakers would be grouped into smaller units or confederations (or mini-autonomous systems). So, a BGP confederation is a mini-AS within a larger AS.

Imagine that number of BGP speakers in Figure 4.12 has been quadrupled. Instead of 4, you now have 16. Without configuring route reflectors and confederations, each of the 16 BGP speakers must maintain BGP sessions with the other 15. Applying the formula of $N*(N-1)/2$, where N is the total number of BGP speakers, it yields 105 internal BGP sessions in the new imaginary AS with 16 BGP speakers. Add to it one or more external peers for each speaker and the number of BGP peering sessions becomes even larger, sufficiently large to avoid showing it in an illustration.

Continuing with the imaginary AS with 16 BGP speakers, now take the 16 BGP speakers and break them into 4 groups of 4 speakers each. Each group of four BGP speakers becomes a confederation (a mini-AS within an already defined AS). The requirement of a confederation is that the BGP speakers within a confederation maintain a full mesh. However, the confederations themselves do not have to be fully meshed, just linked together for connectivity. What this translates into is that each confederation would have a total of six peering sessions,4*(4-1)/2=6, and at least three peering sessions would be required to link the four confederations together. Adding the numbers, this translates into 4*6 + 3 or 27. That's quite a reduction from the 105 calculated previously. BGP confederations are defined via router configuration commands.

BGP path

BGP is considered to be a *path-vector* routing protocol. A path represents a series of steps that must be taken between a point of origin and a point of destination. Imagine yourself hiking through a varied countryside. Part of your hike may be through mountainous terrain, part of it through a forest, and part through an open valley. Different rules may apply to hiking through the various types of terrain. Describing the full path to someone may not be simple, because no single uniform description can apply to all the different segments of the path.

The different portions of the hiking path correspond to autonomous systems that a BGP update packet will cross. The *BGP path* is a series of AS numbers that a packet crosses, or that a packet carrying user data must cross, to reach its destination. These AS numbers are displayed when you view the BGP-derived routes in a router's routing table. However, a series of AS numbers does not represent the complete BGP path.

The complete BGP path is described by a group of attributes. Only one of those attributes is the list of AS numbers that a BGP update packet will cross. This attribute is referred to technically as the AS_PATH attribute or variable. Because AS numbers represent a direction, and direction is associated with vector, the *path-vector* appellation of BGP is derived from the fact that its update messages carry lists of AS numbers that they have crossed. All the BGP path attributes are carried in the *update* messages exchanged between BGP speakers.

BGP derives its robustness and versatility from the flexible structure of its update messages. In Figure 4.14, for example, concentrate on the portion of the message that the variable length path attributes.

The variable size of the update message and the breakdown of the BGP path description into individual attributes allows for new extensions (new attributes) to be developed and implemented as the demands of the exploding Internet dictate. Path attributes allow BGP to deal with technical issues related to the protocol performance, as well as with routing policies that may be economical or political in nature. For example, the implementation of BGP confederations, which improves performance by reducing the mesh level between BGP speakers, relies on modifying and adding to the BGP path attributes.

BGP as specified in RFC 1771 (see RFC 1771, Appendix A) uses the seven attributes shown in Table 4.3.

Additional attributes have been implemented by router and software vendors. For example, Cisco's BGP implementation includes a *weight* attribute. Both Cisco's and GateD (a UNIX daemon) implement the *community* attribute in their BGP implementations. *Originator ID* and *Cluster ID* are other attributes implemented by Cisco to prevent looping in routing environments with route reflection. Confederations are implemented by adding two type codes to the AS_path attribute.

TABLE 4.3 *BGP attributes*

ATTRIBUTE	DESCRIPTION
origin	the origin of the destinations carried in Network Layer Reachability Information (NLRI)
AS_path	series of AS numbers
next_hop	IP address of the next router to reach destinations in NLRI
multi_exit_disc	choice of an exit from an AS if multiple exit points exist
local_pref	degree of preference for a route received via EBGP
atomic_aggregate	indication of a less-specific route selection from overlapping routes advertised by a BGP peer
aggregator	IP and AS number of a BGP speaker that did route aggregation

FIGURE 4.14 *BGP update message structure*

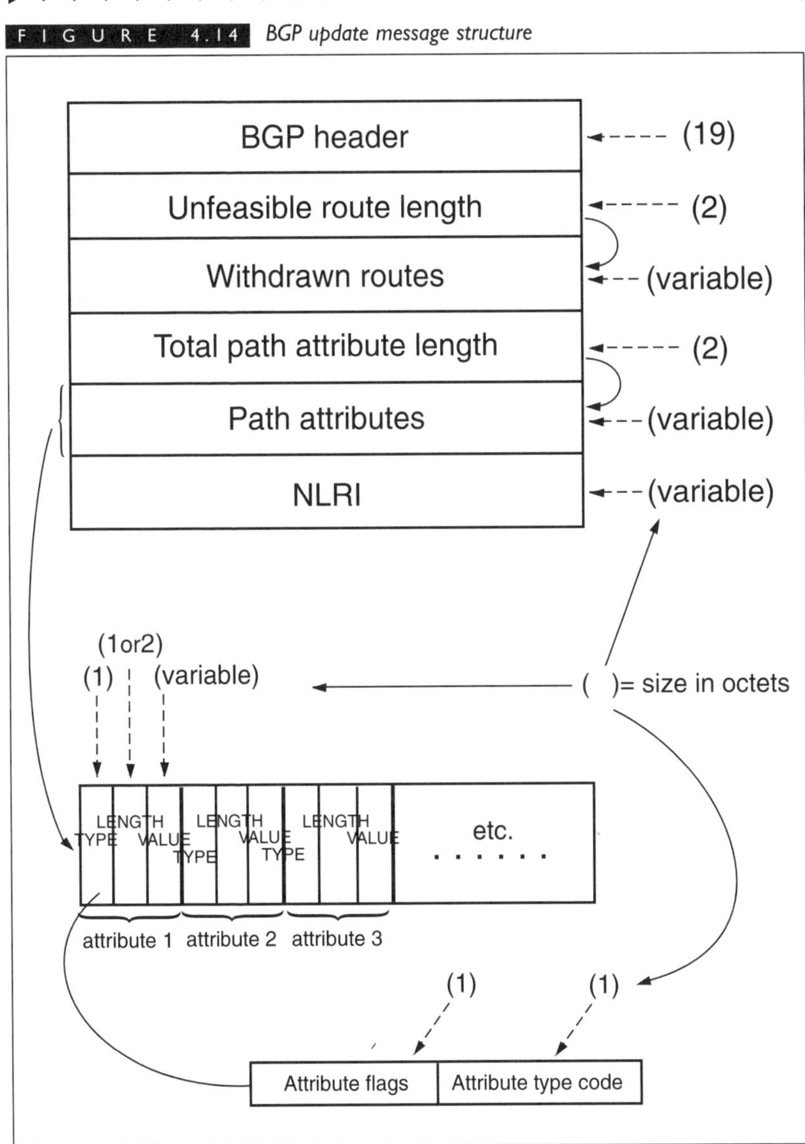

The origin attribute

The *origin* attribute indicates from where the destinations carried in the Network Layer Reachability Information (NLRI) came. The network destinations in the NLRI field are what BGP routing is all about. These are the network numbers that can be reached if the BGP path is followed. There are three possibilities for the origin attribute.

If BGP has learned about the network numbers carried in its NLRI field from one of the IGPs (RIP, OSPF, or IGRP), its origin attribute will be set to an IGP. Dynamic redistribution from any IGP into BGP will set the origin attribute in the BGP update message to an IGP. The IGP origin is typically represented with the letter *I* when the BGP process information is displayed.

The second possibility for the *origin* attribute is EGP. BGP may have learned about the destinations in NLRI from its ancestor, the EGP that has been relegated to history, but, just like RIP, it may still be implemented in some locations. The *origin* attribute is set to EGP in that case and is represented with a letter *E*.

The last possibility is that BGP does not know exactly from where the destinations in NLRI came, in which case the *origin* attribute is considered to be "incomplete," often indicated with a question mark (?). One example of when the *origin* attribute is set to incomplete is when static routes are redistributed into BGP.

The AS_path attribute

The BGP *AS_path* attribute is a series of autonomous systems that a BGP update message has crossed. When a BGP speaker sends routes to an external neighbor, it prepends its AS number in the *AS_path* attribute. When the neighbor receives the route update, and passes it on to another external neighbor, it does the same. Consequently, a series of AS numbers accumulates in the *AS_path* variable. The *AS_path* variable is instrumental in ensuring a loop-free routing environment in BGP, since the BGP speaker ensures that its AS number is not in the *AS_path* variable before prepending the AS number to it. The *AS_path* is displayed in the BGP routing table as a series of AS numbers.

The next_hop attribute

When a BGP route is installed in a routing table for the network addresses that are carried in the NLRI field, the incoming packets with user data must know what is the next step to take in their journey. The *next_hop* attribute is the IP address of a BGP peer to whom packets will be forwarded. The concept of a next hop is not new. All the routing protocols discussed so far are based on the concept of "hop-by-hop" routing. Next-hop is present in the RIP routing table entries as the IP address of a router from whom a RIP update was received for a given network destination. In OSPF, the next hop is derived from the link-state database through the Diijakstra algorithm. In BGP, the next hop manifests in the form of the *next_hop* attribute and it is a component of the BGP update message. Next hop is displayed in a BGP routing table as an IP address.

The multi_exit_disc (MED) attribute

The *multi_exit_dis*criminator attribute represents a measure of choices for an ASBR in one AS to get into a neighboring AS. Imagine a scenario where an ASBR in one AS has multiple external BGP peering sessions with three ASBRs in another AS. It might be an issue of redundancy. The AS with the three routers might be an ISP providing redundant links to a client requiring continuous uptime. The three routers in the ISP's AS are configured with varying values of the MED attribute. The configured values of the MED are now passed by each one of the three ISP's ASBRs to their single neighbor in the client AS.

The MED values will now play a role in determining the best route (which the ISP's ASBR will become the entry point into the ISP's AS) when the client has traffic to send to the ISP networks or beyond. Given that all other route-selection conditions are equal (BGP has a fairly complex mechanism for that), the client ASBR directs traffic to the ASBR in the ISP's AS that was configured with the lowest MED value.

Frankly, this attribute should be renamed from *multi-exit-discriminator* to a *multi-entry-discriminator*. It could save some confusion, because it really has to do with how traffic will enter a neighboring AS as opposed to how it will exit it. However, you could argue the point that MED should remain a *muti-exit-discriminator* because, from the perspective of an AS, MED announces the preference of the exit points from this AS to a neighboring or a client AS. Once these exit points have been announced, however, they become the points of entry for the traffic coming from an ASBR in the client AS. It's the client ASBRs that use the MED value in their decision-making process.

The MED value is passed between neighboring autonomous systems, but it is not carried through a transit AS. The MED attribute is considered to be a non-transitive attribute (because it does not transit multiple autonomous systems) and an optional attribute (because it does not have to be configured on a router). MED value is represented by a 4-octet positive integer. A lower value of MED is given preference in the route-selection process. Typically, the MED value is displayed in the BGP routing table under a "metric" heading.

The local_preference attribute

Again, given a choice in renaming the BGP attributes, the *local_preference* attribute should be called the *multi-exit-discriminator*. Anyway, the *local_preference* attribute is a metric internal to an AS (maybe that's where the "local" comes from). When internal BGP peers use IBGP to exchange routing information, they have the option to include the *local_preference* attribute in the path variable of the update message. When multiple exit points exist (ASBRs) in an AS X whose BGP speakers are advertising routes to the same destination in AS Y, the ASBR in AS X configured with a higher *local_preference* metric will be selected for sending traffic to AS Y. The values of *local_preference* are displayed in a BGP routing table.

The atomic_aggregate attribute

The *atomic_aggregate* attribute is not set through configuration. It is updated by BGP based on the presence of overlapping routes. An example of overlapping routes might be 192.168.0.0/16 and 192.168.32.0/19 using the CIDR notation of a prefix followed by a number of bits in the mask. These two destinations overlap, with 192.168.32.0/19 being more specific. If a BGP speaker chooses to advertise only the less-specific route, it must set the *atomic_aggregate* attribute as an indication to other BGP speakers that it had a more specific route, but it chose not to advertise it.

The aggregator attribute

Remember the route aggregation discussion? If a BGP speaker performs route aggregation, it sets the *aggregator* attribute. It's that simple. The value of the aggregator attribute will be the IP address and the AS number of the speaker performing the aggregation.

Having delved into a lot of technical details of BGP (by the way, in reality we've just scratched the surface), you may still be wondering why BGP is called the long-distance runner. It's because BGP is a very strong routing protocol, capable of propagating routing information between the farthest reaches of the Internet. Operating between and within the autonomous systems (which are the building blocks of the Internet), BGP is singularly responsible for giving all Internet users the abilities of virtual travel, even to Mars, that we have today.

However, even BGP is not immune from anomalies when it comes to implementing routing policies based on economic and political factors, as opposed to just the best way of getting to a destination based on physical connectivity.

The issues of BGP and BGP policy are discussed along with the subjects of ISPs and NAPs in Chapter 10. At the point where even the most robust technology meet politics and economics, don't be surprised if certain absurdities are the end result.

What's Next for Routing Protocols?

The increasingly complex and creative features of the routing protocols discussed in the preceding sections represent the Internet engineering community's response to the ongoing evolutionary demands for an effective means of communication between the growing number of routers participating in Internet routing. These demands stem from the phenomenal growth of the Internet which is traced in Chapter 10. The question that comes to mind is, what's next in store for the routing protocols? Will they become a historical footnote, or do they have a future as the Internet races at a break-neck speed into the 21st century?

It's routing protocols that allow the Internet routers to maintain an awareness of the Internet's topology. It's this awareness that's needed to get your packets to their destinations. But there is a price to pay for this awareness. As the Internet grows, the level of exchanges between routers increases to a point where it begins to interfere with the forwarding of user packets. So, how are the protocol developers and the Internet engineering community coping with these issues? Several trends are in the works.

The existing protocols continue to be upgraded in incremental ways to make them more efficient. New BGP attributes, a recent RFC 2178 (see RFC 2178, Appendix A), updating the OSPF specification, RIP version 2 and RIPng are all examples indicating that the tweaking of routing protocols will continue. It appears they are here to stay for a while. But they are also getting help from other sources.

Faster router hardware and an increasing bandwidth capacity of the transmission media (see Chapter 7) are helping routing protocols to keep up with demand for fast and efficient communications between routers. Distributed router architecture in high-performance backbone routers which is discussed in Chapter 9 is also assisting routing protocols with their job. And several new and exciting integration techniques between the routing and switching layers (layers 3 and 2) described in Chapter 11 are also helping to solve the dilemma. These newer techniques are enabling the routing protocols to cooperate with the faster lower layer technologies to the greatest benefit of guess who? You, the Internet users.

So, now that you've been told many details about routing protocols and what's in store for them, it's time to consider how their features are put to practical use. That's accomplished through router configuration discussed in the next chapter.

CHAPTER 5

Router Configuration

Just because we have beautiful languages in the world does not mean that everyone who speaks them is considered a great speaker or an orator. Think of a router as a speaker of one or more languages, the routing protocols. How effective a router will be in communicating with other routers and consequently directing your traffic to its intended destination will ultimately depend on the router configuration. Most routers come with some default configuration. The default configuration may be equivalent to knowing how to say, "How are you?" or, "Where is the nearest bathroom?" when you are in a foreign country, but not much more.

Router configuration is the responsibility of network administrators. How well routers are configured may well depend on the skill level of the administrator. It is generally recognized in the industry, however, that routers are not plug-and-play devices. Because they interconnect physically different networks (both locally and across long distances), router configuration requires some knowledge of the routable protocols, the routing protocols, and the Data-Link Layer technologies of a router's interfaces.

FIGURE 5.1 *Rear panels of Cisco's 2500 series models (courtesy of Cisco Systems, Inc.)*

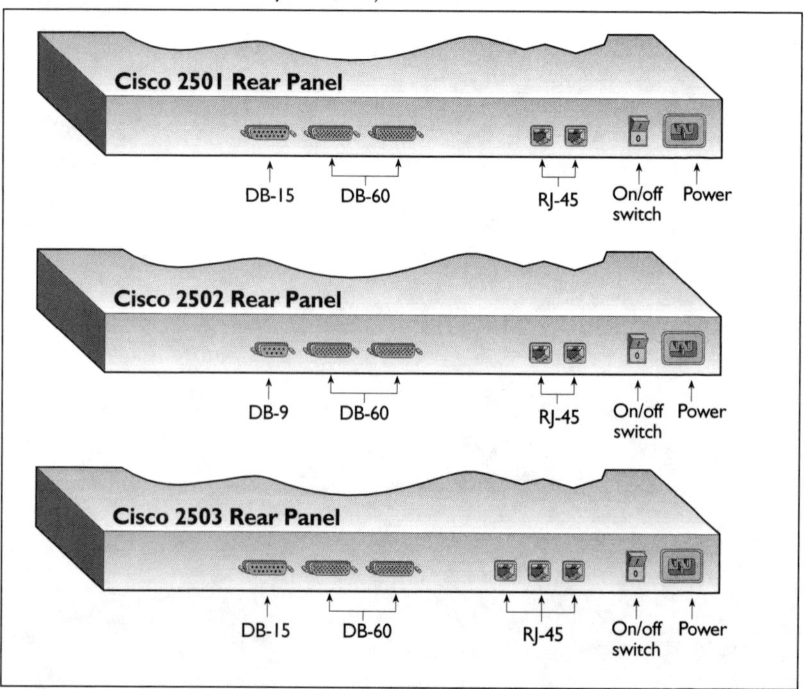

There are multiple approaches to router configuration. How a router is configured may depend on what kind of router it is. A router may be a dedicated, standalone box with its own CPU, random-access memory (RAM), and some form of nonvolatile storage, but with no hard drive or monitor display. A router may be a server like a NetWare sever with multiple NICs and responsibilities for many other functions on the network than just routing. A router may be a workstation with multiple NICs (just like a server), but with no other responsibilities except that of routing packets. So, not all routers are created equal. There are advantages and disadvantages to deploying a router in any of these forms. However, this discussion focuses on routers in the form of dedicated boxes. Additionally, all the router configuration commands used and shown apply to Cisco routers.

A typical *dedicated router* is a box with a number of interfaces and a console port. Figure 5.1 illustrates the rear panels of a number of routers from the Cisco 2500 series.

FIGURE 5.1 (*continued*)

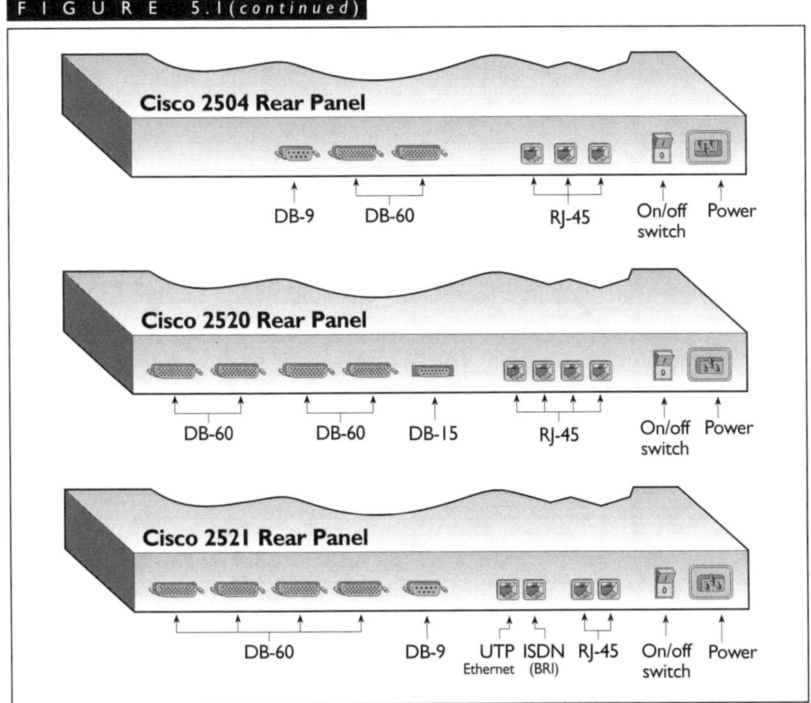

To configure a router like the one shown in Figure 5.1 requires access to another computer that will interface to the router via the console port. A special cable is required that connects the router's console port to a personal computer's serial port. The personal computer must be put into a terminal-emulation mode. Under DOS, any modem communication program such as PROCOM or Quicklink allows you to put a personal computer into a terminal-emulation mode. Other operating systems (such as UNIX or Windows NT) come with their own terminal emulators.

With a router connected to a personal computer through a serial cable (and the personal computer is in a terminal-emulation mode), the router goes through some form of a power-on-self-test (POST) when it is started up. The router then displays an initial configuration screen. One of two approaches to configuration can be taken at that point, depending on the vendor implementation:

- The router goes into a menu-driven configuration mode
- The router goes into a command-line interface mode

Cisco routers allow for either approach. Other routers may or may not support a command-line approach and the entire configuration may be done through a series of menus. The command-line approach to router configuration is a very powerful technique, but it requires the most active knowledge on the part of the network administrator. Normally, extensive help features are available from the command-line interfaces to help administrators navigate through the maze of configuration commands.

Whichever approach is taken to router configuration, the bottom-line objective is to configure a router correctly so that it does its job well. The command-line approach has the added benefit of enabling network administrators to configure a router by way of script configuration files, which contain all the router configuration commands you normally must type from the command-line interface prompt. However, script files can be created by using a text editor and uploaded to a router either via the console port or from a network server. The use of script files for router configuration offers a powerful network-management tool in larger networks, if their locations can be centralized and they can be uploaded to routers via the network as configuration changes dictate.

In the configuration examples that follow (see Figure 5.2 for a hypothetical network scenario), the focus is on the configuration commands themselves and their effect on the router. This discussion does not focus on whether the commands were entered by typing them in from the command-line interface, by using a menu, or by uploading them from a script file.

FIGURE 5.2 *Scenario for router configuration*

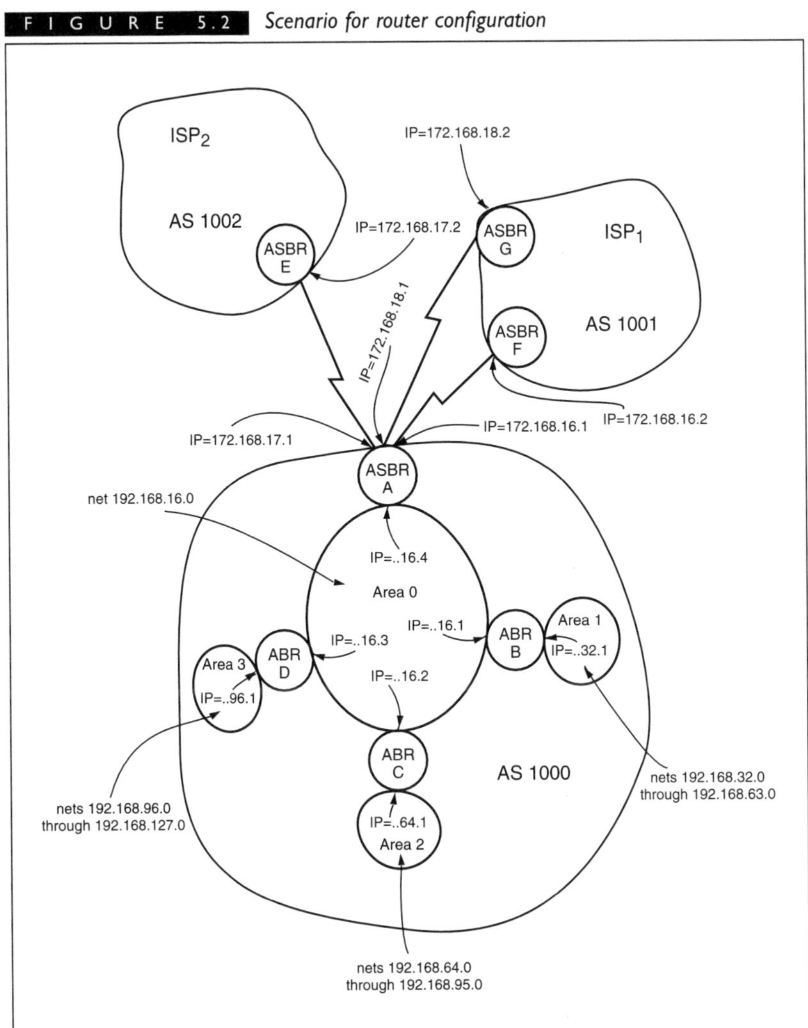

As a reminder, all the IP addresses used in Figure 5.2 and in all other examples throughout this book come from the private reserved address range (see RFC 1918, Appendix A) and should never appear in configuration files on the real Internet.

Physical Interfaces

Routers have physical interfaces corresponding to the Data-Link Layer technologies of networks they interconnect. The physical interfaces fall into two general categories: LAN interfaces and WAN interfaces.

LAN interfaces

In a local-area environment, a simple router connecting an Ethernet network to a Token Ring network would have one Ethernet and one Token Ring interface.

Assume that in Figure 5.2, area 0 (or the backbone) with the network number of 192.168.16.0 is connected via Ethernet. Physically, area 0 could appear as an Ethernet concentrator with four cables going to the four routers, A, B, C, D. Assume that the network 192.168.32.0 in area 1 (which is connected to area 0 via the ABR B) is a Token Ring network. The initial interface configuration for the two interfaces on router B might be as follows:

```
interface Ethernet0
 ip address 192.168.16.1 255.255.255.0
 ip broadcast-address 192.168.16.255
 description Ethernet connector to area 0
interface Tokenring0
 ip address 192.168.32.1 255.255.255.0
 ip broadcast-address 192.168.32.255
 ring-speed 16
 early-token-release
 description first token ring connector to area 1
```

By no means do these commands represent the entire interface configuration of router B. However, they enable B's interfaces to become active, assign to them the IP addresses with the appropriate masks, and assign the IP broadcast addresses for the networks on which the interfaces reside. Because many networks numbers are available in this example, notice that we are working with default subnet masks on each network, rather then subnetting the class C networks shown in Figure 5.2.

Additional parameters are specified on the Token Ring interface like the speed of the ring (16 Mbps, as opposed to 4 Mbps on the earlier version of Token Ring), and the Token Ring option for the *early token release option*, which means that the transmitting workstation does not have to wait until the transmitted frame circles the ring and comes back to it with a confirmation receipt bit set. The early token release option improves performance on a Token Ring network.

The description command under the interfaces is an administrative tool that identifies the interfaces in a more graphic way. Imagine that you have a router where instead of one Ethernet and one Token Ring interfaces, you have ten Ethernet and five Token Ring interfaces. It would be very nice to identify them in the configuration in a way that indicates the function or location of networks to which those interfaces belong. There are no WAN interfaces on the ABR B in Figure 5.2.

WAN interfaces

Router A in Figure 5.2 acts as an ASBR, which interfaces the AS 1000 to AS 1001 and AS 1002. We will assume that the interfaces between the autonomous systems are over T1 point-to-point serial links. Note that Figure 5.2 is a logical diagram of the network and devices such as channel service units/digital service units (CSUs/DSUs) are not shown on the serial links. Router A has at least three serial interfaces connecting it to its neighbors in the other autonomous systems, and at least one Ethernet interface connecting it to the OSPF backbone area in AS 1000. The initial configuration of the interfaces for router A might be as follows:

```
interface Ethernet0
 ip address 192.168.16.4 255.255.255.0
 ip broadcast-address 192.168.16.255
 description Ethernet connector to area 0
interface Serial0
 ip address 172.168.16.1 255.255.255.0
 ip broadcast-address 172.168.16.255
 description Connection to ISP1 - ASBR F
 encapsulation ppp
!
interface Serial1
 ip address 172.168.18.1 255.255.255.0
 ip broadcast-address 172.168.18.255
 description Connection to ISP1 - ASBR G
 encapsulation ppp
```

```
!
interface Serial2
 ip address 172.168.17.1 255.255.255.0
 ip broadcast-address 172.168.17.255
 description Connection to ISP2 - ASBR E
 encapsulation ppp
```

These configuration statements would activate the interfaces in ASBR A, assign the IP addresses to the interfaces, assign broadcast addresses to the networks on which the interfaces reside, describe the interfaces in the context of the internetwork topology, and, for the serial interfaces, define the *WAN protocol encapsulation*. The WAN protocol encapsulation defines the Data-Link Layer protocol operational on the WAN link that will be responsible for creating frames.

Routing Protocol Configuration

If you stopped router configuration with just the activation of a router's interfaces and the assignment of IP addresses to them, you would deprive the routers of their primary responsibility in life — the forwarding of packets. So, the next step is to define the routing protocols that will be operational on each router. Based on the discussion of routing protocols in Chapter 4, you may be guessing by now that the two protocols that will be operational on the internetwork in Figure 5.2 are OSPF and BGP. The internetwork in Figure 5.2 lends itself to configuring the concepts discussed in Chapter 4.

OSPF configuration

Router B in Figure 5.2 is an ABR connecting area 1 to the OSPF backbone. After completing router's B configuration, you should follow the same steps to come up with the configurations for router C and router D.

Initial OSPF configuration

The initial configuration statements that would activate the OSPF process on router B and assign its interfaces to the two different areas would be as follows:

```
router OSPF 88
 network 192.168.16.1 0.0.0.0 area 0
 network 192.168.32.1 0.0.0.0 area 1
```

The number following OSPF in the *router* command is an OSPF process number. A process number is needed because it is possible to have multiple OSPF processes running on the same router. The network statements under the OSPF process assign router interfaces to an OSPF area. These network statements are not to be confused with those used for injecting IGP routes into BGP. A single interface is assigned to an OSPF area when a mask of all 0s (0.0.0.0) is used. This mask is not a subnet mask. It is called an *inverse mask* because a mask of all 0s is the most specific, whereas with subnetting the mask of all 1s is most specific. The inverse mask is a shortcut tool. In this example, only routers with one interface per area are used, so you may as well assign the interfaces to the areas with the most-specific inverse mask of all 0s. However, if you had 32 interfaces on router B that belong to area 1, and you wanted to use the inverse mask of all 0s, then you would have to use 32 *network* statements. That's a lot of typing.

Since you actually have a range of 32 contiguous networks in area 1, assume for a moment that router B had a physical interface to each one of them. Can you still assign all the 32 interfaces to area 1 with a single *network* command? The answer is yes, but it does involve some binary arithmetic, not unlike what you did in Chapter 4.

You must find the common part of all of the network numbers. If you converted all 32 networks from area 1 into binary and then looked for the common part, you would come up with 1100 0000 1010 1000 001 as the common part. Converting it to decimal gives 192.168.32.0. To come up with the inverse mask, you would set the common part (the previous result) to binary 0 and the remainder (13 remaining bits) to binary 1, which would yield (in decimal) an inverse mask of 0.0.31.255. So, the hypothetical 32 interfaces on router B in Figure 5.2 could be assigned to area 1 with a single network statement using 192.168.32.0 for the network number and 0.0.31.255 for the inverse mask. So much for shortcuts.

OSPF summarization configuration

Since you have 32 contiguous network numbers in area 1, the next decision is whether you want to advertise them all individually onto the OSPF backbone, or you want to group them together to minimize the size of routing tables in other routers on the OSPF backbone. Remember summarization from Chapter 4? Conditions are ideal for summarization. If there were multiple networks in the backbone area, you might consider summarizing them as well. Because you only have one network on the OSPF backbone, only the networks in the areas 1, 2, and 3 will be summarized.

The mechanics of summarization are not unlike what you just went through with assigning router B's hypothetical interfaces to area 1, except that the mask once again will be normal. You must find the common part of the networks to be summarized. In the hypothetical example above we already calculated the common part for the networks in area 1 to be 1100 0000 1010 1000 001 in binary. Translating this into decimal gives a summary network number of 192.168.32.0. The rest is a matter of masking. In the case of summarization, the mask is the normal (as opposed to inverse) mask. You use binary 1s for the common part of the networks and binary 0s to the rest, which yields a mask of 255.255.224.0.

In the context of summarization, the mask you just came up with (255.255.224.0) is called the *summarization mask*. The idea behind summarization, however, is to advertise the summarized route to other routers. So, after the summarized route has been advertised by router B via the OSPF link-state exchanges, the summary mask that is used in B's configuration will, in effect, become a subnet mask in some other router's routing table for the summarized route of 192.162.32.0. The summarization command implementing summarization for area 1 would be as follows:

```
area 1 range 192.168.32.0 255.255.224.0.
```

That's it. Again, much ado about nothing.

Following summarization, configuration, router's B OSPF section would look like the following:

```
router OSPF 88
 network 192.168.16.1 0.0.0.0 area 0
 network 192.168.32.1 0.0.0.0 area 1
 area 1 range 192.168.32.0 255.255.224.0
```

Because the OSPF protocol supports authentication (which is not covered anywhere in this book), there could be some additional configuration statements in the OSPF section. However, in contrast to the conceptual complexity of OSPF, the configuration commands seem very simple. Given the symmetry of internetwork topology in Figure 5.2, routers C and D would have almost identical configuration statements. What would differ between the three routers, B, C, and D, are the IP addresses of the interfaces and network numbers being summarized. Consider now the protocol configuration on router A.

BGP configuration

You may be guessing by now that router A will be configured for both OSPF and BGP because it has one interface in the OSPF backbone area in AS 1000 and three interfaces to ASBRs in other autonomous systems. Without delving into the steps of configuring OSPF on router A, the initial OSPF configuration would look like this:

```
router ospf 99
 network 192.168.16.4 0.0.0.0 area 0
```

With no summarization, no authentication, and only a single interface in an area, the OSPF configuration is trivial.

Initial BGP configuration

The BGP configuration on router A will be more involved. First, the BGP process must be started, then the BGP neighbors must be defined, then aggregation and redistribution performed, then any remaining configuration statements put in to implement a desired BGP policy. Still, compared to the operational complexities of the routing protocols, this configuration seems relatively simple.

The initial BGP configuration on router A would look like this:

```
router bgp 1000
 neighbor 172.168.16.2 remote-as 1001
 neighbor 172.168.18.2 remote-as 1001
 neighbor 172.168.17.2 remote-as 1002
```

Notice that the number in the router statement activating BGP is the AS number in which router A is located (1000). The numbers in the neighbor commands correspond to the AS numbers in which the neighbors are located. Neighbor commands define the router A BGP neighbors by specifying their IP addresses and AS numbers.

Redistribution and BGP aggregation configuration

The next step in the BGP configuration would be to let router A know which are the networks in AS 1000 that can be advertised to the other autonomous systems. This is the *redistribution* process into BGP. As you recall from Chapter 4, redistribution can be either static or dynamic. It is also possible to inject specific networks into BGP via a *network* command. Let's explore all options.

Whether you perform static or dynamic redistribution into BGP, you must know the network numbers inside AS 1000 if you are planning to configure router A to do route aggregation as well. Redistribution and aggregation are configured via separate configuration commands, but the concepts of redistribution and aggregation are closely intertwined. In the case of OSPF summarization, you were looking at the network numbers within an OSPF area. For route aggregation, you should be looking at *all* of the network numbers in AS 1000. Looking at Figure 5.2, each of the three OSPF areas has a contiguous range of network numbers. Area 0 stands out with a single network number.

You can use two methods to figure out the aggregate network number for AS 1000. You can list all the networks individually in binary and find their common part. Or, you can summarize each area first, and figure out the common part (prefix) from the OSPF summary network numbers that would be advertised onto the OSPF backbone by routers B, C, and D. If you follow the process of finding the summary networks and masks for areas 2 and 3 (as you did for area 1), the summary networks that will appear on the backbone will be 192.168.64.0 with a mask of 255.255.224.0 from router C and 192.168.96.0 with a mask of 255.255.224.0 from router D. The summary net from A is 192.168.32.0 with a mask of 255.255.224.0. Taking these three summary network numbers plus the OSPF backbone network of 192.168.16.0 and aggregating them together yields an aggregate network number of 192.168.0.0 with a mask of 255.255.128.0. Translating this into the CIDR notation gives 192.168.0.0/17.

Now, armed with the aggregate network number for AS 1000, you can configure both redistribution and aggregation on router A. Start with static redistribution. Adding the static redistribution commands to the existing BGP configuration, the configuration would look as follows:

```
router bgp 1000
 neighbor 172.168.16.2 remote-as 1001
 neighbor 172.168.18.2 remote-as 1001
 neighbor 172.168.17.2 remote-as 1002
 redistribute static
!
 ip route 192.168.0.0 255.255.128.0 null0
```

The *ip route* configuration command creates a static routing table entry that is injected into BGP via the *redistribute static* command. Notice that the network number and mask in the *ip route* command are what you came up with in the previous aggregation exercise. The *null0* at the end of the *ip route* indicates an interface. Normally, interfaces are like *serial0* or *ethernet1* and so on. The *null0* actually means that if a packet arrives for the advertised aggregate network, it will be discarded. Confused? If you think about it some more, it does make sense. The advertised network is not a valid network. It's only a mechanism of advertising the entire supernet of AS 1000. Other, more-specific network numbers that match this supernet will exist in the IP routing table for router A. For one, all the OSPF summary networks will exist in the routing table for router A. It's just that BGP will not be advertising them specifically to its neighbors, because you have not told it to do so — not yet, at least.

In the next example, you combine dynamic redistribution with aggregation. In the case of static redistribution, there was really no need for aggregation because only one static route was being injected into BGP for the purpose of advertising it to routers in other autonomous systems.

With dynamic redistribution, you will remove the static route from the router's configuration and modify the router's BGP section to perform route aggregation and redistribution. For clarity, both the BGP and OSPF sections of Router A's configuration might look like this:

```
router bgp 1000
 neighbor 172.168.16.2 remote-as 1001
 neighbor 172.168.18.2 remote-as 1001
 neighbor 172.168.17.2 remote-as 1002
 aggregate-address 192.168.0.0.255.255.128.0 summary-
only
 redistribute ospf 99
!
router ospf 99
 network 192.168.16.4 0.0.0.0 area 0
```

The *redistribute* command references the OSPF process 99, which is also running on router A. The *redistribute* command causes the OSPF summary routes that have been advertised by routers B, C, and D onto the OSPF backbone to now be injected into the BGP process on A, so that A can advertise them to its peers in the other autonomous systems. The question, however, is: Do you really want A to advertise even the network numbers summarized by the OSPF ABRs?

In the preceding configuration, the answer to this question would have been no because of the *summary-only* at the end of the route aggregation command. Without the *summary-only* at the end of the aggregation command, the aggregate route defined in the aggregation command and the individual OSPF summary routes would have been advertised by A's BGP. With the *summary-only*, only the aggregate route will be advertised. So, by now you might be wondering, what is it about dynamic redistribution that's different from static redistribution? Static redistribution may prove a better approach, especially if the networks are not very stable. However, dynamic redistribution in a stable environment is an acceptable way of advertising internal routes and it's definitely an alternative way of accomplishing the same goal.

Routing tables

A *routing table* is a direction table. Entries in a routing table contain destinations, some cost of reaching the destination (a metric), and the next-hop to go to get to the destination. The routing table can be a combination of static routes, dynamic routes, host-specific routes, and a default route.

A portion of routing table from a Cisco router which could correspond to the table of ASBR A from Figure 5.2 at one stage of its configurations is shown here. Some of the status codes explaining the origin of the routes are also shown.

```
Codes: C - connected, B - BGP O - OSPF, IA - OSPF inter area
       E1 - OSPF external type 1, E2 - OSPF external type 2
C        192.168.16.0/24 is directly connected, Ethernet0
C        172.168.16.0/24 is directly connected, Serial0
C        172.168.18.0/24 is directly connected, Serial1
C        172.168.17.0/24 is directly connected, Serial2
O E2 192.168.32.0/19 [110/100] via 192.168.16.1, 00:20:29, Ethernet0
O E2 192.168.64.0/19 [110/100] via 192.168.16.2, 00:15:11, Ethernet0
O E2 192.168.96.0/19 [110/100] via 192.168.16.3, 00:12:19, Ethernet0
B        172.168.20.0/24 [20/0] via 172.168.16.2, 00:15:52
B        172.168.22.0/24 [20/0] via 172.168.18.2, 00:11:11
B        172.168.30.0/24 [20/0] via 172.168.17.2, 00:19:31
```

These routing table entries show networks to which router A has direct interfaces, the OSPF summary networks that have been injected onto the OSPF backbone area by routers B, C, and D, and some networks not listed in

Figure 5.2 (which A has learned about from its neighbors). There are no static, host-specific, or default routes listed in this sample table. The IP address following the word "via" in the table is the next hop that a packet must reach on its way to the destination network, which is the first IP address on each line.

Static routes

Static routes are routes put into the router's routing table by an administrator. An example of placing a static route in the IP's routing table appeared in the discussion of redistribution. There are advantages and disadvantages to static routes. The big advantage is that when routers are configured with static routes only, routers must not exchange the administrative traffic needed to build their routing tables dynamically. This results in less pressure on the routers CPUs and on the network bandwidth.

In environments concerned with security, the additional advantage of static routes is the lack of routing information zipping across the network. When dynamic routing is enabled, someone could put a protocol analyzer on a network and listen to routing traffic being exchanged between routers. By finding just one router on the network and analyzing its routing table, it is actually possible to discover a significant portion of the network topology, which could be considered a security risk. There are certainly ways to guard against these kinds of enterprising endeavors by sophisticated curiosity seekers, but that's a whole separate topic (security). And that's not what this book is about.

The obvious disadvantage of static-based routing is that when a physical link associated with the static route goes down, there is no automatic rerouting of network traffic. A network administrator must correct the problem by reconfiguring a router's routing table, and that could be a serious disadvantage.

Dynamic routes

Dynamic routes are the routes that are created via the routing protocols discussed in Chapter 4. Whatever is the complexity of a routing protocol, the end result is basically the same. Routing protocols do all of their work so that they can place entries into a router's routing table. This way, packets can find their way to their destinations.

The obvious advantage to dynamically created routes is the redundancy that's created in case of physical link failures on routers. In a way, that's what the visionaries of packet-switched networks from the early sixties had in mind: a network environment where traffic flow could be dynamically adjusted as a result of changing networks conditions. Dynamic routing, however, can become a potential bottleneck in very large networks, especially if those networks are not very stable.

Host-specific routes

A *host-specific route* is a route that's defined by an IP address as the destination associated with a full subnet mask of all 1s. There is no ambiguity about the destination. It's an IP address assigned to some specific interface. It could be a host or it could be a router's interface (such as on a serial point-to-point link). However, the destination is a device on a network rather than the network itself.

Default routes

The *default route* stands in contrast to the host-specific route. A default route is typically designated with a destination of 0.0.0.0 and mask of 0.0.0.0. It means it will match any destination. The default route is looked at last by the routing process. If the address in an arriving packet with user data does not match any of the other routing table entries, the default route kicks in. It's like a router saying to an arriving packet, "These are the destinations that I can send you to through these doors (interfaces). If you don't want to go to any of the places that I have listed, then you will have to exit through this door (an interface associated with the default route), as I do have to pass you on. I am a store-and-forward device. I can accept you inside of me for a very short while but then I must send you either to one of the places I know about, or out through this specific door."

A default route is not the same as a default router. A *default router* is configured on hosts through configuration files. A default route is an actual entry in a router's routing table. In Figure 5.2, a good example of a default route would be a route injected into OSPF by ASBR A for reachability of networks outside of AS 1000.

The router at the other end — is it configured to talk to you?

The configuration example in Figure 5.2 focused on configuration of a couple of routers in AS 1000, which is under your administration and control. However, do you think that without cooperation and working together with the network administrator from the other autonomous systems, AS 1001 and AS 1002, everything would work smoothly? The answer is no.

The routers at the other end (ASBRs E, F, and G) must be configured to talk to ASBR A. All three of them must define A as their neighbor. Additionally, the scenario in Figure 5.2 lends itself to configuration of the MED metric. The idea behind configuring a MED value on F and G is to give A the option of selecting the ASBR with a lower MED value when sending traffic to destinations reachable through the AS of ISP1.

The configuration examples discussed so far are only the beginning. In complex autonomous systems, configurations could include route reflection, confederations, load balancing, and other policy-related issues. Some of those policy issues are taken up in Chapter 10.

Have you heard about bridges?

Bridges are devices that make their forwarding decisions based on the hardware addresses at the Data-Link Layer. In contrast to routers, bridges are simple and are generally considered to be plug-and-play devices. Bridges have evolved to relieve congestion on broadcast LANs, and are intended to connect similar Data-Link Layer technologies. A bridged network remains a single logical network. A bridge helps to control the size of "collision domains," but not of "broadcast domains." Ultimately it will be the size of the broadcast domain that determines the physical size of an internetwork. You might be drawing a conclusion at this point that bridges are not very scalable, which is indeed the case. You can't build a large internetwork based on bridges only. The global Internet could not function without routers.

However, the concepts and principles of bridging have their place even in the Internet. The issue of bridges is introduced because, in recent years, they have become known as layer 2 switches which are assuming a greater and greater role in forwarding Internet traffic where the traffic volumes are very high. This subject is discussed in more detail in Chapter 11.

CHAPTER 6

Routing Support Under Major Network Operating Systems

Routing support under a major Network Operating System (NOS) can be broken down into routing implementations at the clients (the user workstations) and at the servers. At the workstation, routing implementations tend to be very simple regardless of the NOS running on a server. In the context of the OSI Reference Model, a workstation is an end system. Its primary routing function is to figure out what to do with packets it originates. When a workstation receives packets that are destined for it, there are no routing decisions to be made in processing those packets. From the workstation's point of view, the decision process of where to direct packets it wants to send to another end system is the extent of its involvement in routing.

If a workstation must communicate with a server or another workstation (another end system), it must first determine if the other end system is on the same physical subnet. If two devices are on the same physical subnet, they can communicate directly without going through a router. If two devices are on different physical subnets, their communication will be through at least one router. The workstation software must perform an adjacency test to determine if the device it wants to communicate with is on the same physical subnet.

The adjacency test involves comparing the results of two *binary ands*. The first *binary and* is "my address" *and* "my mask." The second *binary and* is "his address" *and* "my mask." If the result of each of these is the same, it implies that the adjacency test passed and the recipient is on the same subnet.

For example, assume you are a workstation with an IP address of 192.168.33.1 and a subnet mask of 255.255.255.0. You want to establish a TELNET session with a server whose IP address is 192.168.34.1. You must determine if you and the server are on the same physical subnet. Doing a *binary and* between "my address" (192.168.33.1) and "my mask" (255.255.255.0) yields 192.168.33.0. Doing a *binary and* between "his address" (192.168.34.1) and "my mask" (255.255.255.0) yields 192.168.34.0. The results are not the same, which implies that the adjacency test has failed. The workstation's software now knows that to establish this TELNET session, it must get involved in some level of routing. Otherwise, it would have proceeded with an ARP request to get the Data-Link Layer address of the server, followed by setting up the TCP connection for the TELNET session.

When a router receives a packet, it consults its routing table to determine what to do with it. Depending on where a router is located in the Internet, its routing table may contain anywhere from a few to tens of thousands of entries. A workstation sitting on a small network someplace on the edge of the Internet does not need to know explicitly how to get to every location in the Internet (it does not have to have a routing table). It does, however, need to know how to get to at least one router, which can then take over the routing of the workstation's packets to their final destinations.

A workstation running TCP/IP applications is typically configured with a *default gateway*, which is an IP address of the nearest router (router on the same physical subnet as the workstation) that serves as a door to the rest of the Internet. Default gateway can be specified statically by a network administrator in a configuration file or it can be discovered dynamically via the Router Discovery Protocol (RDP) specified in RFC 1256 (see RFC 1256, Appendix A), should RDP support be implemented on the workstation's operating system. Default gateway is where a workstation will forward its packets if it determines through the adjacency test that the end system it wants to communicate with resides on a different subnet. A default gateway can be implemented in combination with a few static routes if there is more than one router attached to the same physical subnet. Such a scenario, however, requires that a network administrator be very much aware of the traffic patterns originating from the workstation.

In general, a conclusion can be drawn that at the end system level, there is no need to implement dynamic routing (discussed in Chapter 4), which can place considerable demands on the network bandwidth and CPU cycles of participating devices.

The routing support discussed in the following sections deals with the routing at the servers. When a server's NOS supports routing protocols and a server is equipped either with multiple NICs or WAN interface cards, it can be used as a router in addition to acting as a server. A considerable amount of discussion and controversy permeates the industry regarding *server-based routers*. This discussion should not add to the controversy. However, this discussion should make you aware that, with all its pros and cons, the possibility of using your server as a router does exist.

Routing Support on UNIX Servers

The UNIX environment is a "natural" for routing. This relationship extends way back to the ancient days of computing history (the early 1980s) when the TCP/IP protocols were implemented as part the BSD UNIX. At that time, the star routing component of UNIX was the "routed" daemon, which offered support for RIP. The premier routing program in today's UNIX environments is the GateD daemon, which incorporates into it the support for all of the routing protocols discussed in Chapter 4 (RIP, OSPF, and BGP), in addition to a few more such as EGP and HELLO.

The criteria to determine if a particular flavor of UNIX would allow you to create a very capable server-based-router is simple: Does it support GateD? If GateD is supported, then it's really up to you as to what kind of an IP router you want to create. The process of "creating" a router involves deciding the following:

- What hardware interfaces the router will have
- What routable protocols the router will route
- What routing protocols will be configured to run on the router

Additionally, since an NOS (UNIX or any other) is only a piece of software, it's up to you to match it with an appropriate hardware platform that it supports to create a server. To turn that server into a server-based-router will require installing the additional hardware (either LAN or WAN cards) and configuring the routing software (such as GateD for UNIX). By default, this chapter discusses routing IP.

In the case of UNIX, a representative NOS that implements GateD is the Berkley Software Design, Inc. (BSDI) UNIX. BSDI is a commercial provider of the BSD-based (Berkeley Software Distribution) UNIX NOS, in addition to networking and Internet technologies. With its full support for GateD which incorporates even the latest BGP-4 support, it is my opinion that BSDI NOS is the NOS of choice for creating server-based TCP/IP routers. Support for BGP via GateD sets it apart from other server-based routers.

For more information about other features of the BSDI NOS, point your browser to the BSDI Web site at `http://www.bsdi.com`.

Routing Support on NetWare Servers

The NetWare NOS provides rich support for routing several routable protocols including its native IPX, Appletalk's DDP, and IP. This discussion focuses on the routing support for IP. Static and dynamic routing support for IP is implemented in the NetWare NOS via the implementation of RIP, OSPF, and EGP. A nice feature of NetWare's support for IP routing is its ease of implementation via the INETCFG utility, a menu driven configuration utility that facilitates the configuration of all communication protocols on a NetWare server (not just the routing protocols). A few representative snapshots from INETCFG shown in Figure 6.1, Figure 6.2, and Figure 6.3 provide a sense of this utility's capabilities.

FIGURE 6.1 *Initial INETCFG configuration screen*

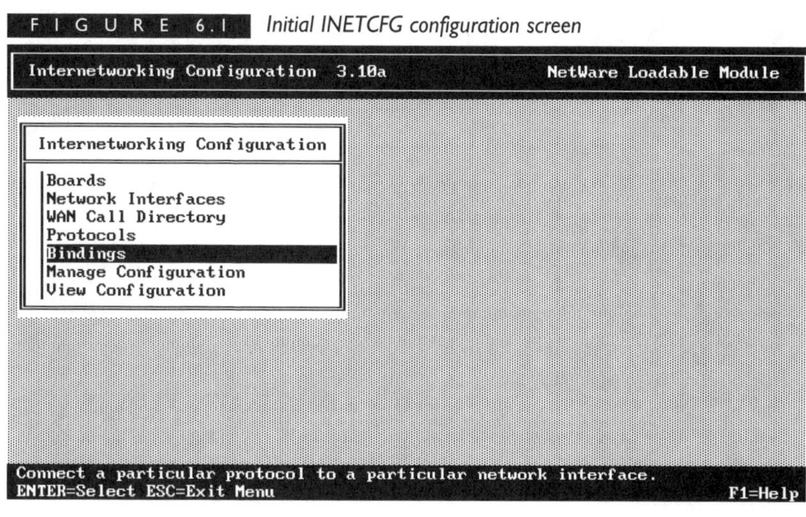

FIGURE 6.2 *TCP/IP protocol configuration screen in INETCFG*

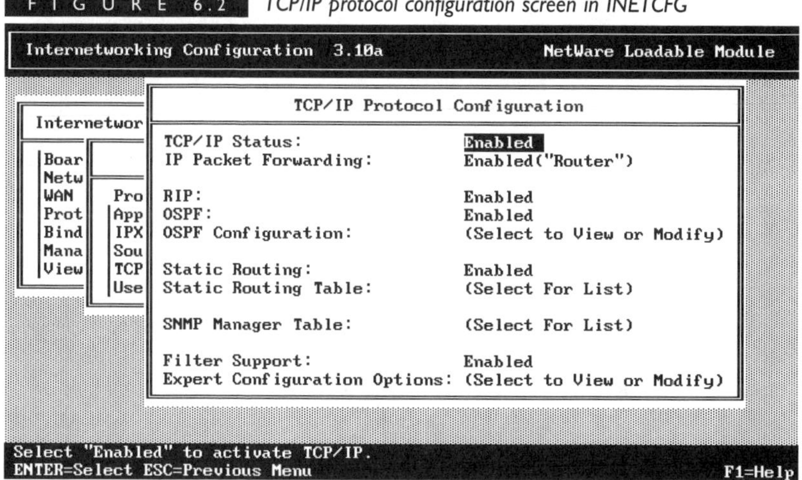

The initial INETCFG configuration screen in Figure 6.1 shows that the utility allows for the configuration of LAN and wide-area networking (WAN) interface cards, binding of the interface cards to the appropriate drivers, and the configuration of communication protocols to operate on those cards.

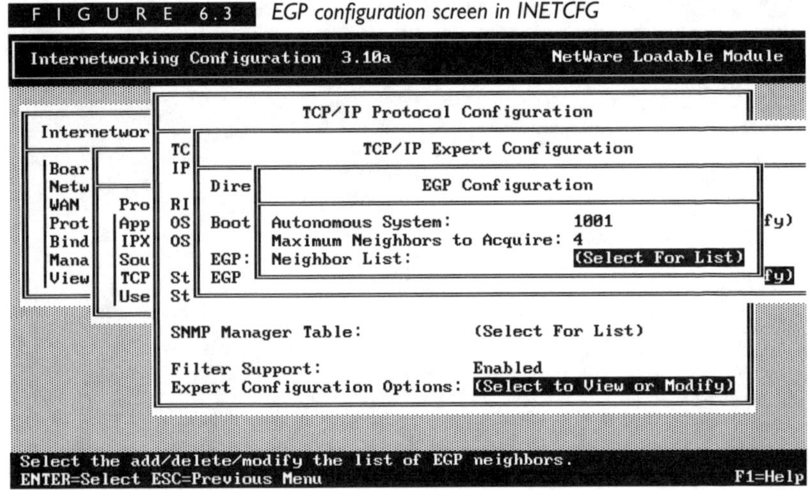

FIGURE 6.3 *EGP configuration screen in INETCFG*

Figure 6.2 shows the main configuration screen for the TCP/IP protocols, with the OSPF configuration having further options. The "Expert Configuration Options" expand into a configuration screen shown in Figure 6.3. This screen allows for the configuration of EGP, the precursor to BGP. The support for EGP allows a NetWare-based router to be configured as an ASBR, which means that NetWare-based routing scales all the way to the level of autonomous systems. If the economics of your particular situation are such that the cost of dedicated routers is out of range (and you already have a significant investment in NetWare), then using NetWare-based routers may be an alternative. See Siyan in Appendix B for a reference on implementing TCP/IP internetworking in NetWare and the use of the INETCFG utility.

Additional support for TCP/IP routing in the NetWare environment is provided via the IntranetWare MultiProtocol Router (MPR) 3.1. The MPR is fully integrated into the latest release of IntranetWare and it's also available as a separate product for NetWare 4.1 and below. The MPR represents a whole family of products that further enhance the routing capabilities included with the earlier native NetWare NOS (4.1 and below).

MPR's features include wide hardware support for both LAN and WAN environments. In the LAN environment, MPR supports the traditional Ethernet, Fast Ethernet (100 Mbps), Token Ring, FDDI, and that persistent (but little-known) player in the LAN industry, ARCnet. On the WAN side, MPR's support extends to frame relay, X.25, Asynchronous Transfer Mode (ATM), Switched Multimegabit Data Service (SMDS), Integrated Services

Digital Network (ISDN), and synchronous and asynchronous Point-to-Point Protocol (PPP). Some of these Data-Link Layer protocols are discussed in Chapter 8. Additionally, MPR supports extensions for routing Systems Network Architecture (SNA) traffic, and a more bandwidth-efficient NetWare Link Services Protocol (NSLP) routing protocol for routing IPX traffic. Initially, IPX traffic was routed via the IPX-RIP.

For more information on MPR, point your Web browser to the Products section of the Novell Web site at `http://www.novel.com`.

Routing Support on Windows NT Servers

Up until mid-1997, Windows NT offered the most limited routing support out of all of the network operating systems discussed here. However, Microsoft was not about to be left behind in the internetworking field. In partnership with Bay Networks, Microsoft has developed routing software for Windows NT known as Routing and Remote Access Services (RRAS). RRAS is occasionally referred to as "Steelhead," which was its code name during development and beta testing.

RRAS currently supports RIP version 1 and 2, OSPF, IPX-RIP, static routing, dial-up access, and some additional features. With RRAS, Windows NT 4.0 (and higher) platforms can be turned into full-fledged routers, effectively competing with low-end and mid-range dedicated routers. RRAS replaces several communication components available under Windows NT thus far: Remote Access Services (RAS), RIP and SAP services, and the dial-up interface. These components turned Windows NT platforms into general-purpose communication servers, but only offered a limited routing support.

It may not be long before RRAS for NT becomes what GateD has become for UNIX. RRAS has been written with standard Application Program Interfaces (APIs). This allows third-party developers to write additional features and routing protocols to be incorporated into RRAS. Microsoft is also releasing an RRAS development kit to make it easy for other vendors to enhance RRAS with new capabilities.

The big advantage of RRAS is that a Windows NT server can be configured as an IP router via the standard Windows interface. To configure RRAS, you still must be familiar with IP addressing, subnetting, and RIP or OSPF parameters, but a familiar GUI can make the configuration task less daunting. RRAS also offers a command-line interface and scripting for those who feel more at ease using non-GUI configuration techniques.

Before RRAS, routing support under Windows NT was limited to static routing and RIP. It's important to remember, however, that Windows NT is not just a server platform; it's a workstation platform as well. The static routing and default gateway configuration on a Windows NT workstation is easy and plenty adequate to meet an NT workstation's requirements for communication with the rest of an internetwork.

A tool that can be used to create and maintain a static routing table on a Windows NT server (when RRAS is not deployed) is the *route* command-line utility. The *route* utility allows for the addition, deletion, printing, and changing of routing table entries on a Windows NT server or workstation. Route costs in the *route* utility are based on the concept of RIP cost metric, or the number of hops (routers) a packet must go through to reach its destination. RIP is also supported by installing the "RIP for Internet Protocol" service from the services option available under the Network icon in the Control Panel.

Before doing anything with the *route* utility, the RIP service, or RRAS, you should first determine if it is necessary for a Windows NT server to be acting as a router. Whether or not you choose to deploy a Windows NT server as a router, you must still configure its NICs with the correct IP addresses and subnet masks if you want to deploy TCP/IP services on it. That's accomplished by loading the necessary TCP/IP components for Windows NT during the installation, and then using the configuration options available under the Network icon in the Control Panel. For more information on Windows NT configuration, see any number of references on the subject that are available from your local bookstore.

Server-Based Routers

All the operating systems discussed in this chapter offer robust support for server-based routing. The clear advantage of server-based routers is their cost and relatively easy configuration. If you already have the server hardware and routing software (GateD for UNIX, MPR for NetWare, or RRAS for Windows NT), then your cost will be limited to the extra NIC(s) that must be installed in the server to be configured as a router. If you've configured the server NOS, then you are already familiar with the configuration interface for a given operating system. This saves you the time that would otherwise be needed to learn a new configuration interface on a dedicated router. Incidentally, these interfaces vary from one router vendor to another.

The disadvantage of server-based routers is that servers perform many other functions. A heavily utilized server configured as a router can become a serious bottleneck for the routable traffic. Also, whenever a server comes down — either by crashing or for hardware/software maintenance — you are without a router. Consequently, server-based versus dedicated routers must be considered in the context of the business requirements for your installation.

CHAPTER 7

Transmission Media: The Cyber Pipes and Connectors

All the routing protocols, router configurations, and network operating systems discussed thus far could not fulfill their reason for being without a physical mechanism over which to communicate. That mechanism represents collectively the transmission media, or the cyber pipes and connectors that link together all the routers, servers, and user workstations composing the Internet.

Imagine yourself without any skin. It's a pretty dramatic picture. Yet, all the wonderful systems composing the human body could not function if they were not restrained or confined by a layer of skin. It's hard to see, however, what's going on inside a human body without the aid of very specialized instruments.

In the same context, the next time you look at a router cable that appears inert and static from the outside, just think about the action that's taking place inside that cable. The electrons must be doing quite a dance to keep up with all the features of the routing protocols using that cable to exchange update packets between routers. The instruments that allow network troubleshooters to glimpse these behind-the-scenes cable activities are signal meters and protocol analyzers.

How Routers Relate to the Cyber Pipes and Connectors

The transmission media represent the Physical Layer (Layer 1) of the OSI Reference Model (see Figure 3.1 in Chapter 3). Occasionally, the transmission media are considered to be a sublayer of the Physical Layer and have been referred to as the Media Layer, or Layer 0. Terminology aside, routers span the bottom three layers of the OSI Reference Model and use physical transmission media to exchange packets with user data and routing updates.

Routers reduce packets to bits at the Physical Layer. Various encoding techniques are used to convert the bits into electrical and optical signals. Those signals are then propagated along the transmission media. How much information can be packed into those signals and how far they can travel depends on the encoding techniques and the physical characteristics of the transmission media.

Engineering details of encoding and signal propagation are beyond the scope of this book. Suffice it to say, however, that the electrons and photons that are the instruments of signal propagation "get tired" as they carry encoded information along the transmission media. Consequently, they begin to distort the signals they are propagating. Eventually, the distortion reaches a point where the signals no longer resemble their original state and cannot be decoded by the receiver into meaningful information. Signal distortion caused by propagation over transmission media is called *attenuation*.

Attenuation necessitates cable length limits between communicating devices. However, when signals must travel long distances (which would result in their distortion beyond recognition), they receive a periodic boost before reaching the unrecognizable state. Devices responsible for signal boosting are called *repeaters*. They take a distorted (but still recognizable) signal and regenerate it into its original state before sending it farther along the transmission media. Repeaters are considered Physical Layer devices and are associated with the Physical Layer (Layer 1) of the OSI Reference Model. Since routers span the bottom three layers of the OSI Reference Model (the Physical Layer, Data-Link Layer, and Network Layer), they also perform repeater functions.

Routers interface to the physical transmission media via built-in connectors, media-access modules (discussed in Chapter 9), and Physical Layer devices such as CSU/DSUs. What's important for network administrators to understand about the Physical Layer are connector specifications and cabling rules. DB9, V.35, and RJ-45 are examples of connector types at the Physical Layer. A single connector type can be used with different Data-Link Layer technologies and different connector types can be used with the same technology. A DB9 connector is one of several connector types for a Token Ring port; a V.35 connector is used for WAN serial ports; and an RJ-45 connector can be used with Ethernet, Token Ring, or an ISDN port.

Referencing a router port type is typically Level 2 (or Data-Link Layer) speak. When referencing a connector type, it's Level 1/0 (or Physical Layer) talk. Following proper cabling rules when installing an internetwork is like building a house on a solid foundation instead of building it on quicksand.

Cabling Rules

Proper installation of a cable plant is vital to the successful operation of an internetwork. Some estimates are that up to 70 percent of all network problems are related to cable-plant and the Physical Layer. Nicks, bends, cuts, twists, crossed wires, bent pins, and poor cross-connects are only some of the nemeses of cables and connectors used between internetworking devices such as routers.

Considerable attention is often given to the frequency response characteristics of certain cables. For example, unshielded twisted-pair (UTP) Category 5 (Cat 5) cable is rated for 100 MHz at distances of up to 100 meters when used with 100BaseT, and for 155 MHz for use with ATM. However, the use of Cat 5 or any cable — especially for high bandwidth applications — without regard to the cabling standards will not deliver the expected performance.

For quite some time, proponents of cabling standards have included the Electronics Industry Association (EIA) and the Telecommunications Industry Association (TIA). The recent cabling standard adapted by these associations and the American National Standards Institute (ANSI) is known as the ANSI/TIA/EIA-568-A. Adapted in 1995, it's referred to as "structured wiring." This standard updates the earlier 1991 version and incorporates several other industry-accepted wiring-related standards.

The topic of structured wiring covers issues related to cabling distances, cable proximity to sources of electromagnetic interference (EMI), cable cross-connects, cabling in user work areas, backbone cabling, color coding of cables and connectors, cabling in equipment rooms (ER) and telecommunications closets (TC), and more. Bear in mind that structured wiring is a big topic that can easily qualify as a book on its own. Structured wiring covers both copper and fiber-optic cables.

Most WAN and LAN Data-Link Layer technologies (see Chapter 8) support copper and fiber cabling. Fiber's properties to deliver high bandwidth over long distances make it a medium of choice for long-haul backbone connections. Copper tends to be less expensive (the price gap between fiber and copper is closing), is more familiar to many network administrators, and still predominates in LAN installations.

Copper Cabling

The varieties of cables in the internetworking field seem limitless. They come in all shapes and sizes and with numerous types of connectors. Only a few copper cable types are discussed here. They are commonly found in router installations and represent the most popular cable categories.

Twisted-pair cables

The most notable among the twisted-pair cables are the Cat 5-compliant UTP variants. When used according to 568A, a Cat 5 cable consists of 4 pairs of color-coded (solid or stranded) 22- or 24-gauge copper wire and is terminated with an RJ-45 connector. The same 586A cables can be used with different networking technologies, including Ethernet, ISDN, Token Ring, and ATM. Different pairs are used by different technologies.

For reference, the colors of wires assigned to the RJ-45 connector pins 1 through 8 in the 568A pinning are white with green stripes, solid green, white with orange stripes, solid blue, white with blue stripes, solid orange, white with brown stripes, solid brown. The four pairs, 1 through 4, correspond to pins 5-4, 3-6, 1-2, 7-8, respectively. The first pin listed in each pair is for transmit; the second for receive. Figure 7.1 shows RJ-45-terminated cables.

FIGURE 7.1 *RJ-45 connectorized twisted-pair cables (courtesy of Interface Technology)*

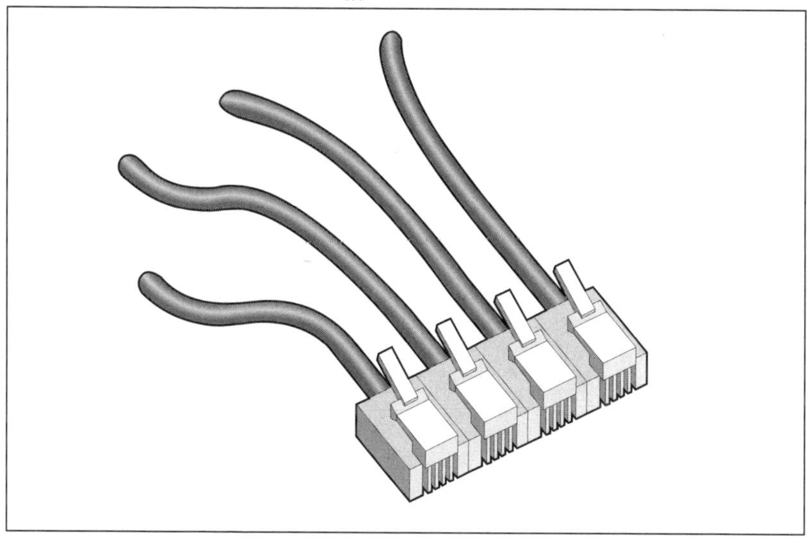

However, not all RJ-45-terminated Cat 5 cables are the same. There are "straight-through" and "cross-over" cables. For example, a *straight-through cable* can be used to connect an Ethernet device such as a router or workstation into an Ethernet concentrator. A *cross-over cable* is used to connect two Ethernet devices together, such as an Ethernet-NIC-equipped server to an Ethernet port on a router. (In the context of this example, an Ethernet concentrator is not considered an Ethernet device.)

If you work in Ethernet environments, keep your cross-over and straight-through cables separate, or have a clear way of differentiating between them. Otherwise, hours of troubleshooting can result.

In a straight-through cable, the same wires connect to the same connector pins at both ends of the cable. When a 568A cable is used for 10BaseT, only pairs 2 and 3 (pins 3-6 and 1-2) are used. In a cross-over cable, the positions of the transmit and receive wires are swapped between the pairs. A 10baseT cross-over cable would have the following pin mating between the straight and the cross-over connectors: 1—>3, 2—>6, 3—>1, and 6—>2.

Another 568 variant is known as 568B. The difference between 568A and 568B is that different wires are assigned to different pins. Still another RJ-45 connectorized variant is a 10BaseT cable that only has pins 1, 2, 3, and 6 connectorized, and can only be used in Ethernet installations requiring two pairs. The pinouts for 568A and 568B "straight-through" cables are graphically represented in Figure 7.2.

FIGURE 7.2 *EIA 568A and 568B pinouts (courtesy of Interface Technology)*

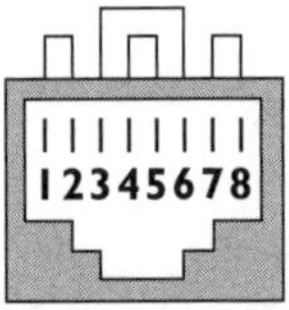

12345678

EIA 568A

Pair ID	Pol	Pin #	Color Code	
T1	+	5	Wh/Bl	> PR 1
R1	-	4	Bl	
T2	+	3	Wh/Or	> PR 2
R2	-	6	Or	
T3	+	1	Wh/Gr	> PR 3
R3	-	2	Gr	
T4	+	7	Wh/Br	> PR 4
R4	-	8	Br	

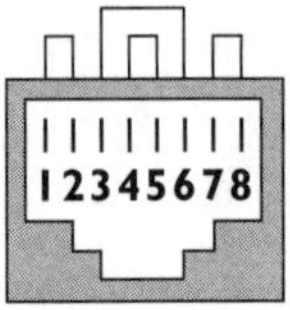

12345678

EIA 568A

Pair ID	Pol	Pin #	Color Code	
T1	+	5	Wh/Bl	> PR 1
R1	-	4	Bl	
T2	+	1	Wh/Or	> PR 2
R2	-	2	Or	
T3	+	3	Wh/Gr	> PR 3
R3	-	6	Gr	
T4	+	7	Wh/Br	> PR 4
R4	-	8	Br	

It's best to use the same wiring standard in all installations, and if possible to standardize on the latest 568A.

Serial cables

Figure 5.1 in Chapter 5 shows the rear panels of all the routers, including serial and console ports. Serial cables used with these interfaces are quite different. The console port uses a variant of an RS-232 serial cable that connects to a personal computer serial port. The console port is used in router configuration and troubleshooting. Notice that the serial cable used with the console port is RJ-45 terminated just like the twisted-pair cables discussed earlier in this chapter. Don't try to use it for Ethernet cabling, however. It won't work.

The serial cable that plugs into the serial ports shown in Figure 5.1 is a V.35 cable. It's a higher-speed serial cable that's used to connect a router to a CSU/DSU, or to connect two routers together. A CSU/DSU provides a router with an interface to a telco-provided service such as a T1 line. A CSU/DSU would use still another high-speed serial cable to connect to telco's outlet, such as an RJ-48 jack in case of a T1 line installation.

Coaxial cables

Coaxial cables (also known as *coax*) are still in use, but their influence in the networking field is waning. Thick coax was first used with Ethernet, but thick coax is now considered a legacy technology. A 93-ohm RG-62 coax was used to wire IBM 3270-type terminals to cluster controllers and in ARCNET networks. Its use has diminished, however, in favor of twisted-pair cabling, just as dumb IBM terminals have been replaced with Ethernet or Token Ring-capable personal computers. ARCNET has also become a legacy technology. It may still be found in very small installations where the 2.5 Mbps bit rate is adequate. It may also be found in very specialized installations requiring longer distances (up to 2,000 feet between hubs or repeaters for a total of up to 20,000 feet). However, it's hard to find a dedicated router with ARCNET interfaces.

Thin coax (RG-58 or cheapernet) is still used to daisy-chain small Ethernet clusters. With the use of thin coax transceivers, the Ethernet AUI ports from Figure 5.1 could be daisy-chained together with cheapernet. The length of thin coax between Ethernet devices can be almost twice as much as that of twisted-pair (185 meters versus 100 meters). It's useful in situations where this extra cable length is needed without an intermediate concentrator. Also, thin coax has an economic advantage in very small clusters because it does not require a concentrator like twisted-pair cabling.

However, what stands out about coax in internetworking is that the newer, faster transmission technologies (variants of Fast Ethernet, FDDI, and ATM) do not rely on coaxial cables.

Fiber Technology

In fiber optics, it's the photons that are the ultimate carriers of user packets and updates between routers. Optical fiber is used in local networks and long-haul backbone designs. It is the rule for the Internet backbones spanning the globe as depicted in Chapter 2 and Chapter 10. Fiber is also reaching right to the desktop. Popular LAN technologies such as Ethernet and FDDI support fiber cabling. Fiber is expected to come into wider use on customer premises shortly after the year 2000, when costs of fiber installation equal those for copper for the local telephone loops.

Fiber-optic technology has the following technical advantages over copper:

- Bandwidth is extremely high.
- Distances between nodes or repeaters are greatly extended.
- Fiber is immune to EMI, cross-talk, and electrostatic discharge (ESD).
- Fiber-optic bundles are lightweight and small.
- Optical fiber does not radiate and is inherently secure.

Overall, fiber optics provides the best solution for internetworks that must combine high bandwidth, long distance, and high security. Fiber-optic infrastructure can be upgraded easily if planned for in advance. These properties translate into advantages for users, network administrators, network planners, and ISPs. Understanding fiber helps explain why the Internet relies on strands of glass the size of a human hair for so much of its long-distance communications and high-speed LAN access.

Fiber Types

Optical fibers can be made of plastic, plastic and glass, or entirely of glass. In most cases, the fibers used in data communications are all-glass construction. Optical fiber is not hollow. It is actually two types of glass joined coaxially, one wrapped around the other. The geometry is cylindrical. The center glass region is called the *core*. The outer region is called the *cladding*. The cladding is usually deposited in a variety of polymeric coatings, PVC, or both that dress the fiber as one might expect wires to be dressed in a cable. An anatomical section of fiber is shown in Figure 7.3

FIGURE 7.3 *Anatomical section of fiber (courtesy of Optical Cable Corporation)*

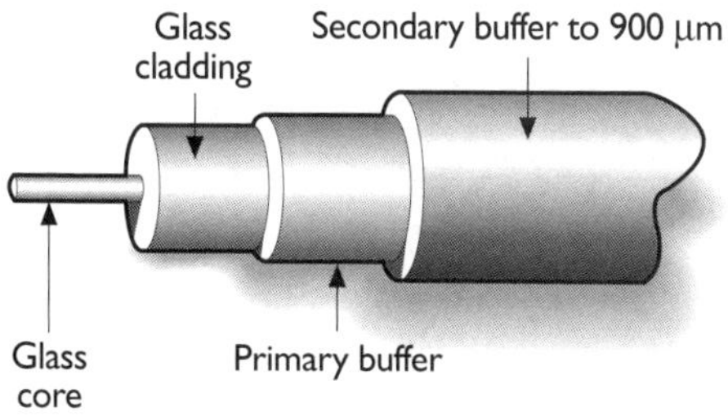

The two types of optical fiber are referred to as *single-mode* and *multimode*. In multimode fiber, a number of light rays (or modes) are allowed to propagate through the fiber. That's because the core diameter of a multimode optical fiber is large relative to the wavelength of light injected into the fiber. Light wavelength is used to represent the data.

Multimode fiber

Typical core diameters for multimode optical fiber are 50 microns and 62.5 microns. (A micron is one one-millionth of a meter.) A typical outer diameter of multimode fiber is 125 microns. Multimode fibers can have core diameters up to 1,000 microns, but larger diameter fibers are low in bandwidth and lossy. They are used only in special applications or when distances are small.

As the light rays travel inside a multimode fiber core, they interfere with one another. This interference forms modes or standing waves inside of the wave guide, which is defined by the inner diameter of the cladding layer. Typical core and cladding diameters for single-mode and multimode fibers are shown in Figure 7.4. The first fiber cross-section in Figure 7.4 is single-mode, the remaining are for multimode fibers

FIGURE 7.4 *Typical dimensions (in microns) for single-mode and multimode fibers (courtesy of Optical Cable Corporation)*

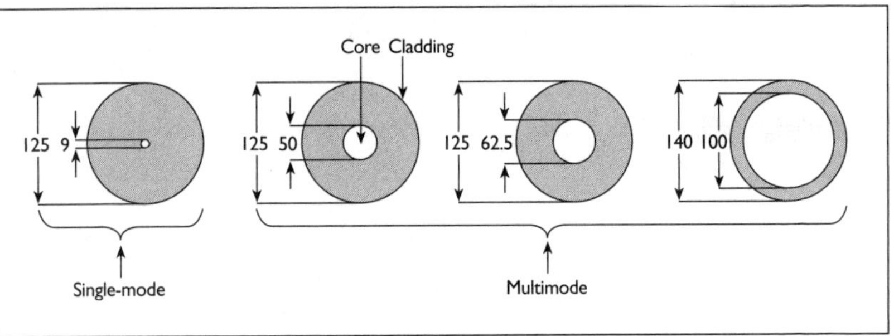

Mode formation can be viewed as a kind of turbulence in the flow of the optical signal in the light pipe. Ultimately, it limits the distance that light pulses (representing the data) can travel in the wave guide before their meaning is lost to the receiver. This process is called *modal dispersion* in fiber-optics literature.

Modal dispersion is shown graphically in Figure 7.5. The axial ray (straight ray) reaches the end of the fiber before any of the angular rays. Keep in mind that all the rays represent the same bit of information but are seen in the optical receiver as arriving at different times because they take differing length paths. Consequently, they smear or broaden the detected width of the light pulse. Broader pulses at the receiving end mean fewer pulses can be received per time interval. Fewer pulses per time interval mean less information arriving per time interval. This translates into a lower bandwidth capacity.

The step-index fiber as shown in Figure 7.5 has a uniform index of refraction. The same index of refraction throughout a fiber strand results in a largest spread between the distances traveled by light rays (emanating from an initial input pulse) before reaching the receiver. Compare this to a graded index multimode fiber.

In a *graded index multimode fiber*, the index of refraction varies between the center of fiber and the edges. As the speed of light varies when it travels through the portions of fiber with a different index of refraction, the net result is a more uniform arrival time for all the light rays at the receiver. The rays that travel longer distances near the edges travel faster. The rays traveling shorter distances near the center travel slower. This variance in the speed of light through different portions of a fiber strand creates a smaller dispersion. This leads to a less spread-out output pulse and, consequently, a potential for higher bandwidth. Multimode graded index fibers are more common now than the multimode step index, which represents an older technology.

FIGURE 7.5 *Mode formation in a multimode step-index and graded index fibers (courtesy of Optical Cable Corporation)*

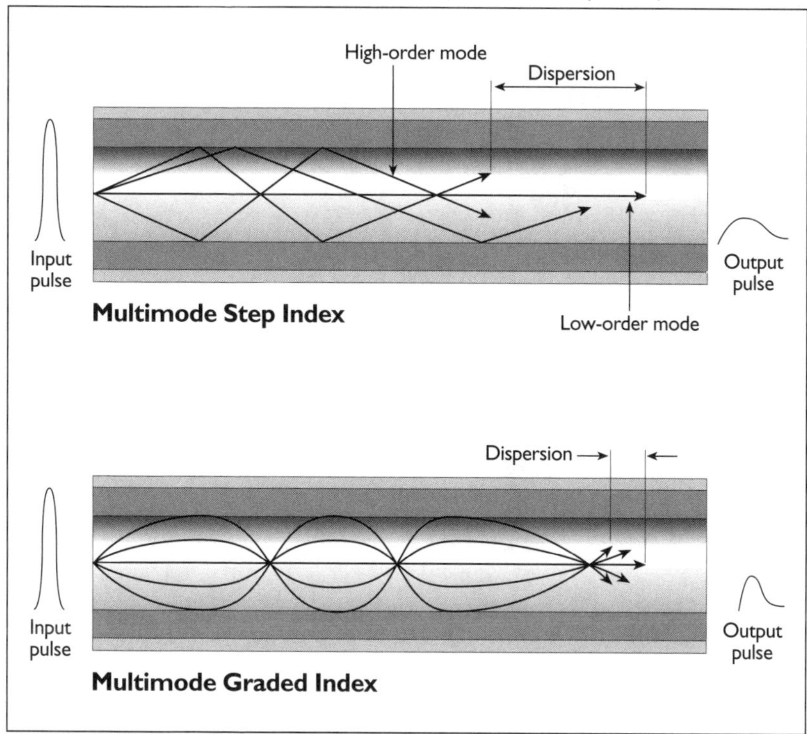

In general, multimode optical fibers allow pulse broadening and, hence, lesser bandwidth as an accepted consequence of the large core. The prime advantage of a large core is a higher coupled power into the fiber and relaxed tolerances for connectors and splices, all of which makes the installation process easier. Multimode optical fiber is favored in local applications and LAN systems. Typical modal bandwidths for multimode fibers range 500 MHz kilometers (62.5 µm) to 1,500 MHz kilometers (50 µm). Very large core fibers will be much less.

Single-mode fiber

The construction of single-mode optical fiber is similar to multimode, except that the core diameter of single-mode is typically 9 µm. This eliminates the formation of modes in the wave guide and greatly enhances datum pulse discreteness. The net effect is that single-mode optical fiber has many times the information-carrying capacity of multimode and a fraction of the loss (decibels/kilometer).

Light pulses injected into a single-mode fiber do not create modes because the light wavelength is much closer to the core diameter (there isn't much room for the light rays to bounce around). This is shown in Figure 7.6, where only a single light ray is the result of a light pulse with the consequence of minimal or no distortion at the opposite end.

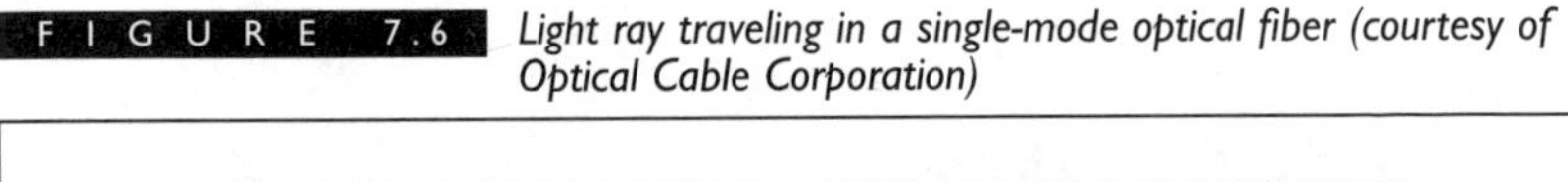

FIGURE 7.6 *Light ray traveling in a single-mode optical fiber (courtesy of Optical Cable Corporation)*

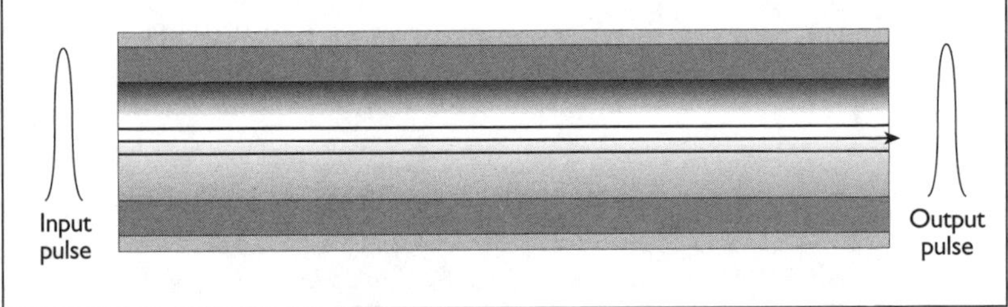

The main disadvantage of single-mode fiber is the higher tolerance for connectors and splices. Matching two 9 µm spots is not easy. System performance is limited by the interaction of light and glass in what are usually called *chromatic dispersion* and *wave guide dispersion*. In this regard, the optical and electrical qualities of the terminal equipment are central in determining the overall behavior of the fiber-optic system.

It would not be difficult to show how the telephone companies might couple 32,000 voice or modem circuits onto a solitary single-mode optical fiber using ordinary off-the-shelf laser diodes and optical receivers. The limitation of the system (as though 32,000 channels is not enough) is not in the optical fiber. It's in the terminal equipment — the lasers, photodetectors, and electronics.

The ultimate data-rate capacity of single-mode fibers in use today is unknown. Currently, experimental 10 Gbps systems are being designed for deployment in networks in the next few years. Even those rates will likely be exceeded in a more-distant future. Keep in mind that this data rate is per single optical fiber!

Optical fiber cables

The three basic designs of optical fiber cables are loose-tube, tight-buffer, and ribbon cable. Submarine and aerial cables are also used, but they are considered a specialty. Each of these cable types may have multimode, single-mode, or both fibers present in the cable. It would be unusual to build a submarine cable with multimode fiber, but it can be done. Some specialty cables might have electrical conductors in them, as well, to create hybrid applications, or to power repeaters.

Loose-tube cables

Loose-tube cables are generally considered outdoor cables. The construction is designed so that the cabling materials do not connect or pull directly on the glass fibers. In this way, the cable designer hopes to prevent any stress-related losses in the fiber from thermal or mechanical expansion or contraction. In a loose-tube cable construction, all the fibers are free to move independent of the cable structure and are housed inside large diameter tubules. Fiber counts may exceed 100 in loose-tube cables. Figure 7.7 shows a cross-section of loose-tube cable.

FIGURE 7.7 *Loose-tube cable cross-section (courtesy of Optical Cable Corporation)*

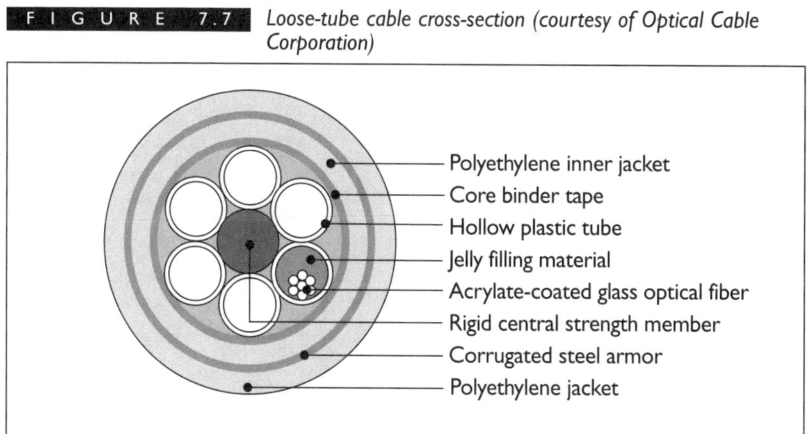

Another common feature of loose-tube cables is the presence of a silicone-based hydrophobic gel in the tubes that house the fiber bundles. This gel is meant to exclude moisture (and ice) from the fiber. Loose-tube cables are used in long-haul backbone applications. They can be buried, pulled through ducts, suspended in aerial applications, and laid through rivers and lakes.

Tight-buffer cables

Tight-buffer cables are more like the twisted-pair copper cables used in LAN applications. These cables are small in diameter, usually low in fiber count, and used in indoor applications. Tight-buffer cables may be composed of multimode or single-mode fibers. Usually, tight-buffer cables have multimode fibers because they are used in buildings where multimode is common. As data rates increase in LAN applications, this will change. Single-mode fiber is becoming the rule in backbone wiring of campus networks. Figure 7.8 shows a cross-section of tight-buffer cables.

FIGURE 7.8 *Tight-buffer D-series cable cross-section (courtesy of Optical Cable Corporation)*

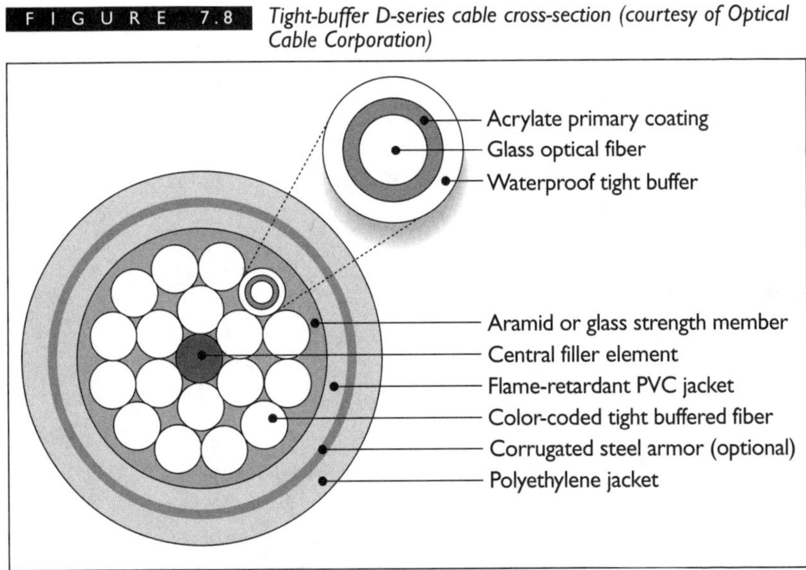

The small cross-section of tight-buffer cables makes them easier to pull through partially filled ducts and cable trays. Some cables are rated for plenum applications in buildings, and many are rated and approved in the NEC for building wiring. Tight-buffer cables generally do not withstand extreme temperatures like light loose-tube cables. That's because the cable components of polyvinyl chloride (PVC), glass, and steel are right on top of one another and pull on one another as different rates of thermal expansion and contraction take over. Consequently, these cables are used in places where temperatures are reasonably stable and not extreme (such as walls, ceilings, false floors, and wiring closets).

Ribbon cables

Ribbon cables are not as popular as either tight-buffer or loose-tube designs. Ribbon is usually single-mode fiber bound together in linear arrays of 8 or 10 fibers. These flat fiber-optic ribbons may be stacked to form a two-dimensional array of fibers. An array of fibers is normally placed in a cable either alone or with other ribbons to form a single-mode optical cable with unparalleled fiber count. Cables of 1,000 single-mode fibers have been built this way. Imagine the bandwidth!

One advantage of the ribbon cable is that it's possible to splice all fibers in a one-dimensional element at one time. This is very economical in installations that require a large number of fibers. The main drawback of the ribbon cable is that it (usually) has marginal thermal properties and thus cannot be deployed in all environments. It is also somewhat difficult (or unusual) to handle.

Splicing and joining of optical fiber

The joining of optical fibers is accomplished by using either a splice or a connector. Splices may be mechanical (friction), chemical (epoxy), or fusion (melting the glass). Connectors are solely mechanical devices. All these techniques involve some preparation of the fiber ends prior to joining them.

Mechanical splicing

Mechanical splicing is a commonly used method to join fiber cables. It's often used for quick connections and restoration work. Mechanical splices hold the fiber ends together and "pot" the joint with a gel or epoxy matching the fibers' refraction index, thus lowering the light pulse loss at the optical boundary between fibers. A mechanical splice life expectancy is around 20 years and its cost is minimal. It's anticipated that mechanical splicing will be used in local phone loop applications as fiber comes closer to homes and businesses in the near future.

Fusion splicing

Fusion splicing of the fiber ends yields the lowest signal loss and is strong enough to last an average human lifetime. It's also the most expensive of all the splicing techniques. Fusion splicing is not economically feasible, unless a fiber-installation project involves hundreds of splices to offset equipment costs. In fusion splicing, two fiber ends are placed in an electric arc and the glass is melted, forming a fusion joint between the two fibers. Fusion splicing is the rule for long-haul network connections.

Fiber-optic connectors

Connectors and couplers for fiber-optic systems are unavoidable. They are used with both multimode and single-mode fibers. Usually found indoors in wiring closets and patch panels, they are commonly used in all implementations of fiber-optic LANs and telecommunications interconnects. Figure 7.9 shows a couple of commonly used connectors and couplers.

FIGURE 7.9 *Fiber-optic connectors and couplers (courtesy of Interface Technology)*

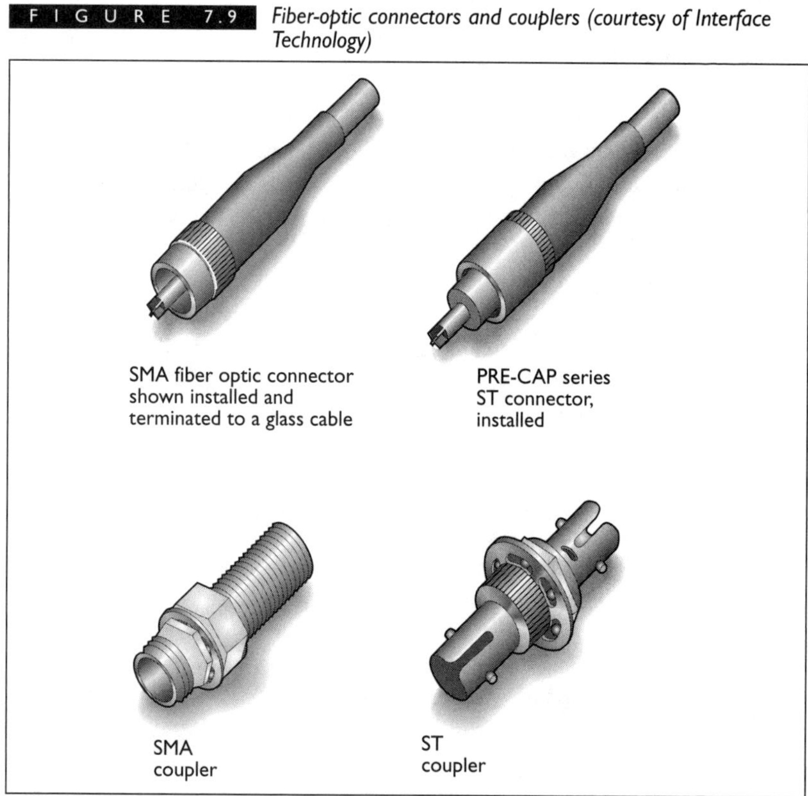

Multimode connectors are usually applied by hand by a technician. Single-mode fiber tolerances, however, are so tight (9 micron core) that it is not always advisable to apply these connectors manually. Rather, it's advisable to buy preterminated single-mode connectors with pigtails and splice them into line with the fiber.

Fiber optics and routers

If you wonder what all of the details about fiber optics have to do with routers and routing, the answer is just about everything. Consider the thousands of miles of fiber-optic cables spanning the globe. These are the Internet cyber pipes interconnecting thousands of routers into the global Internet. Just like the arteries and veins that carry blood to vital organs throughout the human body, the cyber pipes carry routing updates and user traffic between routers, enabling the Internet to function. Anywhere along the way, a break, a poorly executed slice, or an improperly applied connector could result in loss of connectivity or decreased performance for thousands of Internet users.

Wireless Media

Physical media, like copper and fiber-optic cables, are very tangible to our physical senses. A cable can be seen, touched, and smelled (most cables smell pretty bad). Cables are referred to as *bounded media*. Fiber-optic cables are particularly impressive in carrying high-bandwidth data streams over long distances, but their deployment is not always possible or practical for traversing two or more points in a network.

The alternative to cables is the air we breathe or the vacuum of outer space. Electromagnetic waves of varying frequencies become the carriers of information between the line-of-sight terrestrial transmitters or satellites. These wireless transmissions are generally considered unbounded and are deployed where it's not practical (or possible) to use the bounded media (cables).

Terrestrial microwave

Microwave links are commonly used in network design and are considered a basic building block in WANs and long-haul systems. In a simple case, the microwave link can be two antennae separated by a distance of many kilometers in a direct line-of-sight path. More complex systems might require several antennae in succession, and span tens of kilometers, forming a kind of trunk (or backbone) from which signal channels can be added (or dropped) as needed. Some very long microwave links of several hundred kilometers have been deployed.

The direct line-of-sight nature of the microwave systems make them attractive in situations where cabled applications might be hampered or undesirable because of terrain, installation expense, construction timetables, or availability of certain services or materials in the local area.

Ordinary microwave links operate in the 2 GHz to 8 GHz regions (or bands) of the electromagnetic spectrum although up to 24 GHz is defined and allowed. Distances between towers are normally on the order of 30 to 60 kilometers. The object of the game is to pass multiplexed data (usually) from tower to tower without great loss or introduction of noise.

The frequency bands used for communications in the microwave region for both analog and digital applications are rigidly defined by the International

Telecommunications Union-Radiocommunications sector (ITU-R), formerly known as the International Consultative Committee for Radiocommunications (CCIR). Bit rates run from 2 Mbps (T1/E1) up to 280 Mbps, which is enough to accommodate 4,032 voice channels. Direct line-of-sight microwave links for T1/E1 applications are very common.

Several factors affect the performance of microwave links, including antenna design, beamwidth, noise, interference, atmospheric effects, weather, defraction, fading, and reflection. Designers often apply a fade margin as a safety factor to the designs because of some or all these factors. Space and frequency diversity are used to further boost the performance of the microwave link.

One of the most popular digital microwave systems in use today for long- and medium-haul applications are the 140 Mbps high-capacity radio systems used in trunking and backbone links in urban and suburban areas. The growing demand for bandwidth has pushed this system to a new level of performance at 565 Mbps.

Naturally, interest in using digital microwave at these rates for LAN applications is quite keen. It can be found in rural areas (spur routes) or in metropolitan area networking where a company might connect several buildings together in a private network without referencing the public network. In either case, distances are short, on the order of 2 to 20 kilometers.

Lower-capacity digital microwave links are also in demand today. These links are also short (2 kilometers to 20 kilometers) and are common in inner cities and rural areas alike. Two frequency bands that are used for these systems are the 1.5- to 2.5-GHz band, and the 14- to 24-GHz band.

Of the two bands, the low-frequency band is the more common. Components are available to make use of the high band but a complete fade analysis must be done for high-band deployment to account for the worst-case weather conditions. Rain and other atmospheric disturbances can seriously affect the higher-band signals.

Satellite microwave

The big difference between the terrestrial and satellite transmissions is the distance traveled by the electromagnetic waves between the transmitting and the receiving stations. In the line-of-sight transmissions between terrestrial microwave towers, the distance is typically in tens of miles. A geocentric satellite is positioned at approximately 22,300 miles above the Earth's equator. It orbits the Earth at an angular velocity equivalent to the Earth's rotational velocity, which gives it the appearance of being stationary when observed from the Earth's surface.

At 22,300 miles above the Earth's surface, a geocentric satellite's speed is approximately 7,000 miles per hour. It's the satellite's "height" above the Earth's surface, however, that results in a round-trip signal delay of approximately a quarter of a second — even for electromagnetic waves traveling at the speed of light. Though seemingly insignificant from an everyday life perspective, this delay must be taken into account by computer applications using satellite transmission paths.

The advantage of using satellite transmitters over terrestrial microwave towers is that a very large portion of the Earth's surface can be reached from a single satellite. Three equally spaced geocentric satellites are sufficient to cover most of the Earth's surface. Since the 1960s, when the first communication satellites were put into orbit, they've been used for telephone voice circuits and television transmissions. Today, satellites are also deployed to afford access to the Internet. A portable transmitter/receiver set up at the most remote or inaccessible regions of the planet can now be used to gain access via satellite to the Internet. Another advantage of satellite links is their transmission speed.

An example of a practical satellite application on the Internet is Hughs Network Systems' DirectPC. It's aimed at a market where high-speed physical line connections to the Internet are not available, or simply too expensive. A DirectPC kit includes an interface card for a personal computer, a 21-inch satellite dish, and software.

DirectPC still relies on the use of a modem for traffic leaving your personal computer. If you think about it, this makes a great deal of sense. Most of the traffic leaving your personal computer when surfing the Web is minimal compared to what's coming in. Outgoing traffic consists mostly of requests to connect to different Web sites. Web traffic tends to be asymmetric — you send out small requests and download large files. DirectPC capitalizes on this concept to drastically improve transmission time for the larger volumes of inbound traffic. Instead of the typical 28.8 Kbps or 33.6 Kbps modem rates, DirectPC supports inbound transmission rates of 400 Kbps. The inbound traffic arrives via satellite.

When you make a request to download a file from a Web site using DirectPC software, the data that you would normally be receiving over your modem line is forwarded to a DirectPC Network Operations Center (NOC). From there, it is beamed up to a DirectPC satellite and down to the satellite dish on your house roof or garage wall. It's not totally wireless. From the satellite dish, there is a cable that transmits that data to a receiving interface card in your personal computer. It's all happening about 14 times faster than if you were using a modem.

DirectPC is ideal for those who want a faster response from the Net and for companies looking at fast distribution of digital information to multiple locations. Simultaneous distribution of information through the Internet to multiple locations is referred to as *multicasting*, which is gaining popularity in Internet applications. With satellites now involved in passing Internet traffic, the Internet is not just a terrestrial network; it's a celestial network as well.

CHAPTER 8

Data-Link Layer Protocols

In the context of the OSI Reference Model as discussed in Chapter 3, the Data-Link Layer protocols operate at the second layer of the model. These protocols interface with the Physical Layer (Layer 1) protocols and Network Layer (Layer 3) protocols.

Historical Perspective

The Data-Link Layer protocols fall into two categories: LAN and WAN. There was a time in the ancient history of computing — early- to mid-1980s — when the characteristics of the Data-Link WAN and LAN protocols were clearly defined. The WAN protocols operated over long distances, they were slow, and typically connection-oriented. A *long distance* would qualify as anything in excess of 2,500 meters, which was the maximum Ethernet range with no bridges or routers between cable segments. *Slow* was in the range from 9.6 Kbps to 64 Kbps, and *connection-oriented* meant that a circuit had to be set up before data transmission could commence (not unlike a telephone call).

The LAN protocols, on the other hand, operated over short (local) distances. They were fast and typically connectionless. A *short distance* meant anything less than 2,500 meters. *Fast* meant anything from 1 Mbps to 10 Mbps, and *connectionless* meant that delivery was not guaranteed. With no guaranteed delivery, the protocols make the best effort to reach a destination, but that's it. Today, the high-speed LANs of the mid-1980s are affectionately called the *legacy LANs*.

Today's Perspective

It's more difficult now to draw the line between the WAN and LAN protocols. Protocols such as Frame Relay or the X.25 recommendation are very much considered WAN protocols. Variants of Ethernet and Token Ring are distinctly LAN protocols. In the historical context, however, a few hybrids have emerged — protocols such as FDDI and ATM. They operate over long distances, and at very high speeds.

Asynchronous Transfer Mode (ATM) is not only available to the desktop at 25 Mbps, but also can operate at long distances spanning the globe at speeds of up to 622 Mbps and beyond. So, where does ATM fit in? Is it a WAN or a LAN protocol? The answer is that it doesn't matter. ATM is used where it best fulfills the internetworking needs.

The Data-Link protocols selected for the discussion in this chapter are commonly used in today's Internet and represent a spectrum of Internet connection speeds and types. Most home users access the Internet through a dial-up modem connection to a local ISP. The modem connections are the bottom end of Internet connection speeds. They are slow. The majority of dial-up connections used by millions of Internet users are set up using the Point-to-Point Protocol (PPP). Major metropolitan areas in the U.S. offer ISDN access, but trying to get ISDN in less populated rural areas is nearly impossible.

Frame Relay is used by smaller ISPs to interface their routers with larger routers upstream. ATM is used to carry aggregate Internet traffic along the major Internet backbones. And FDDI is also used at the Internet exchanges to switch between backbone traffic (see Chapter 10). Since entire volumes are available on the topics of Frame Relay, FDDI, and ATM, the treatment of these protocols here is only in the context of their common functions and how they relate to routers.

Generic Functions

All Data-Link Layer protocols share common generic functions. First and foremost, they are responsible for creating the Data-Link Layer communication vehicles called *frames* and *cells*. This function is referred to as *framing*. Frames and cells encapsulate and then transport user data and higher-layer protocol overhead.

The next function is *addressing*. The addresses at the Data-Link Layer are hardware addresses as opposed to logical addresses at the Network Layer. In LAN environments, hardware addresses are also known as Medium Access Control (MAC) addresses. They are burned into the NICs.

Error checking is another function of the Data-Link Layer protocols. Error checking ensures that frames and cells are not malformed when they arrive at their destinations. The structure of a generic Data-Link Layer frame reflects the protocol functions. It's normally composed of four groups of fields: addresses, error checking, payload (user data plus higher-layer protocol overhead), and control information.

Data-Link Layer protocols are implemented in routers, bridges, and switches. When they are implemented in routers, a mechanism is needed to map their hardware addresses to the logical addresses supported by network protocols such as IP or IPX. This function is generically called *address resolution*. Its implementation varies from one Data-Link Layer protocol to another. However, it's a vital link between the Data-Link Layer and Network Layer.

Point-to-Point Protocol (PPP)

The Point-to-Point Protocol — as the name indicates — is intended to frame and transport packets over dedicated serial lines (such as point-to-point links), but it's also widely used in switched environments such as dial-up modem connections to the Internet. PPP is considered to be a member of the family of Data-Link Layer protocols collectively known as the High-Level Data Link Control (HDLC). However, the HDLC family is not to be confused with a specific International Standards Organization (ISO) protocol also known as HDLC. The development of PPP as a standard to encapsulate IP packets over point-to-point links was driven by the explosive growth of the Internet since the mid-1980s. Today, PPP is widely supported by router vendors and is defined in the IETF standards-track RFC 1661 (see RFC 1661, Appendix A) and several other companion documents.

PPP applications

PPP can operate over any Data Terminal Equipment/Data Circuit-terminating Equipment (DTE/DCE) interface, which makes it very popular in WANs where routers are connected over dedicated leased lines. On a leased circuit, the Data Service Units/Channel Service Units (DSUs/CSUs) assume the roles of DTE/DCE devices. In a PC configured for dial-up Internet access, the DTE/DCE interface is the interface between the PC — acting as DTE — and the modem acting as the DCE. PPP is widely used with IP, but not limited to supporting only IP. PPP is able to carry packets that originate with other Network Layer protocols such as DECnet or Novell's IPX.

PPP functions

The key function of any Data-Link Layer protocol is to create and transport frames. PPP incorporates the Link Control Protocol (LCP) and a family of Network Control Protocols (NCPs) to support functions other than framing. LCP is responsible for setup, testing, monitoring, and termination of logical Data-Link Layer links. LCP ensures that a link is operational (at the Data-Link Layer) and has an adequate quality to warrant the transmission of network packets over it.

A physical cable may be present between two devices, but it may be damaged or plugged in wrong. LCP will not be able to create a logical link between these devices. It's also possible for electromagnetic interference (EMI) to render the link quality so low that it's unusable for transmission. This can happen after the initial link has been set up. Because LCP monitors the link quality, it detects when the link condition has degraded below an acceptable level and tears down the link.

LCP also terminates a link as a result of user-initiated actions. Issuing a router interface-level *shutdown* command or turning off the power on a router at one end of the physical link causes LCP to terminate the logical link from the other end. LCP terminates a link if it's idle for too long (such as when no packets are flowing over it). A more drastic way to terminate a link is to break, damage, or unplug a cable. From LCP's point of view, it's comparable to turning off the power. LCP detects the carrier loss and logically terminates a link. In addition to link management, LCP also is responsible for negotiating the maximum packet size to be used for transmission across a link.

The primary job of the NCPs is to negotiate between the PPP devices what kind of Network Layer packets will be transmitted in PPP frames. PPP has the ability to multiplex different Network Layer (Layer 3) packets over a single link. It uses several different frames for the setup, maintenance, and the negotiation of link options. These frames may be of interest to those programming PPP implementations, but the frame that's of most interest to network users is the frame that carries their data. In PPP, this frame is called an *informational frame* and its relatively simple structure is shown in Figure 8.1.

FIGURE 8.1 *PPP informational frame structure*

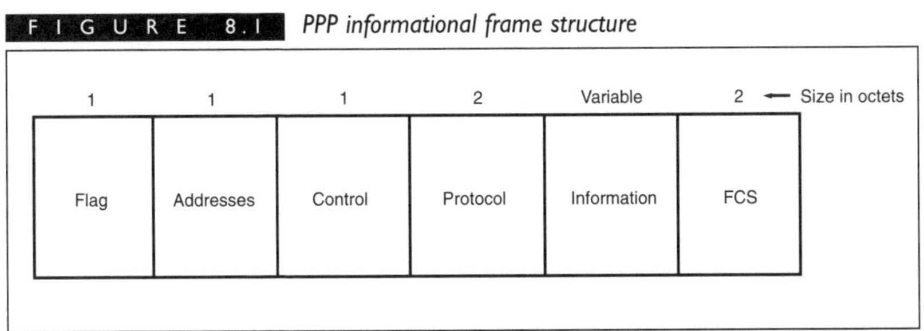

The *protocol field* identifies what type of Network Layer packet is encapsulated inside the data portion of the frame. (It's typically IP for Internet access.) The *information field* carries your data. The Frame Check Sequence (FCS) supports checking a frame's health after transit between devices (error-checking function). The *address field* is set to a broadcast value and is not used by PPP. The remaining fields are used to manage the transmission process itself.

PPP router configuration

Chapter 5 presented an example of activating PPP. *Encapsulation PPP* is all it takes to make PPP active on a serial interface. Other options relating to link quality and security can be configured. However, vendor router manuals are the best source for the syntax of PPP configuration options.

Frame Relay (FR)

Frame relay has become a very popular WAN protocol, partially because of an increase in the reliability of the transmission media. Prior to Frame Relay, one of the key protocols for carrying WAN traffic was X.25, which is an umbrella expression for a series of recommendations developed by the Consultative Committee for International Telegraphy and Telephony (CCITT). Frame relay is commonly considered to be a successor to X.25, even though the design assumptions for Frame Relay are diametrically opposed to those of X.25. This all has to do with the changing computing landscape over the decades.

The evolution

If you can think back to the days of the 1970s when the X.25 protocols were being specified by CCITT (currently renamed to International Telecommunications Union-Telecommunications Standardization Sector, or ITU-TSS, also abbreviated as ITU-T), the computing landscape was quite different than what it is today.

The end-user devices were typically dumb terminals and the transmission media were mostly copper. The end-user devices did not have much intelligence and the transmission media had a significant potential to cause errors. These conditions translated into the development of communication protocols that had to compensate for the deficiencies in the physical infrastructure. X.25 protocols perform error checking on user's packets between any two successive packet switches. If a packet passes through multiple X.25 switches, it is checked multiple times for errors.

Because the end devices had no intelligence to check for errors and the transmission media were error-prone, something had to do it. So, the communication protocols picked up the slack. The net result was communication protocols that were more complex and operated at slower speeds (such as 56 Kbps).

The computing environment had changed drastically by the 1990s. So, the Frame Relay design was based on the assumptions opposite from those of

X.25. The transmission media were more reliable which meant that there were fewer errors in the first place. Secondly, if errors did occur, the communicating devices had sufficient intelligence and processing power to initiate any necessary error correction. The result was a simple and relatively fast WAN protocol.

As a natural successor to the X.25 family of protocols, Frame Relay is commonly used by smaller ISPs and corporations connecting to the Internet. Typical Frame Relay speeds vary between 56 Kbps and 2 Mbps. Frame Relay providers rely on the statistical nature of network traffic to allocate bandwidth to network users.

The statistics

Network traffic tends to be erratic. Bursts of traffic occur during operations such as downloads and file transfers, while very little may be happening at other times. When a corporate network is connected to the Internet through Frame Relay, these kinds of traffic patterns from individual users translate into an average bandwidth use per site. Over a period of time, a Frame Relay provider can come up with an aggregate average bandwidth demand from all its client sites. This is where statistics come in.

The vast majority of the Frame Relay clients do not need a continuous dedicated bandwidth equivalent to their occasional peak usage. What they really need (and care about) is that all their traffic gets through. So, why not offer them bandwidth that's equivalent to their average use, but also assure them that their occasional peak traffic has a very good chance of getting through (though it's not an absolute guarantee)? There are economic incentives for both sides in this type of scenario.

Assume that an organization's average bandwidth use is 50 percent of their occasional peak use. Also assume that this same organization can get a Frame Relay circuit for 25 percent less than it would have to pay for a dedicated point-to-point circuit. The point-to-point circuit would have to be sized for the peak usage, even though most of the time it would be underutilized. When a dedicated, leased point-to-point circuit is underutilized, it's like making a long-distance call and then not saying anything, but also not hanging up.

So, with a reasonable assurance from the Frame Relay provider that the occasional peak traffic will go through, guess who wins? Everyone! No wonder that Frame Relay has really taken off in the 1990s, a decade of win-win scenarios.

For those readers who are more mathematically inclined and contemplating Frame Relay installations, you can plug some numbers into the just-described scenario to see who the real winners are and why. Thanks to statistics, the Frame Relay client may be getting a good deal. That doesn't mean, however, that the Frame Relay provider is not getting an even better deal.

Applying some technical terms to the preceding discussion, the client's average bandwidth usage is referred to as the *Committed Information Rate (CIR)*. The Frame Relay provider guarantees to pass the client's traffic equivalent to this bandwidth usage. In the preceding example the peak usage would have been twice the CIR. It's called the *oversubscribed CIR*.

Most of the time — thanks to the law of averages and the Frame Relay providers having some extra capacity in their networks — the client's network traffic exceeding the CIR will go through. However, it will be marked with a discard eligibility flag in the Frame Relay frames. If a statistical anomaly results from everyone using the network at the same time, the frames marked with discard eligibility flags can be sent to the bit buckets or be discarded. When frames are discarded, higher-layer protocols must detect that condition and retransmit the data. Otherwise, users don't get the expected results.

Frame relay router configuration

Frame relay protocol relies on the use of Permanent Virtual Circuits (PVCs) and circuit identifiers known as *Data-Link Connection Identifiers (DLCI)* to move traffic across a Frame Relay network. DLCIs have a local significance and can be compared to the hardware addresses in LANs or the Virtual Path Identifiers/Virtual Circuit Identifiers (VPIs/VCIs) in ATM. Basic Frame Relay configuration is not much different than that of PPP, as Frame Relay (like PPP) is a Data-Link Layer protocol encapsulating network packets.

The following Cisco configuration commands can be used to configure a serial interface for use with Frame Relay. What needs to be remembered, however, is that Frame Relay routers must be configured at least in pairs.

```
encapsulation frame-relay ietf
frame-relay map ip x.x.x.x yyy broadcast
```

In these configuration commands, the first command indicates that Frame Relay is the encapsulation protocol. The *ietf* option at the end of that command means that the Internet Engineering Task Force (IETF) variant of Frame Relay encapsulation is used. Cisco has its own variant of Frame Relay encapsulation.

In the second command, the *x.x.x.x* is the IP address of an interface on the neighboring router. The *yyy* is the DLCI assigned by the Frame Relay provider to the neighboring router. The neighboring router will have to use the same kind of commands, except that the IP address and DLCI will correspond to the router's interface configured with these commands.

Asynchronous Transfer Mode (ATM)

The discussion of ATM in this section can be compared to describing a patch of land 20 miles long by 20 miles wide as viewed from a jet traveling at 400 miles an hour at an altitude of 37,000 feet. If you had to walk through that land, it might take you 10 hours and you would observe many more details than viewing it for 3 minutes from a high-flying plane. For a walk-through discussion of ATM, refer to works listed in Appendix B; for a high-flying view stay with me.

ATM has become an umbrella expression for many standards and sub protocols that comprise this service — almost like X.25. In the context of the OSI Reference Model, the ATM layer is placed above the Physical Layer and below an ATM Adaptation Layer (AAL). The AAL interfaces the ATM layer with the protocols at the Network Layer. However, ATM's addressing structure and quite complex "routing" protocols give it the appearance of a Layer 3 service. So, it's important not to get caught up in semantics when talking about the OSI Reference Model. After all, it's only an imperfect reference model.

ATM functions

The responsibilities of the ATM layer have to do with creating cells, establishing circuits between communicating devices, moving cells along the established circuits, managing the flow of cells, and looking after the well being of cells by checking their headers for errors. The functions that differentiate ATM from other Data-Link Layer protocols have to do with how the circuits are set up and the cell flow managed along those circuits. These functions have significant implications for the successful performance of user applications over ATM. Setting up an ATM circuit permits a quality of that circuit to be determined at setup time.

Quality of Service (QoS)

If you could see data from user applications reduced to bits and translated into signals that are moving along the transmission media, it might be difficult to tell which application originated which bits and why. After the bits are reconstructed by the user applications at the end systems, however, they take on a different meaning. The bits can suddenly become an image of a friend, the voice of a boss, or an e-mail message.

I participated in a videoconference at a recent computer show. I carried on a conversation and saw my partner on a video monitor as though he were standing right next to me, even though he was 2,000 miles away. The bits that carried our digitized images probably did not look any different than the bits that carry millions of e-mail messages exchanged daily on the Internet. However, it was important for the bits carrying our voice and images to move right along. If they decided to slow down, stop for a break, and so on, it wouldn't have been much of a videoconference. The bits behaved the way they did because the ATM circuit over which this videoconference was taking place was set up with an *a priori* knowledge that it had to meet certain criteria.

The much talked about Quality of Service (QoS) feature for ATM circuits is something that can be determined and controlled at the time a circuit is being set up by the ATM hardware. Different applications can request different levels of the QoS from the ATM hardware to make these applications operate properly. Proper operation of a videoconference means no delays. If you check your e-mail once a day, a delay of a few minutes in the delivery won't be noticed.

QoS has to do with the bit rates on ATM circuits. In the ATM jargon, there are several bit rates: *Constant Bit Rate (CBR), Variable Bit Rate (VBR), Available Bit Rate (ABR),* and an *Unspecified Bit Rate (UBR).* UBR offers no QoS guarantees at all, and with ABR, it's basically a best-effort delivery service. Would you want to do video conferencing with an ABR or a UBR QoS? I wouldn't. If no one else is using the ATM network, a videoconference over ABR might work. Otherwise, forget it. The CBR or a variant of the VBR for real-time applications would work much better in videoconferencing.

ATM's universal appeal

ATM is a service that is most widely deployed in the core of the Internet. With the future of the Internet going in the direction of real-time audio and video applications, the integration of ATM with the IP is receiving a great deal of attention from the major players in the router business. Some exciting new techniques aimed at better integration of IP and ATM are discussed in Chapter 11. ATM is also available to the desktop. What makes ATM so universal?

As a technology, ATM is somewhat of a hybrid between the traditional datacom technologies deployed mostly in LAN environments and the telecom technologies deployed in the traditional telco WANs. The datacom LAN traffic tends to be bursty and erratic, and is carried in variable-sized frames. Any business environment with computerized accounting and customer support functions might be considered a traditional datacom environment. The telco WAN traffic used to carry voice is a steady flow of fixed-size frames. ATM uses fixed-size cells to carry all traffic: traditional datacom, voice, images, and real-time video.

The ATM overhead is not insignificant. If you consider that 5 bytes out of every 53-byte cell are used for a header, then, by percentages, this represents almost 10 percent of overhead carried in every cell. Now consider a maximum size Ethernet frame with 1,500 bytes of payload and 18 bytes of overhead for the header. The overhead percentage is barely more than 1 percent. So, why is ATM so efficient for carrying real-time applications traffic (such as voice and videoconferencing) despite its high byte overhead?

The fixed and small cell size enables ATM to switch cells very quickly in hardware. Also, ATM is not dependent on any particular transmission media. When used with fiber, it can take advantage of the almost unlimited bandwidth potential of fiber-optic cables (as explained in Chapter 7) to achieve extremely high throughput rates. Through the use of ATM, some Internet backbones already operate at 622 Mbps; others are planned for higher rates — in gigabits per second. Combine these factors with ATM's QoS capability and it begins to sound like a universal panacea for all internetworking needs.

The interfaces

Because ATM can be deployed in a wide spectrum of internetworking environments (from the desktop to the core of the Internet), different types of interfaces are used between ATM equipment. Those interfaces include the User to Network Interface (UNI) and the Network to Network Interface (NNI). A UNI can be either public or private. Since both UNI subtypes begin with a P, it's hard to create another acronym.

A UNI exists between the customer equipment and the provider equipment. A *public UNI* is used when a customer's ATM host is interfaced to a provider's ATM switch. It's also used when a customer's switch is interfaced to a provider's switch. A *private UNI* is used to interface an ATM host to a switch in a privately operated network.

You might have guessed that the NNI is an ATM interface between the providers' equipment (that is, ATM switches operated by telco companies, or NSPs operating Internet backbones). The UNIs and NNIs have been standardized by the ATM Forum and ITU-T. These standards define addresses, signaling for circuit setup, and structure of the ATM cells.

ATM circuits

ATM uses addresses and circuit identifiers. A circuit identifier is a combination of the Virtual Path Identifier (VPI) and the Virtual Circuit Identifier (VCI). The values of these fields are stored in the 5-byte header of an ATM cell and are used in moving cells along an ATM circuit established between two end systems. VPI/VCIs have local significance comparable to DLCIs in Frame Relay. An ATM switch is like a cross-connect in a telephone closet with incoming and outgoing combinations of VPI/VCIs.

Several standards have been proposed for ATM addresses. Exploring the address structure is beyond the scope of this work. The easiest way to think about ATM addresses is to compare them to phone numbers. In fact, the E.164 standard for NNI addressing uses a phone-number-like address structure. When a phone is installed, a phone number is assigned to you. Phone numbers used in the U.S. are composed of an area code, a prefix (local exchange), and a local number. It's a hierarchical structure. ATM's addresses also have a hierarchical structure and are assigned through the American National Standards Institute (ANSI).

When an ATM host wants to communicate with another ATM host, it's almost like making a phone call. The address of the end host must be known by the host initiating contact. ATM signaling is used to establish an end-to-end circuit that's composed of segments identified by VPI/VCI values. This kind of on-demand circuit is called a *Switched Virtual Circuit (SVC)*. It is set up and then torn down by ATM hardware as needed. Other ATM circuits are called *Permanent Virtual Circuits (PVCs)*. These circuits are set up once by network administrators and stay up all the time. Once an SVC or a PVC is set up, data can begin to flow over it. Network Layer packets are converted into ATM cells, which then move along the established circuit.

ATM configuration

Configuring ATM in routers is no small task, and the specific details are beyond the scope of this book. You should be aware of a few issues, however. ATM is normally supported in mid-range to high-end routers as described in Chapter 9. If ATM is to be configured over a router's high-speed serial interface, another piece of equipment is needed — an ATM DSU. Conceptually, it's comparable to a CSU/DSU used in a T1 installation. Mid-range and high-end routers also support modules with direct ATM interfaces.

All the parameters related to issues discussed in the preceding sections must be known to configure ATM on a router. This includes the ATM addresses, VPI/VCI values for PVCs, the signaling techniques for SVCs, the encapsulation technique for Network Layer packets, address resolution techniques, and more. Happy taming of ATM!

Fiber Distributed Data Interface (FDDI)

FDDI has been a major player in the high-speed internetworking field since its standardization by ANSI in 1988. It's a mature standard combining the most desirable characteristics of traditional LANs and WANs: high speed and long operational distances. FDDI's nominal throughput speed approaches 100 Mbps and the operating distance is up to 100 km (approximately 62 miles) when used with fiber as its transmission medium.

FDDI plays a major role as a LAN technology in the Internet's infrastructure. It's used at the Internet exchange points where high-performance FDDI switches interconnect major providers' backbone routers and switch traffic between them (see Chapter 10). The newer high-speed LAN technologies (variants of 100BaseT or 100VG-anyLAN) operate at speeds comparable to FDDI. However, FDDI derives its uniqueness and robustness from its greater maturity, better fault tolerance, and longer operational distances.

FDDI's fault tolerance

FDDI's fault tolerance stems from its ability to support a Dual Attachment Concentrator (DAC), a Dual Attachment Station (DAS), and dual-homing. An FDDI DAC is a concentrator that attaches to both FDDI rings. Imagine two circles, one inside another. That's the simplest logical representation of FDDI's logical topology of two fiber rings, one used for traffic, the other as a hot standby.

In a typical FDDI implementation, several DACs are connected to both rings. They aggregate traffic from other FDDI devices, such as a Single Attached Station (SAS) or Single Attached Concentrator (SAC). If the primary ring is broken, a DAC automatically redirects the traffic onto the second ring. Should both rings fail at the same physical location, the DACs on both sides of the failure reconnect (wrap inside themselves) the broken ring ends, creating a single larger ring. If the maximum distance of 100 km is used for the individual rings, the total distance of a single ring following a failure could be up to 200 km.

FDDI workstations are good candidates for a SAS. As long as they are plugged into a DAC, they have the benefit of the DAC's ability to recover from ring failures. A FDDI-interfaced backbone router would more likely be a DAS.

A DAS attaches to both FDDI rings, but no other FDDI devices are plugged into it. DAS devices are usually backbone routers or servers — devices that must be up all the time.

When a FDDI device is multihomed it means that it is a DAS or DAC, which is plugged into two different concentrators. This fault tolerance technique guards against concentrator failures. Connection to one concentrator is active, while connection to another concentrator is passive. Should the active connection fail, the passive connection becomes active without disrupting the device operation. FDDI modules for mid-range and high-end routers support both SAS and DAS interfaces. Modules with DAS interfaces can be dual-homed. High-performance FDDI switches offer the same interface capability.

FDDI router configuration

Configuration of FDDI routers can be as simple or as complex as network administrators choose to make it. The simplest way to configure FDDI is to activate its interface with an *Interface FDDI #* command and assign an IP address to it. That much must be done. Numerous FDDI timers and ring-management parameters can also be configured, provided that network administrators understand the implications of changing their default values.

The more important aspect of FDDI configuration is to understand its physical cabling rules and the use of different FDDI ports. Four different FDDI ports have been specified (A, B, M, S). The slave (S-port) is normally used to connect an SAS into a master (M-port) on a concentrator. The A-port is for connection to the primary ring and the B-port is for connection to the secondary ring. The A-port and B-port can be used to interconnect two DACs, but this is only the tip of the iceberg.

How Routers Relate to the Data-Link Protocols

Routers absolutely rely on the correct implementation of Data-Link Layer protocols in their operating systems. The interface ports on a router's physical media interfaces are a good indication of which Data-Link Layer protocols a router supports. Choosing the appropriate ports is one of the key selection criteria for network administrators making router purchasing decisions.

The physical media interfaces and the ports are closely coupled for the LAN Data-Link protocols. One media interface corresponds to one Data-Link protocol. You can't run Ethernet on a Token Ring port, or FDDI on a Token Ring port. On the WAN side, however, the same physical media interface can be used with several different Data-Link Layer protocols. For example, PPP and Frame Relay can both use a router's serial interface.

The bottom line is that the primary purpose of routers is to interconnect networks with different Data-Link Layer technologies. Routers come into their own when they correctly implement support for multiple Data-Link Layer protocols. Otherwise, they might as well be bridges.

CHAPTER 9

Vendor Examples

Hundreds of router and switch vendors do business in the United States and throughout the world. This chapter discusses representative routers from three major categories: *access routers*, *mid-range routers*, and *high-performance backbone routers*. These router categories are aimed at a wide spectrum of internetworking needs, from home and small office environments to Internet backbone interconnections.

The edge or access routers typically come with a fixed number of physical media interfaces. Once you buy a unit, adding extra ports to it is not an option. The mid-range routers tend to be modular. Modular design allows for the addition of new interfaces without having to purchase a new router. It also offers more initial configuration choices. The high performance backbone routers are definitely modular, offering a wide range of options to access high-speed transmission media.

Access Routers

Examples of access routers are Cisco's 2500 series (discussed in Chapter 5), Ascend's Pipeline series, or 3Com's OfficeConnect series. There are usually many models in a series, mixing and matching combinations of LAN/WAN interfaces and routing protocols. The typical WAN interfaces allow for use of PPP Frame Relay, or dial-up ISDN. You will not find an ATM interface or a High-Speed Serial Interface (HSSI) on these kinds of products. Typical LAN interfaces on access routers are Ethernet or Token Ring. FDDI interfaces are typically reserved for higher-end products.

In LAN environments, access routers provide connectivity between different Data-Link Layer technologies. Suppose an installation has a combination of Ethernet and Token Ring networks running IP-based applications. Access routers with Ethernet and Token Ring interfaces are ideal to interconnect these networks. Bridges and switches can't be used to interconnect differing Data-Link Layer technologies. Of course, there are exceptions to every rule. Some "bridges" have been engineered to convert between Ethernet and Token Ring, but with no routing capabilities.

In WAN environments, access routers are typically used to provide connectivity from remote offices to a central site. A remote office may have one or two LANs that connect to an access router's LAN ports. The WAN port on the access router is then used to interface to a WAN port on the central site router. This design also works for small ISPs connecting to a larger Internet access provider. A practical example of this configuration is shown in the discussion of local and regional ISPs in Chapter 10. Cables used for this kind of connectivity are discussed in Chapter 7.

Vendors offer access routers in a series in order to provide their customers with a wide range of hardware configurations and increasing capabilities. The access router market is very creative and aggressively priced to allow even a small office or home user to purchase one of these units. Some home users and small businesses want a direct access to the Internet rather than a modem dial-up.

It's a matter of securing an ISDN or a fractional T1 line into the home, acquiring an access router, and making arrangements with a local Internet provider with a comparable setup to assign IP addresses to your connection. You don't even have to set up a network at home. If you have an access router with an Ethernet interface, you will need an Ethernet network card in your personal computer, but you can connect it directly to your router with a crossover cable (as explained in Chapter 7).

A desirable feature in access routers is a built-in CSU/DSU. With a built-in CSU/DSU, a router's WAN port can connect directly into a telco-provided WAN port (Frame Relay, ISDN, and so on). It reduces cabling and the number of different equipment pieces that must be installed to set up a WAN or gain a direct access to the Internet through a local provider.

Mid-Range Routers: Cisco's 4000 series

Cisco's 4000 series routers are modular, mid-range routers that offer a variety of hardware configuration options through the Network Processor Modules (NPMs). The NPMs interface the 4000s to the underlying physical media and Data-Link Layer technologies of networks that these routers interconnect. One way to size up a router is from the number and type of interfaces that it supports. More and higher-speed interfaces usually translate into a higher ticket price and more packets-per-second throughput.

Cisco 4000 series routers support up to 3 NPMs. The NPM interfaces include one-port or multiport 10BaseT Ethernet; one-port single-attachment or dual-attachment multimode FDDI; multiport serial; multiport ISDN Basic Rate Interface (BRI); and one-port single-mode or multimode ATM OC-3c. Figure 9.1 shows the rear panel of the Cisco's 4000 series router with three of the NPMs. Additional NPMs are shown in Figure 9.2 and Figure 9.3.

FIGURE 9.1 *Rear panel of the Cisco's 4000 series router with 3 NPMs (courtesy of Cisco Systems, Inc.)*

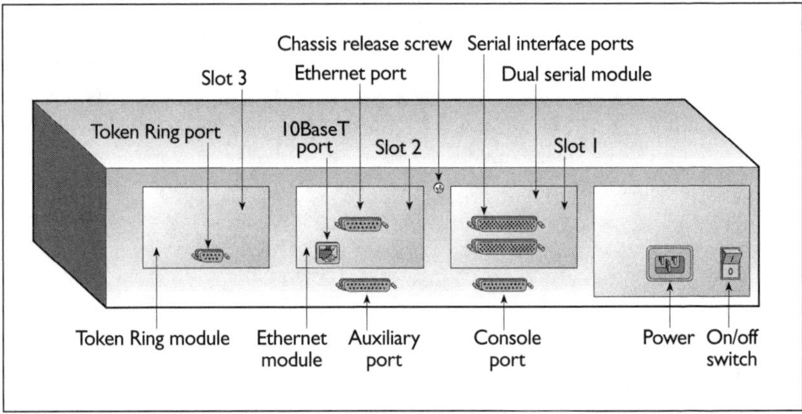

FIGURE 9.2 *One-port dual-attachment, multimode FDDI NPM for a Cisco's 4000 series router (courtesy of Cisco Systems, Inc.)*

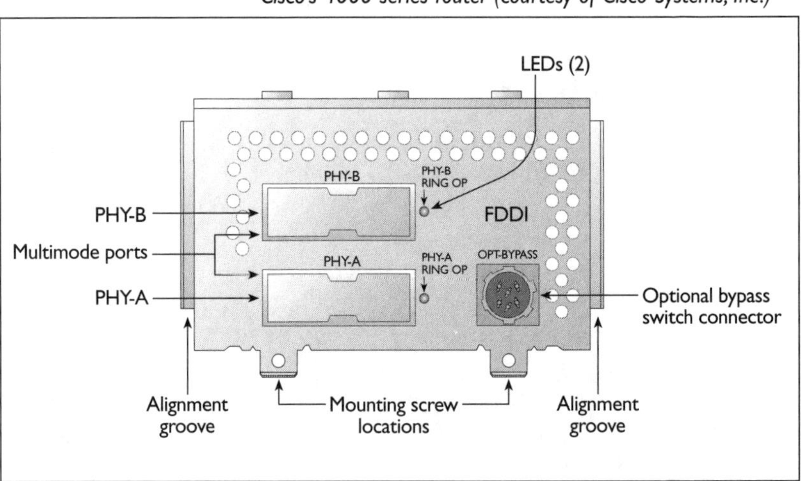

FIGURE 9.3 *Eight-port ISDN BRI NPM for a Cisco's 4000 series router (courtesy of Cisco Systems, Inc.)*

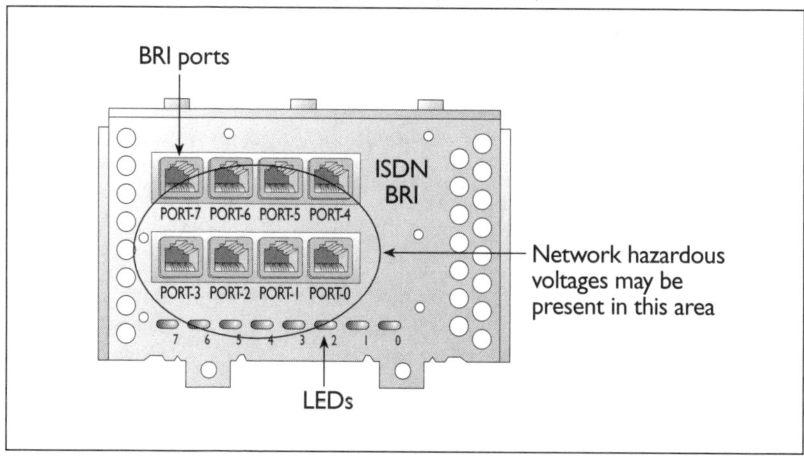

With media interfaces ranging from ISDN to Ethernet and OC-3c ATM, the 4000 series routers are capable of supporting a wide range of internetworking environments, from remote offices to corporate intranets and Internet backbone connectivity. The 4000 series routers use Cisco's flash-upgradable Internetwork Operating System (IOS), which, like the 4000 hardware, also has a modular design.

As the internetworking environment becomes more complex, the number of features supported by router operating systems will continue to increase. Cisco's IOS utilizes the concept of modularity in the IOS design. It is possible to purchase a basic IOS and then enhance it with additional feature sets needed for specific applications and environments where a router is to be deployed. This process requires a good overall understanding of an internetworking environment and the functions a router is expected to perform.

Additional feature sets may support functions such as encryption, routing protocols of other vendors (such as IPX), or connectivity to IBM's SNA architecture. The concept of feature sets is not new. UNIX enhances its kernel by way of daemons and NetWare by way of NetWare Loadable Modules (NLMs). Something to watch out for is that extra memory or specific interfaces may be required to support additional IOS feature sets.

High-End Routers: Ascend's GRF-400 and GRF-1600 Series

Ascend's GRF series products are some of the highest-performance IP switch/routers available on the market. They are aimed at the carrier-class, backbone service providers exchanging traffic at major Internet backbone interconnection points (see Chapter 10). The GRF-400 and GRF-1600 units derive their high-performance characteristics from a distributed-processing architecture combined with a very high-throughput internal switch fabric. The key hardware components of the GRF units are the media cards, the IP switch/control board, and a nonblocking, full-duplex switch fabric connecting the media cards. The GRF-400 can accommodate up to 4 media cards and the GRF-1600 up to 16.

The media cards

The media cards are at the heart of the GRFs' distributed architecture. The media cards interface the GRFs to LANs and WANs. In that sense, they are conceptually comparable to the physical interfaces in the low-end routers, the NPMs in Cisco's 4000-series (see preceding sections) and the interface processor modules in Cisco's 7500 series (see Chapter 10). However, the media cards uniquely differentiate the GRF series routers from other high-end routers because the GRF routers perform additional functions.

All media cards are self-contained IP forwarding processors. Each media card stores a copy of a GRF unit's entire routing table (up to 150,000 entries) and is equipped with its own Pentium chip, memory, and a hardware-assisted search/lookup engine to perform routing table lookups on the destinations of incoming packets. The routing table search/lookup engine implementation on the media cards, which is referred to as the Quick Branch Routing Technology (QBRT), is capable of finding a packet's next hop in less than 2.5 microseconds. According to Ascend's *GRF IP Switch Architecture Guide*, that's about 100 times faster than software-based lookups. The only question is, how do the media cards get their own copies of the entire routing table?

The GRF media cards are controlled by the IP switch/control board that hosts Ascend's BSD-based operating system running the Route Manager. The Route Manager implements the routing protocols (BGP, OSPF, RIP) and maintains the routing information base (RIB) from which it derives the IP forwarding information base (FIB). Throughout this book, the FIB has routinely been called the routing table. The unique aspect of GRF's distributed processing architecture is that the Route Manager periodically synchronizes and distributes the FIB (routing table) between all the media cards.

The delegation of the IP forwarding functions and the routing table search/lookup capabilities to the individual media cards create a high-performance, distributed routing architecture in a single GRF switch/router. The media cards are almost routers in and of themselves. They have a routing table, but they don't create it on their own. However, as long as the routing table on the media cards is updated by the Route Manager operating from the IP control board, the media cards can concentrate on what's important to Internet users — fast forwarding of user packets.

The routing table searches performed by the media cards are different from *route caching*, which relies on storing a portion of an entire routing table (the most frequently accessed routes) in a very high-speed secondary memory. When a packet comes into a router which implements route caching, the cache memory is checked first. If the packet's destination is not found in the cache, then the full routing table must be checked. Frequently missed cache lookups begin to degrade the overall router performance.

The GRF-400 supports up to four media cards. Each media card can support multiple interface ports. The interface ports on a fully populated GRF-400 include up to 16 FDDI ports, 8 HSSI ports, 32 Ethernet ports, 8 ATM OC-3c ports, 4 ATM OC-12c ports, or some combination of all of these. The FDDI media cards support both SAS and DAS interfaces.

In the GRF-1600 the number of supported media cards and ports goes up by a factor of four. Figure 9.4 and Figure 9.5 show the back panels of the GRF-400 and the GRF-1600 units populated with the various media cards and show the details of interface ports.

In the GRF-400, the IP switch/control functions are implemented by using one board, as shown in Figure 9.4. In the GRF-1600, the control board and the IP switch board are separate modules as shown in Figure 9.5. The routing protocols supported by GRF include all the standard protocols, such as BGP-4, OSPF, RIP-1, RIP-2, and more. BGP support includes the latest BGP features, such as route reflection (see Chapter 4), route dampening, and Nexthop-Self (see Chapter 10).

FIGURE 9.4 *GRF 400 back panel (courtesy of Ascend Communications, Inc.)*

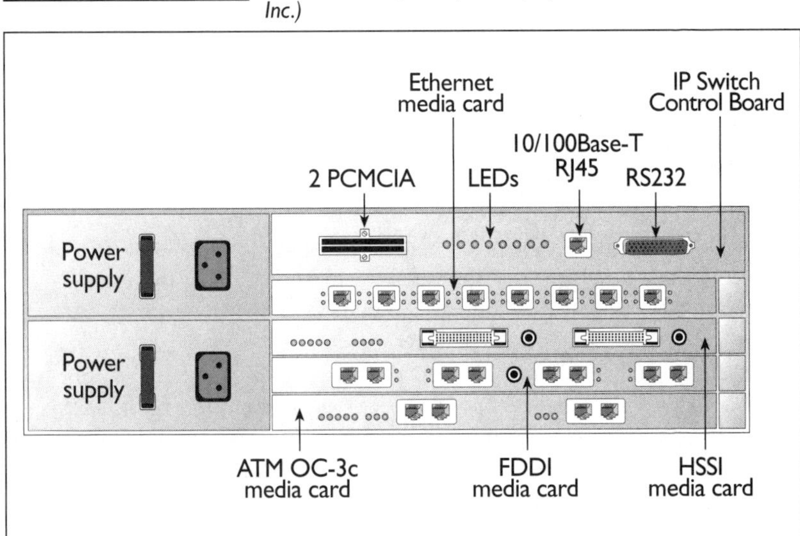

Distributed processing architecture

The traditional router architecture, which is also commonly used in lower-end routers, is based on the following:

- centralized IP forwarding and route maintenance processing
- shared-bus backplane for passing routing updates and user traffic between the media interfaces and the CPU
- caching of the most frequently accessed routes

The distributed processing architecture of the GRF series products stands in contrast to the traditional router architecture.

The GRF architecture splits the responsibility for packet forwarding and route maintenance between multiple components. Processors on the media cards generate the CPU cycles to forward packets and look up their next-hop destinations. The resources to maintain BGP peering sessions and exchange routing updates with other routers are derived from the CPU on the IP switch/control board. Because the route processing is split from packet forwarding, the route update traffic and the user traffic can be handled simultaneously without vying for the same processing resources.

FIGURE 9.5 *GRF 1600 back panel (courtesy of Ascend Communications, Inc.)*

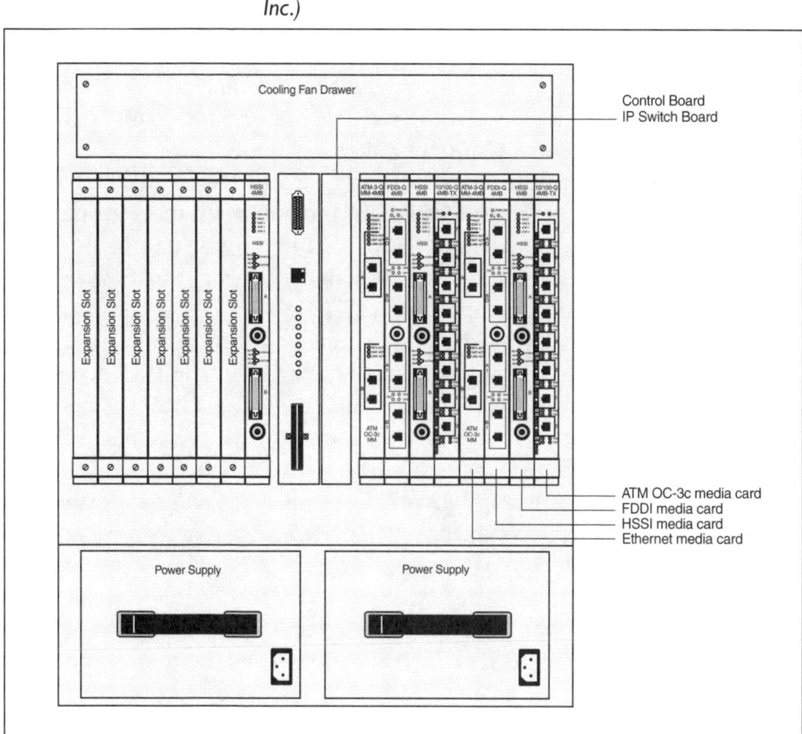

In the centralized processing architecture, when large volumes of user traffic combine with large volumes of routing updates, the net result is delays. Either the processing of routing updates is delayed or the processing of the user traffic is delayed. Routers begin to run out of steam trying to handle the combined user and route update traffic coming their way.

The traditional shared-bus backplane architecture is replaced in the GRFs with a nonblocking switching fabric. The switch fabric is used only to forward the user traffic between the media cards. The nonblocking nature of the switch fabric enables simultaneous transfer of packets between multiple media cards without mutual interference or queuing delays.

The internal switch fabric is not used by the IP controller board to distribute the routing tables to the media cards. Neither is it used to pass the arriving routing updates by the media cards to the IP controller. A separate high-speed communication bus is used for the communication between the media cards and the IP control board.

Route caching in the GRFs is replaced with a microcoded QBRT chip for fast route lookups by each media card. When the hardware-based routing table lookups are combined with distributed IP forwarding and a nonblocking full-duplex switch fabric between the media cards, the net result is Layer 3 routing capabilities at Layer 2 switching speeds.

These departures from the traditional approach to routing afford the GRF routers a significant boost in performance. Combined with the wide range of media access cards accommodating the most sophisticated and fastest Data-Link Layer technologies, the GRFs are fast making their way into the very core of the Internet. Additionally, the distributed GRF architecture allows for the addition of new media cards with linear scalability in performance.

As an aside, one of the configuration commands for the GRF series is a *throttle-peer*. This command is intended to throttle (or regulate) the flow volume of the routing updates between GRF and non-GRF peers. When a large volume of routing updates has to pass between GRF and non-GRF routers, some non-GRF routers reach 100 percent CPU utilization and stop forwarding packets. The *throttle-peer* command on the GRF allows it to moderate the speed at which it passes routing updates to a non-GRF peer.

Other router vendors such as Cisco and Bay Networks also manufacture high-performance backbone routers. Keep your eye on the Cisco's 12000 series Gigaswitch Routers (GSRs). These high-performance routers represent the culmination of all technologies and protocols discussed thus far — the routing protocols from Chapter 4, the physical media from Chapter 7, and the WAN protocols from Chapter 8. A clear understanding of topics that are covered in these chapters is part of the key to a judicious selection and successful router deployment.

PART III

The Internet: Architecture, Routing, and Switching

CHAPTER 10

Internet Routing

The Internet is a dynamically evolving (if not literally a living and breathing) organism. To describe routing or the movement of packets in the Internet (and most importantly, in the Internet's core), it's vital to understand what the Internet and its core are and how they evolved to be what they are.

However, trying to describe the Internet and its core is like trying to describe a moving target. Major milestones in the evolution of the Internet and its core infrastructure can be identified, but the reality is that the Internet transcends itself almost daily. It's nigh impossible for any single person to fully understand all the multifaceted aspects of the Internet. However, a slice, a glimpse, and an individual perspective can be offered.

From the ARPAnet to Internet Backbones

To relate to what's happening with the Net today and what the Internet of the future might be like, you should first understand some of the major stages in the Internet's evolution. The evolution of the Internet in the United States can be broken down into the following major stages:

- Stage 1 (from 1969 through 1983): The ARPAnet
- Stage 2 (from 1983 through 1986): The pre-NSF-backbone Internet
- Stage 3 (from 1986 through 1995): The NSFnet-backbone-dominated Internet

A fourth major stage of the Internet's evolution is the current Internet architecture based on commercial backbones interconnecting at public and private Internet exchanges. It's graphically represented in Figure 10.1, which is a reference point throughout this chapter.

The new Internet architecture officially commenced on April 30, 1995, when the NSFnet backbone service was finally turned off. However, nothing about the Internet is cut and dried. Internet exchanges gradually came into existence even while the NSFnet service was still functional and its dominance of the Internet was gradually waning. The date of April 30, 1995, is used only as a rough marker.

FIGURE 10.1 *The 1995 Internet architecture (Reprinted with the permission of MCI Telecommunications Corporation. Copyright 1997 MCI Telecommunications Corporation. All rights reserved. This material is based upon work supported by the National Science Foundation under grant No. NCR 9321047. Any opinions, findings, and conclusions or recommendations expressed in this publication are those of the author(s) and do not necessarily reflect the views of the National Science Foundation.)*

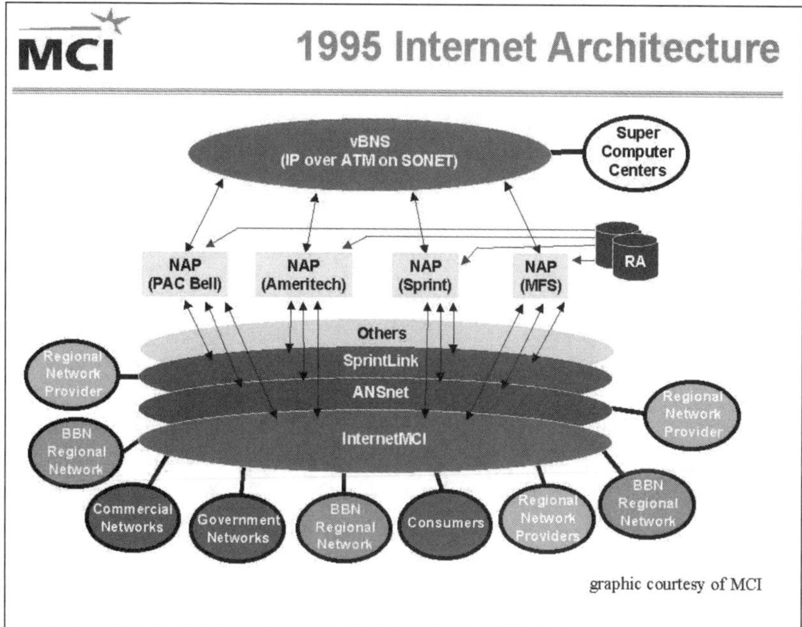

Stage 1 (1969–1983): The ARPAnet

The first stage of the global network (ARPAnet) — from 1969 through December 1982, before it was even called the Internet — was a period of relative obscurity. It was a period of research, development, and experimentation. The ARPAnet was the domain and playground of the few on the frontier of computer communications: universities, research labs, and military bases. This was also a period of the development of the fundamentals that are still bearing fruit and are still in use on the Internet today. This period marked the development of the Department of Defense (DoD) open communication protocols, which are now known as the TCP/IP protocol suite.

In 1974, Vinton Cerf (who is widely considered one of the founding fathers of the Internet) was awarded an ARPA contract to design a new protocol suite for the ARPAnet. Cerf was not new to communication protocols and to the ARPAnet when he landed the ARPA contract. He was a graduate student at UCLA when the first IMP was installed there in 1969, and he's been involved with the ARPAnet ever since. Cerf was also aware of the severe limitations of the Network Control Protocol that was in use on the ARPAnet throughout the decade of the seventies. The NCP allowed only a single packet at a time to be in transit between any two hosts communicating over the network. In today's TCP/IP jargon, you might say that NCP had a "window of 1."

With a "window of 1" protocol, the sending host must receive an acknowledgment for *every* packet that it transmits before it can send another packet to a receiving host. Can you imagine carrying on a conversation with a friend where for every word you say to your friend, your friend must say, "Aha," before you can say another word. It's one way to ensure that your friend is not sleeping through your monologues, but it's also bound to be a painfully slow conversation.

Computers may not experience pain as people do, but on a large network, computers can be drastically slowed down in their communication as a result of using a "window of 1" communication protocol. As the ARPAnet continued to grow in size, it was becoming increasingly obvious that NCP simply would not scale. The "sliding window" mechanism of TCP — a component of TCP/IP that Vint Cerf developed as a replacement for NCP — overcame the "window of 1" limitation of NCP.

Another factor was also driving the need for a new, more robust set of communication protocols for the ARPAnet. When ARPAnet first came online, it was using ordinary telephone wires as its transmission medium. However, the decade of the seventies saw the emergence of other transmission media for use in data communications.

Norman Abramson created the ALOHAnet by using multiple radio frequencies to link dumb terminals to a mainframe at the University of Hawaii. The principles of ALOHAnet inspired Bob Metcalfe to invent Ethernet, which initially used thick coaxial cable as the transmission medium. ARPA was sponsoring the development of satellite-based networks where the satellites were using different slices of frequencies from the electromagnetic spectrum to relay information between one another. The new twist in the satellite networks was that the satellites were acting only as intermediaries or relays between the end hosts.

The idea of a relay (or packet switch) for data communications had arrived. A relay or a packet switch would switch packets from one frequency to another — or from one transmission medium to another — but it would not interpret the packet's data contents.

What ARPA wanted was a set of common communication protocols that would allow computer hosts to communicate with one another across multiple networks using different physical transmission media. This effectively meant that the communication protocols were to be transmission-media independent. The TCP/IP protocols were designed to operate over a very wide media range, some of which were discussed in Chapter 7.

Against the background of ALOHAnet, Ethernet, and satellite-based networks, Cerf, Robert Khan, Jon Postel, Steve Crocker, and many others were developing and testing the new communication protocols (see Chapter 2). What started out as a single ARPA network was about to become a network of networks. A glue was needed to hold it all together — new robust communication protocols and a new breed of devices to connect the different networks together into a larger internetwork.

Interfacing these new technologies into a larger internetwork also meant that the IMPs may have fulfilled their reason for being, and now had to be supplemented and replaced by something more sophisticated. The IMPs of the ARPAnet had played their role in isolating the initial ARPAnet hosts from the network functions. Now there was a need for a new breed of devices to enable all the different networks to interact with one another.

Over the years, these devices have been known by many different names (a *packet switch*, a *relay*, a *gateway*, a *router* — whatever you want to call it), but it had to be a device that would interface networks together and not just interface individual computers to a single network. In the early 1980s, as the ARPAnet was approaching the second major phase of its evolution, these devices became known as *IP gateways*. The majority of the time, they are referred to as *routers*.

Formal specifications for the component protocols of the TCP/IP suite are available on the Internet in the form of RFCs. The IP protocol is specified in RFC 791, the TCP in RFC 793, the ICMP in RFC 792, and the ARP in RFC 826. All these RFCs are from around 1981, when the preparations were getting underway to convert ARPAnet from NCP to TCP/IP. It took almost ten years from the time that the work on these protocols began until they were being formally implemented. With their wide implementation and acceptance, the second major stage in the evolution of the Internet was about to begin.

Stage 2 (1983–1986): The early Internet

In January 1983, more than 200 hosts from major universities and research centers were connected together when the ARPAnet began its formal transition from NCP to the TCP/IP protocol suite. The development and deployment of the TCP/IP protocol suite on the ARPAnet, in fact, marked the birth of the Internet. Anyone who works with computers and has been through a major implementation or transition from one platform to another is well aware that a major transition to a new protocol suite on the ARPAnet could not have been just a singular event. It was a process that started before January 1, 1983, and continued for some time. However, January 1, 1983, has become formally associated with the beginning of a new epoch — the second major stage — in the Internet's evolution.

From January 1983 through early 1986, the Internet began to grow by leaps and bounds, fueled by the wide adoption of the openly specified TCP/IP protocols. During that time, the size of the Internet was still measured by the number of hosts, not the number of networks that were interconnected together. Today, it is the number of networks or rather the number of "prefixes" in the routing tables of backbone routers that's used to gauge the size of the Internet. In just three short years, the Internet grew by an order of magnitude from more than 200 hosts to more than 2,000 hosts by February, 1986. That was nothing compared with what was about to happen.

Several networks were connected to the Internet during the 1983 to 1986 time period, including the Computer Science Network (the CSnet) and the Joint Academic Network (JAnet) of the United Kingdom. However, the killer network that was going to set the stage for an Internet revolution was still to come.

Stage 3 (1986–1995): The NSFnet dominance

In 1986, the National Science Foundation network (NSFnet) was created by using 56 Kbps lines to connect 5 of the NSF-sponsored supercomputing centers (SCCs). The NSF-funded SCCs of that time included the John VonNeumann National Supercomputing Center in New Jersey, Cornell Theory Center, Pittsburgh SuperComputing Center, the National Center for SuperComputing Applications at the University of Illinois at Urbana-Champaign, and the San Diego SuperComputing Center. When the NSFnet became part of the Internet, the number of computers and networks comprising the Internet began to explode — almost like our national debt. The physical outline of original NSF network was quite similar to the outline of the Very High-Speed Backbone Network Service (vBNS), which is the currently NSF-sponsored Research and Education (R&E) network discussed later in this chapter. However, the architectures of the original NSF network and the vBNS are worlds apart.

With an operational 56 Kbps NSFnet, the Internet's architecture and infrastructure were set for the third major stage of its evolution. When the NSFnet first came on line in 1986, the Internet was exclusively an R&E phenomenon and all the Internet traffic was noncommercial. When the NSFnet backbone was eventually shut down nine years later, the estimates are that roughly 50 percent of the total Internet traffic was R&E traffic and the other 50 percent was commercial. Today, the Internet is dominated by commercial traffic.

The third major stage of the Internet's evolution (from 1986 through April, 1995) was dominated by the NSFnet backbone and regional networks. Some of the major regional networks were — and some still are — networks, such as the Michigan Net (MICHNet), the Southeastern Universities Research Association network (SURAnet), the Missouri Research and Education Network (MOREnet), the Pennsylvania Research and Economic Partnership Network (PREPnet) and the Bay Area Regional Research Network (BARRnet). BARRnet, for example, linked such research institutions as the Lawrence Livermore National Labs and the NASA Ames Research Center with several University of California campuses in the San Francisco area.

There was no "one size fits all" formula for the regional networks. Some of the regional networks existed before the NSFnet came online; others were founded and operated by nonprofit corporations for the sole purpose of connecting clusters of regional universities and research institutions to the NSFnet.

As a case in point, the New York State Education and Research Network (NYSERnet) started out as a nonprofit organization serving only the needs of the academic communities. As the commercial pressures on all of the nonprofit regional networks began to mount, they had to adjust to the changing times. For example, the NYSERnet spun off a for-profit subsidiary in 1989, the PSInet, and then turned around and contracted with PSInet to provide services to the NYSERnet clients. Today, PSInet is one of the largest national and international ISPs, recently announcing plans to upgrade its backbone to OC-48 (2.4 Gbps) capability. OC-48 is 1,600 times faster than the operational speed of the PSInet backbone at the time of its founding in 1989. Each one of the regional networks has a fascinating history of its own.

During the late 1980s and early 1990s, the business community began to wake up to the possibilities of using the Internet for commercial purposes. It was during this time in 1991 that the Commercial Internet Exchange (CIX) was founded. CIX was the prototype of today's public and private commercial interconnections and is discussed later in this chapter. However, as the Internet entered the decade of the 1990s, the bulk of its infrastructure was either sponsored and subsidized by the U.S. government (the NSFnet) or operated by nonprofit corporations (the regional networks). A mechanism was desperately needed that would allow the coexistence of both commercial and noncommercial traffic on what was becoming a national and international phenomenon. How this coexistence came about is best illustrated in the context of some of the highlights from this stage of the Internet's evolution.

In 1987 (only a year after the NSFnet became operational), NSF issued a solicitation to have the NSFnet backbone upgraded from 56 Kbps to T1 speeds (1.544 Mbps). The contract to manage the NSFnet backbone and upgrade it to a T1 operational speed was awarded to a Michigan corporation, Merit, Inc. Merit (which stands for Michigan Education and Research Information Triad) is a nonprofit organization with its roots dating back to 1966 when it was formed to interconnect computers at three Michigan universities. By 1988, Merit upgraded the NSFnet backbone to a T1 speed. The Internet continued its phenomenal growth rate. The size of the Internet was estimated at 130,000 hosts and 650 networks in July of 1989. In the three and a half years since the 56-Kbps NSFnet came on line, the number of computers connected to the Internet went from slightly more than 2,000 to approximately 130,000. That's a growth rate of more than 6,000% in three and a half years. Where was this going to stop?

Merit has done an excellent job of documenting the traffic patterns on the NSFnet backbone. If you are interested in number crunching, just point your browser to a Merit server at `http://www.merit.edu/nsfnet/statistic`, for all kinds of interesting statistics about the traffic patterns on the now-retired NSFnet backbone. Also refer to the Hobbes' Internet Timeline by surfing the Web to `http://info.isoc.org/guest/zakon/Internet/History` for additional figures relating to the Internet growth.

In this third major stage of the Net's evolution, the aging ancestor of the now-booming Internet, the ARPAnet was shut down. However, the unabated growth of the Internet continued. In 1990, another nonprofit corporation, Advanced Network and Services (ANS) was founded by IBM, MCI, and Merit to take over the management of the NSFnet backbone. The obvious question might be: Why found another non-profit corporation to manage the NSFnet backbone when Merit was already nonprofit and very successful? In part, the answer stems from the NSFnet's success.

From Merit's perspective, some of the motivation for founding ANS was to have a more nationally oriented organization manage the NSFnet backbone, since Merit's primary orientation was toward serving the Michigan universities. Other reasons for founding ANS had to do with economics and with the ability of the NFSnet to continue to provide a sustained and improved level of service to more and more R&E institutions that were connecting to the Internet through the regional networks.

The bottom line was that the NSFnet backbone had to be upgraded to a higher bandwidth capacity such as a T-3 (which is equivalent to 28 T1 circuits, or approximately 45 Mbps), but the cost of an upgrade to T-3 was going to be astronomical. A formula was needed whereby the NSFnet backbone could increase its bandwidth capacity without breaking the NSF financially. The formula turned out to be the privatization of the backbone service.

The basic premise behind privatization of the Internet backbone was that with commercial pressures for the use of the NSFnet mounting, the Internet backbone could be implemented as a *shared service* — a service shared by R&E and commercial interests. That's quite a departure from having an Internet backbone dedicated only to supporting NSF's goals and being completely subsidized by NSF. The NSF and the NSFnet service would effectively become one of the many clients of this new *shared backbone service*.

To implement the idea of a shared Internet backbone service, ANS founded a for-profit subsidiary, ANS CO+RE Systems. By 1991, ANS CO+RE put in place a new T-3 Internet backbone. ANS was now in a position to sell the new T-3 backbone services back to Merit, which continued to be funded by the NSF to provide academic institutions with access to the NSFnet. ANS was also free to sell access to the T-3 backbone services to commercial users. The profits from commercial sales were helping to defray the costs of operating and maintaining the new T-3 backbone service. The co-existence of the academic and the commercial Internet had begun, marking the beginning of the next stage in the Internet's evolution. The new T-3 backbone operated by ANS became known as the ANSnet and NSFnet backbone services.

If you look at the capacity of the new shared T-3 backbone service as compared to the original NSF 56-Kbps network, the T-3 represented approximately an 800-fold or 80,000% increase in the bandwidth capacity of the NSFnet backbone in just 5 years. Granted, not all of the T-3 backbone capacity was dedicated to the NSFnet, but it was a good indication of where the Internet was heading.

In 1993, the NSF — faced with an undeniable reality that the Internet was becoming more and more commercial — issued a solicitation (NSF 93-52) that effectively defined the structure of the Internet we have today. The key points in the solicitation included the following:

- Creation of a dedicated very high-speed backbone that would continue to serve the academic and research community. This new NSF backbone is known today as vBNS, and is discussed later in this chapter.
- Creation of Network Access Points (NAPs). These would act as the focal points for the interconnection of the components of the NSF high-speed backbone, but would also allow for the interconnection of commercial backbones.
- Assignment of the router arbiter function to an organization separate from the provider of the very high-speed backbone service.

MCI ended up creating and managing the vBNS. Sprint, Metropolitan Fiber Systems (MFS), Ameritech Advanced Data Systems (AADS), and Pacific Bell were awarded the operation of the four NSF-sponsored NAPs. Merit was awarded the router-arbiter component of the NSF solicitation. When ANS shut down the NSFnet T-3 backbone service on April 30, 1995, the next stage of the Internet's evolution was already in full-swing.

Incidentally, sometime in 1995, Advanced Network and Services — the nonprofit parent of ANS CO+RE — sold the ANS CO+RE subsidiary and its assets to America Online (AOL). ANS is now a subsidiary of AOL. Interestingly enough, Advanced Network and Services continues as a nonprofit corporation, but no longer uses ANS as the abbreviation for its name. ANS — the AOL subsidiary — continues to be a major player in providing Internet services to corporate customers through the ANSnet whose infrastructure has evolved from the T-3 shared backbone service. The ANSnet also carries a significant portion of the AOL dial-up Internet traffic.

When the NSFnet backbone service was being turned off, its Internet landscape was composed of 19 major sites to which more than 30 major regional networks were connected. Smaller networks from more than a thousand different institutions were connected to the NSFnet backbone through the regional networks. The structure of the ANSnet at the time that its NSFnet backbone service was being turned off is shown in Figure 10.2. The current structure of the ANSnet is shown in Figure 10.3.

FIGURE 10.2 *The ANSnet at the time of the NSFnet backbone transition (courtesy of ANS Communications, Inc.)*

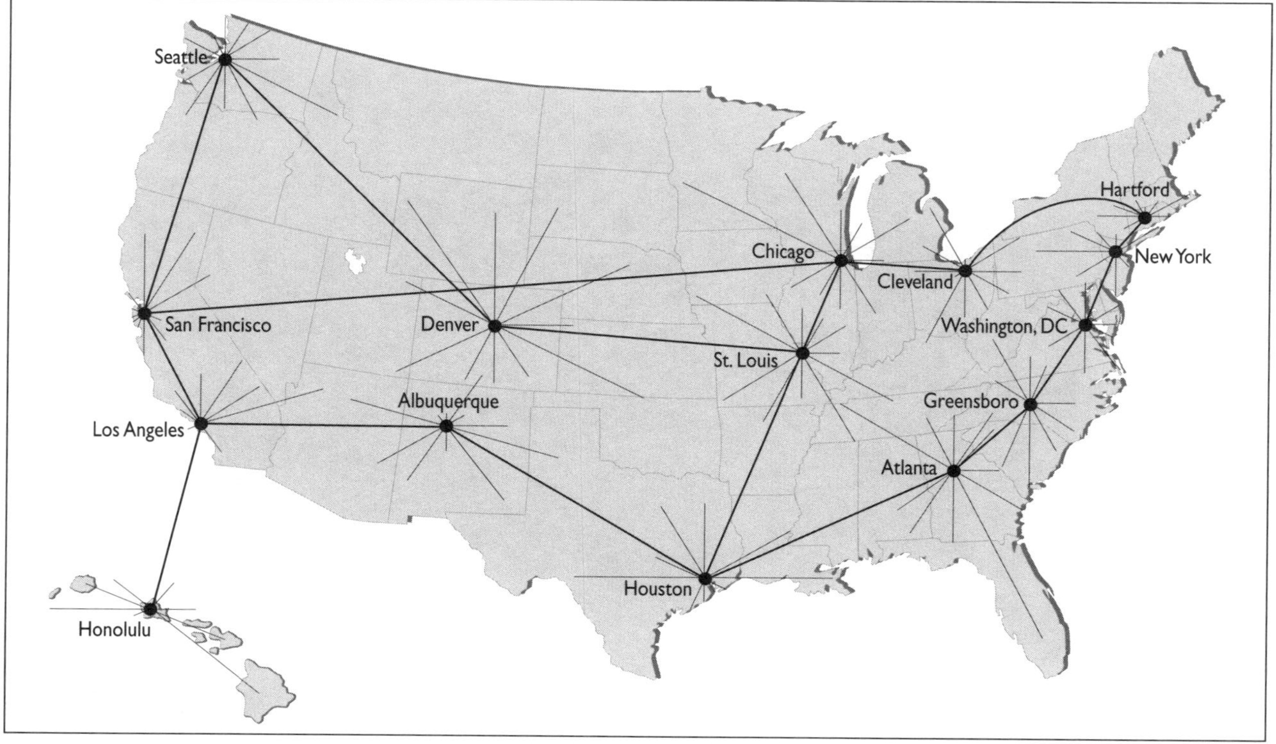

FIGURE 10.3 *Current structure of the ANSnet (courtesy of ANS Communications, Inc.)*

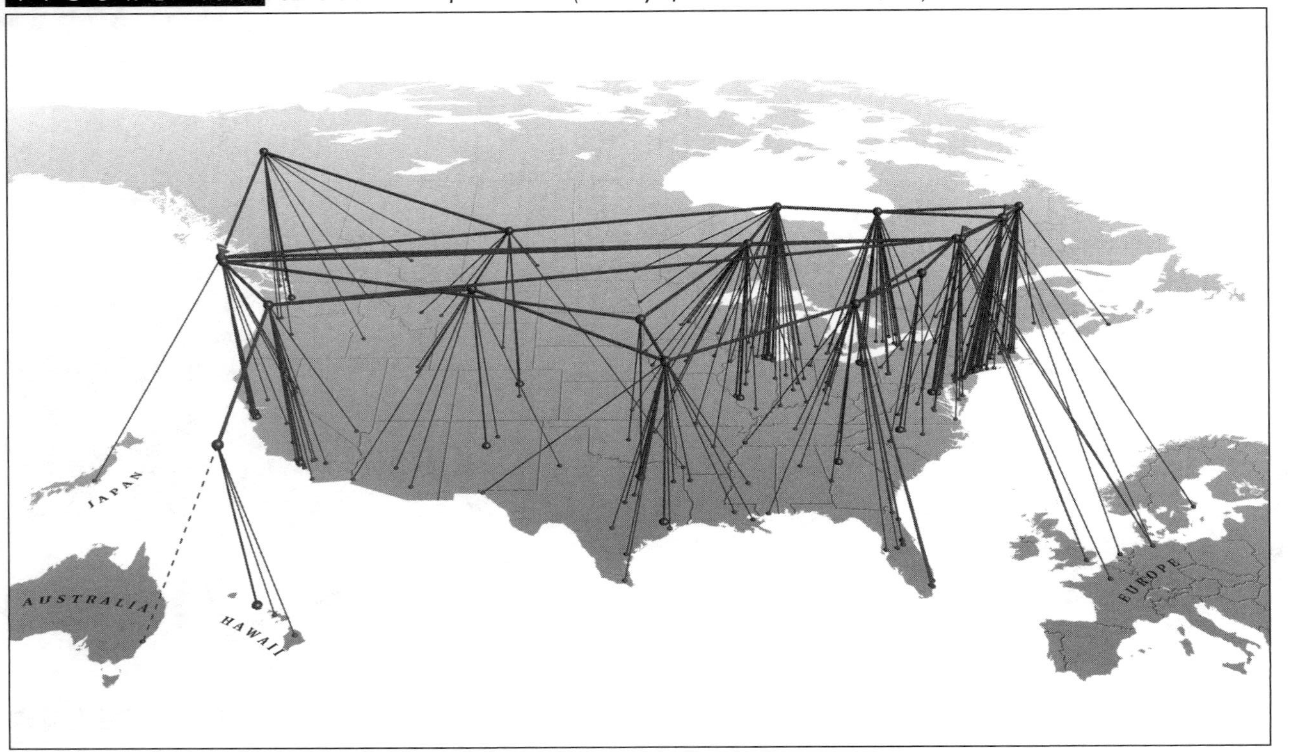

Backbone Interconnections

Recall the travel analogy from Chapter 1 and compare the locations where Internet backbones interconnect to an airport serving many airlines. In this new analogy, an airport is no longer viewed as a router from the point of view of individual packets. This analogy assumes the ability of each airline to bring passengers to this imaginary airport, and then transfer them for further travel to other airlines.

The airlines represent the backbones over which network traffic flows. If you can imagine an airport where every airline has its own runway — converging toward the center of the airport — and the arriving passengers (packets) are shuffled from one airline to another as soon as they arrive, you indeed have a vivid imagination! Imagining this scenario can help you picture what's happening with the packets on the transmission media interfacing with the many high-performance backbone routers at the Internet exchange points.

Now, try to imagine what happens when the only way to reach destination X is through airline A as shown in Figure 10.4. However, airline A says that it will only accept passengers for destination X arriving on airlines B and C. Airline A will not accept passengers destined for X arriving on airline D. So, what happens to those passengers (packets) destined for X, arriving at this imaginary airport on airline D? Their distress is reflected in Figure 10.4. This is where the *peering agreements* between the major Internet backbone operators come into play.

Review the legend in the BBN U.S. map in Chapter 2 (see Figure 2.4). The wavy-line circles where it says "peering locations" are the places where the backbones from the major providers come together. Some of those peering locations are labeled "NAP" or "MAE," and others are labeled "Private." The peering locations are the traffic-exchange points between the backbone service providers. Regardless of a specific label applied to a peering location, their function remains the same: switch user traffic (packets) between the backbones, subject to the *peering agreements* between the backbone operators. If all the backbones coming into an Internet exchange point were owned and operated by a single company, there would be no need for peering agreements. However, the commercialization of the Internet has inspired competition and there are many commercial backbone Internet operators. Sprint, MCI, UUnet, BBN, ANS, and AGIS are some of the major backbone operators. There are several dozen more.

FIGURE 10.4 *Lack of peering agreements analogy*

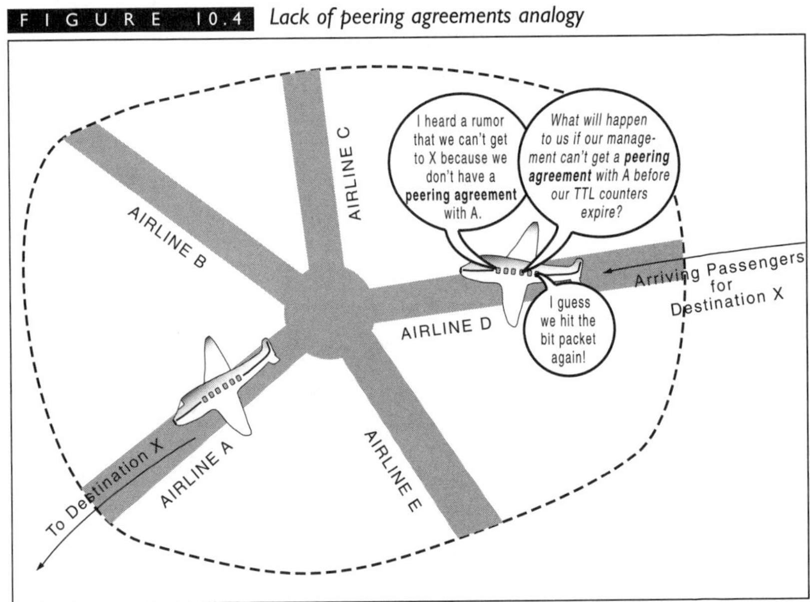

The NSF NAPS

The four NSF-sponsored NAPs resulting from the transition from the T-3 based NSFnet to the new Internet architecture are as follows:

- The AADS operated NAP in Chicago known as the "Chicago NAP."
- The "Sprint NAP" or the New York NAP located in Pennsauken, New Jersey. Just don't ask why it's not called the "New Jersey NAP"!
- The PacBell NAP located in the San Francisco area.
- The Metropolitan Area Ethernet-East (MAE-East) NAP located in Washington, D.C., and operated by MFS.

When the NAPs first came online in 1995, their operation was subsidized by the National Science Foundation and they served as the focal points for the interconnection of commercial Internet traffic and the vBNS. See Figure 10.1 for the logical relationship between the NAPs, vBNS, regional networks, and other Internet providers and users. The NAPs still continue to serve as major interconnection points, but the NSF sponsorship of the NAPs did not last very long.

The four NSF NAPs are now often referred to as *public Internet exchange points,* although the NAP is also still used. Public Internet exchange points are in contrast to the *private Internet exchange points* that are now beginning to dominate the Internet landscape. The former NSF-sponsored NAPs (or the major public exchange points) are still with us — they have not gone away — but already a new model of private exchange points and GIGAPOPs (discussed later in this chapter) is beginning to emerge.

Isn't there something almost prophetic and eerie about the NSF sponsorship of the four NAPs? Doesn't this sponsorship of the four NAPs by the NSF remind you of the original plan for a four-node ARPA network back in 1969? Look at what happened to the four ARPAnet nodes. They turned into millions in less than 30 years. Dare I risk ridicule by saying that the number of Internet exchange points like the NSF-sponsored NAPs, or like the private exchanges, or like the upcoming GIGAPOPs may be in the millions, 30 years from now? Perhaps we'll even see a NAP on the Moon or Mars by then (see Figure 10.5).

FIGURE 10.5 *Futuristic vision of the Internet*

Logical NAP architecture

So, what's really a NAP or a public Internet exchange point? It's more than just a location where the major Internet backbones interconnect. A NAP offers a mechanism for switching the user traffic between the backbones and for exchanging reachability information (routing updates) between the high-end backbone routers located at the NAPs. The two major components of a NAP are high-speed switches and high-performance backbone routers. The logical NAP architecture is shown in Figure 10.6.

FIGURE 10.6 *Logical NAP architecture*

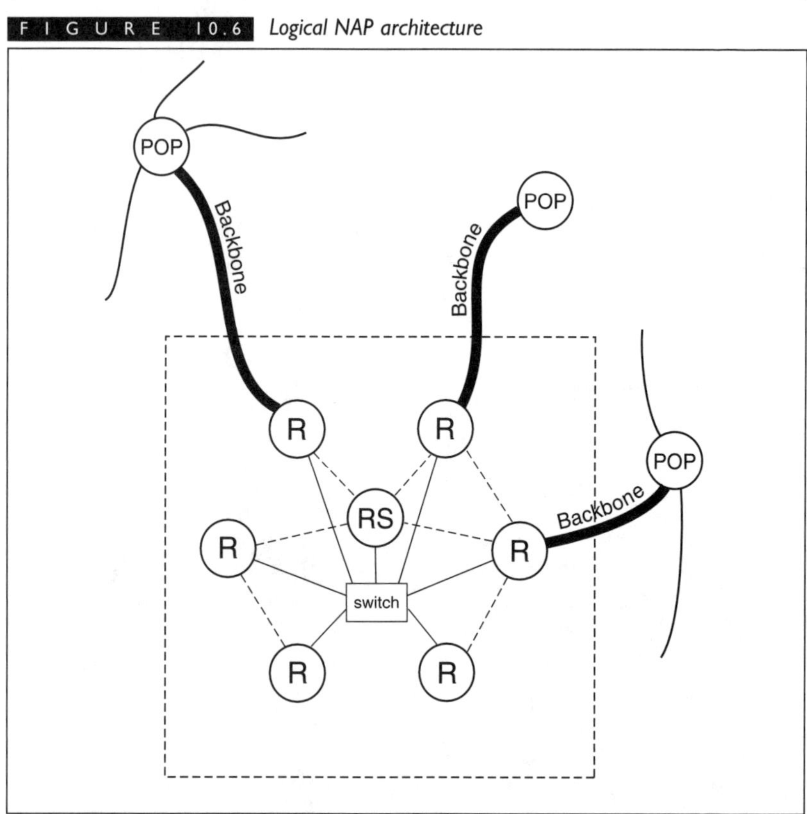

The circles in Figure 10.6 represent the high-performance backbone routers with interfaces to the high-speed switching fabric and to the incoming backbones. Another component at a NAP can be a route server (discussed later in this chapter). The solid lines in Figure 10.6 represent the physical connections from the routers to the high-speed switching fabric. The dotted lines represent the logical peering sessions between a route server and the backbone routers and between routers themselves.

High-performance backbone routers

Some examples of high-performance backbone routers are shown in Figures 10.7, 10.8, and 10.9. Others are discussed in Chapter 9.

FIGURE 10.7 *Front view of the Cisco 7513 backbone router (courtesy of Cisco Systems, Inc.)*

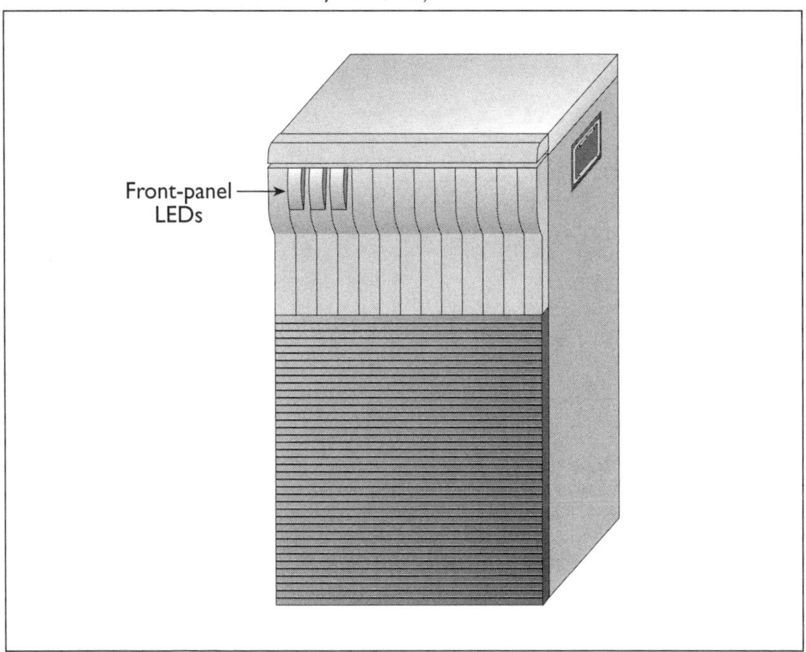

The architecture of the high-performance backbone routers is complex. If you look at Figure 10.8 (the rear view of the Cisco 7513 model), it shows a card cage where interface processor modules plug in. The media interface processor modules represent an acronym city of their own and they support technologies whose detailed discussion is beyond the scope of this book. Some of the media interface processor modules supported by the 7513 are as follows:

- Asynchronous Transfer Mode (ATM) Interface Processor (AIP)
- FDDI Interface Processor (FIP)
- Ethernet Interface Processor (EIP)
- High-Speed Serial Interface (HSSI) Interface Processor (HIP)
- Token Ring Interface Processor (TRIP)

FIGURE 10.8 *Rear view of the Cisco 7513 backbone router (courtesy of Cisco Systems, Inc.)*

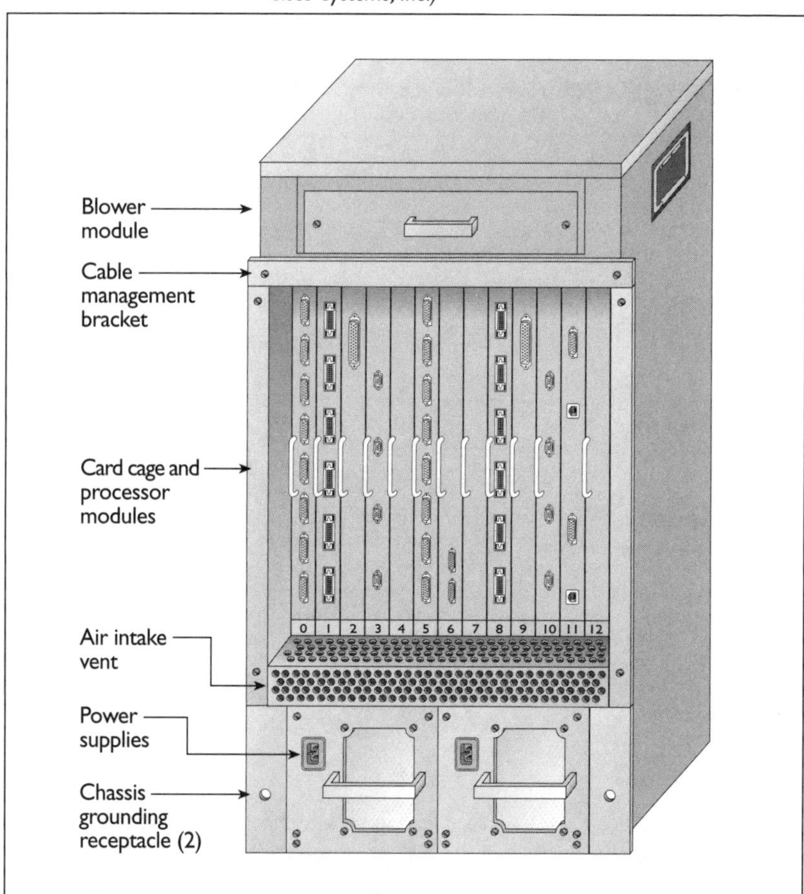

These are just a few of more than a dozen available interface processors for a Cisco 7513. So, if you are looking for a hip internetworking trip, just visit a backbone router at your local Internet exchange. The interface processor modules allow a backbone router to connect to the incoming backbone media, and to the switching fabric at an Internet exchange point such as a NAP.

FIGURE 10.9 *Front view of Bay Networks backbone node (courtesy of Bay Networks, Inc.)*

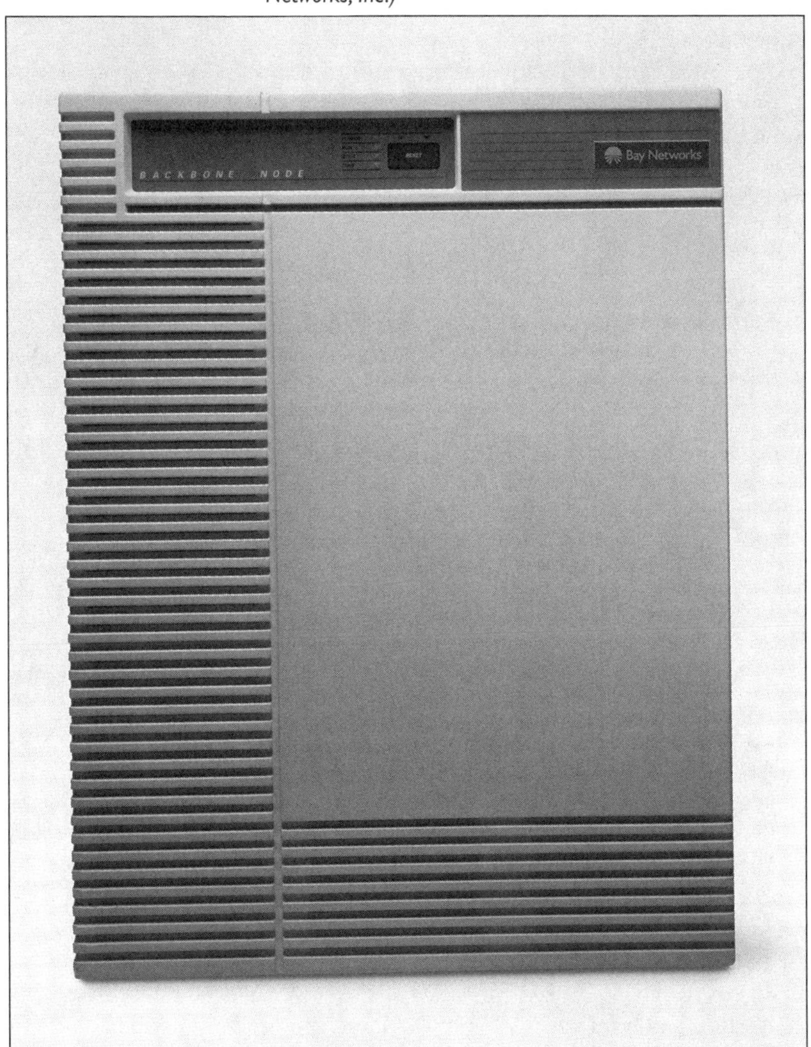

In addition, a backbone router such as the Cisco 7513 supports two Route Switch Processors (RSPs). An RSP is a processor module that combines all the routing and the high-speed switching functions deployed in the Cisco 7500

series routers. The Cisco Internetworking Operating System (IOS) resides on an RSP in the form of flash memory cards. The RSPs (with the IOS) and the interface processor modules are the heart of what makes up one of these backbone routers.

The rest is mechanical stuff: the power supplies, fans, and a chassis. The list of routing and routable protocols supported by backbone routers is extensive. Suffice it to say, all of the routing protocols discussed in Chapter 4 (RIP, OSPF, and BGP) are supported by the operating systems on backbone routers. The routable protocols — in addition to IP — include protocols from Novell, Apple, Banyan, Digital Equipment Corporation (DEC), and Open Systems Interconnection (OSI), just to name a few.

High-performance backbone switches

The switching fabric to which the routers at a NAP interface can be an FDDI switch, an ATM switch, or an FDDI/ATM hybrid. For example, the Sprint NAP deploys a combination of an FDDI switch and a shared FDDI LAN. The FDDI switch is a high-performance DEC GIGAswitch/FDDI, as shown in Figure 10.10

DEC GIGAswitch/FDDI started out as an FDDI switch only, but it is now a multilayer, multitechnology switch with an aggregate switching capacity of 3.4 Gbps. It's a multitechnology switch because it supports FDDI, ATM, and Fast Ethernet. The 3.4 Gbps switching capacity effectively translates into a support of 34 FDDI ports, 34 fast Ethernet ports, 22 OC-3c ATM ports, or some combination of all three technologies. The GIGAswitch is a multilayer switch because in addition to the Layer 2 switching of FDDI, ATM, and fast Ethernet, the GIGAswitch/FDDI also supports IP switching (discussed in Chapter 11). One of the unique features of the GIGAswitch is that it supports the FDDI Full-Duplex Technology (FFDT). FFDT has been developed by DEC and can be licensed from DEC by vendors who want to incorporate it into their high-end backbone router interface modules.

The GIGAswitch supports both *cut-through switching* and *store-and-forward switching*. Cut-through switching is faster because only a portion of a frame is read by a switch on the input port before the frame begins to exit the switch on an output port. To understand cut-through switching, envision a frame as a long string of bits. The bits from the tail end of the frame are still getting into the switch, bits from the middle of the frame are inside the switch, and the beginning bits are already on their way out of the switch through the output port. Imagine a very long snake crossing a very narrow stream, with its head on one side, its tail on the other, and its belly in the middle of the stream. With store-and-forward switching, the entire frame must get inside the switch before it is forwarded on an appropriate output port.

FIGURE 10.10 *High-performance DEC GIGAswitch/FDDI (courtesy of Digital Equipment Corporation, Inc.)*

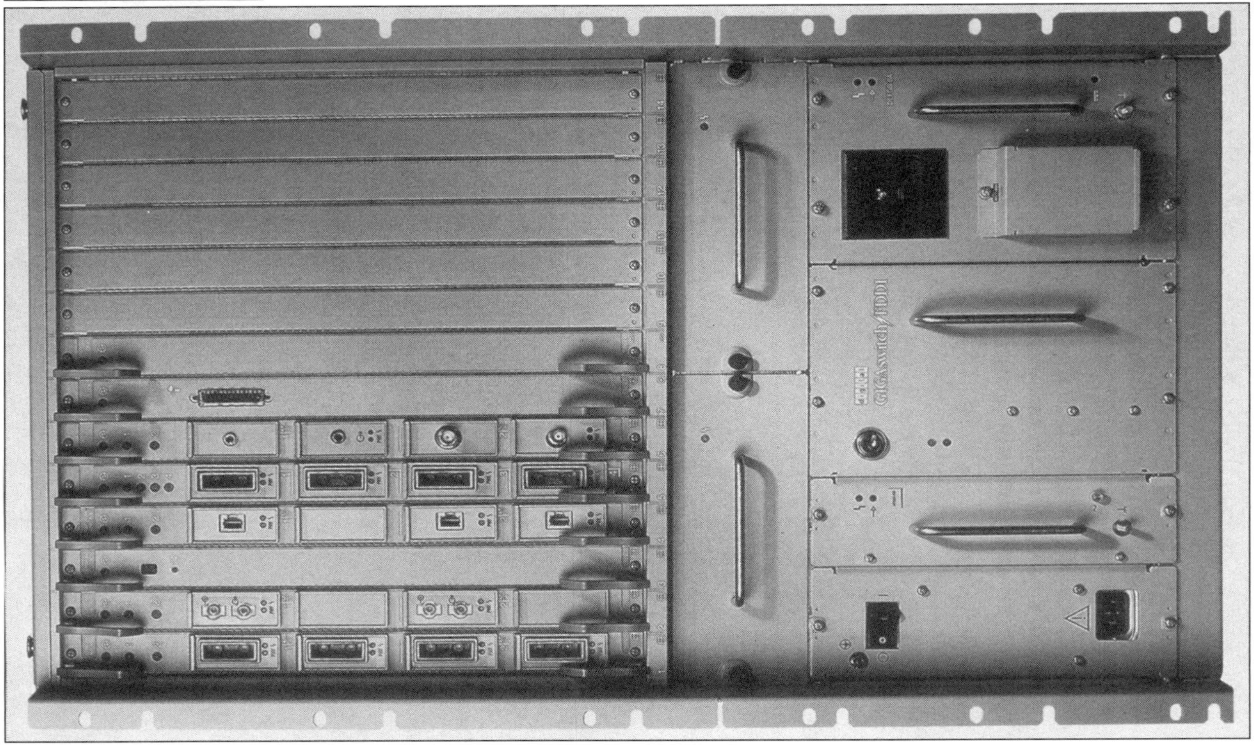

The GIGAswitch uses a *nonblocking crossbar-switching fabric,* which means that traffic from any switch port can be flowing to any other switch port in a full-duplex mode without any interference from traffic between the remaining ports. Even with this kind of switching capacity, if you consider the number of providers that are coming into the NAPs and the bandwidth capacity of their backbones, it is still possible even for very high-performance switches such as the GIGAswitch/FDDI to run out of steam. Several of the GIGAswitch/FDDI units are deployed at the Sprint NAP and at the Digital Internet Exchange (DIX) in Palo Alto, California.

The Chicago NAP deploys a Lucent Technologies Globalview 2000 ATM switch with a switching capacity of 20 Gbps. Some traffic statistics from the Chicago NAP are shown in Figures 10.11 and 10.12.

FIGURE 10.11 *Traffic volume at the Chicago NAP on August 1, 1997 (courtesy of Ameritech Advanced Data Services, Inc.)*

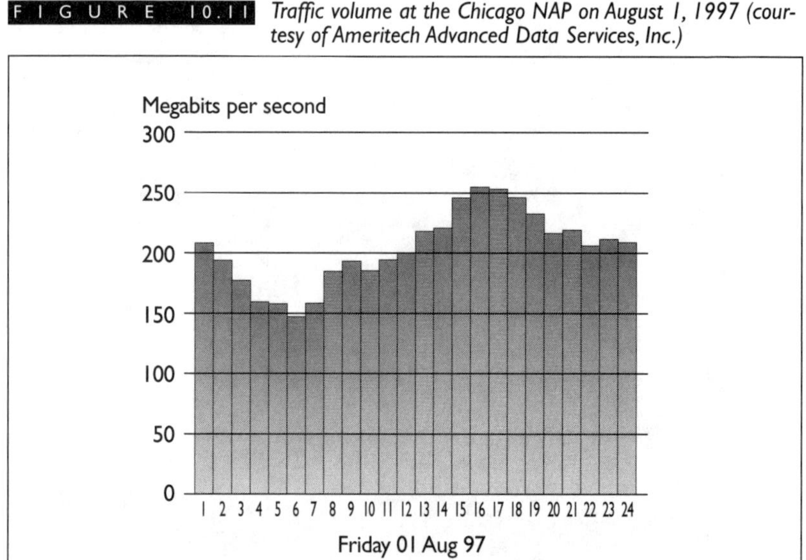

An example may provide an idea of the aggregate volume of information that flows through some of the public exchange points. On Friday, August 1, 1997, between the hours of 3 p.m. and 4 p.m., the volume of traffic at the Chicago NAP ATM switch exceeded 250 million bits/sec as shown in Figure 10.11. These numbers are so staggering that they defy the imagination.

FIGURE 10.12 *Cell loss at the Chicago NAP on August 1, 1997 (courtesy of Ameritech Advanced Data Services, Inc.)*

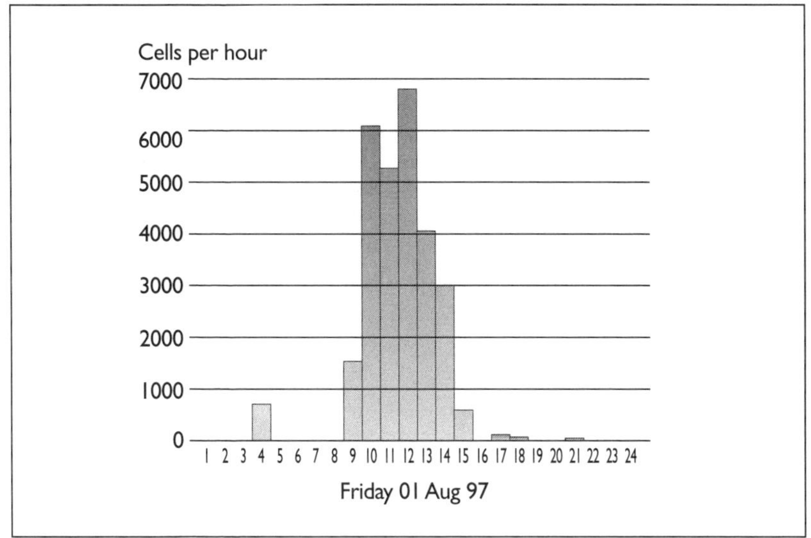

Consider that a single-spaced 8.5-by-11-inch typed sheet of paper contains approximately 54 lines of text with approximately 72 characters per line, which translates into approximately 30,000 bits per page (54 times 72 times 8). This means that the ATM switch at the Chicago NAP is processing the digital equivalent of 8,000 pages per second. In one hour, this would be the equivalent of approximately 30 million pages of single-spaced typed text. If you consider that 250 pages is approximately an inch thick, then 30 million pages would create a stack of paper that's approximately two miles high. How long would it take you to read a book that's two miles thick? Chances are it would take longer than an hour! That's just to give you an idea of the volume of information that flows through some of the Internet exchange points. And the Chicago NAP is not even the busiest exchange!

Figure 10.12 shows a reflection that at times under load conditions, even a high-power ATM switch will drop some cells. When cells are dropped by a switch, it means the higher-layer protocols must get involved to ensure that the information contained in those cells is re-transmitted. It's like being in a conversation where people are speaking really fast. Every now and then you may have to stop and ask someone to repeat something — request a retransmission — because the original message simply did not register in your brain (somehow it was dropped). If you can think of the human brain as a high-performance switch — receiving information through one of its components and then passing that information to another component for further processing — then what takes place in daily life is not that far from what takes place at the most critical points of the Internet. Just like a human brain that gets overloaded, so do the switches at the NAPs. It never fails to amaze me how the technology resembles the working habits of its creators.

The four NAPs sponsored by the NSF when its T-3 backbone was retired were not enough to accommodate the increasing commercial pressures on the Internet. Other public peering locations and private interconnects have come about as a result of sustained Internet growth. There are also smaller Internet exchange points popping up at the local level. The presence of the initial NAPs introduced a certain level of hierarchy into a relatively flat Internet based primarily on the NSFnet backbone. However, with the increase in the number of the private exchange points, this hierarchy seems to be flattening out again. The effects of this evolution are yet to be seen.

Route servers

Chapter 4 introduced the concepts of designated routers in the discussion on OSPF. In the discussion on BGP, Chapter 4 also introduced the concepts of the route reflectors and confederations. All those techniques — selection of designated routers in OSPF, BGP route reflectors and confederations — were designed with the idea of minimizing the exchange of the routing updates traffic between routers. After all, in an ideal world, routers would concentrate on forwarding your traffic, not on talking with one another about how to forward it. The more routers talk with one another about *how to forward* traffic, the less they are able to concentrate on *forwarding* it.

A component of the NSF solicitation (NSF 93-52) was for a qualified organization to assume the role of a routing arbiter. This component of the NSF solicitation has become known as the Routing Arbiter Project. One of the elements of the Routing Arbiter Project is to create and maintain a database from which routing configuration for the NAP routers can be derived. Another element of the Router Arbiter Project is a route server. Merit, which was awarded the router arbiter component of NSF's solicitation, cooperated with the Information Science Institute (ISI) of the University of Southern California on the routing database and the route server projects.

The fundamental idea behind a route server at an exchange point (such as a NAP) is that instead of all the provider routers at an exchange establishing BGP peering sessions with one another, the provider routers would peer only with the router server. The route server would accept routing updates from each provider router, and it would pass these routing updates to all of the other routers. It sounds like a perfect plan!

The net result would be if every provider router peered with the route server only, each provider router would have to maintain only one peering session to the route server (as opposed to maintaining a peering session with all the other provider routers). The route server effectively becomes a very powerful router, but with one major exception. The route server would not be involved in forwarding any user traffic.

This is where the route server contrasts with the designated routers in OSPF and the route reflectors in BGP, which, despite their somewhat "special" status, are also involved in forwarding user traffic. The route server would peer with the provider routers for the purpose of reducing the BGP mesh inside a NAP, which in turn would reduce the level of routing updates traffic on the switching fabric connecting all the routers. Ideally, the route server would become the singular focal point for the exchange of routing information, which would enable the provider routers to concentrate on their primary responsibility (the forwarding of user traffic). Instead of the provider routers exchanging routing updates with one another, they would exchange it with the route server only. Frequently, however, there is a gap between the ideal and the real.

The Internet is not an environment where everyone does things the same way. Peering with a route server at a major exchange point like a NAP is optional. It is possible for provider routers to peer with the route server only. It is possible for providers to peer with each other and not with the route server. It is also possible for provider routers to peer with each other and with the route server at the same time. Consequently, there is some potential for chaos at the NAPs and the initial idea behind the route server reducing a BGP mesh at an exchange point has not come into full fruition.

In a way, noble ideas become victims of advances in technology. When the route server project was being proposed, many backbone routers had a significant limit on the number of simultaneous BGP peering sessions they could maintain. This limitation seems to have receded as vendors have upgraded the operating system software for their high-end backbone routers, enabling those routers to maintain more peering sessions than the providers would care to have in the first place. Even if the route server is not used to reduce the BGP mesh at a NAP, or it is not relied on by providers for routing updates, it still serves a very important function of collecting routing statistics if enough providers decide to peer with it. Route server implementation has a backup route server for redundancy.

The route server component (just like the operation of the NAPs) was initially subsidized by the NSF in the form of a financial grant to Merit. At this time the NSF subsidy has been phased out and providers who want to use the route server pay Merit directly.

vBNS

The NSFnet backbone may have been "shut down" in the logical sense in April 1995, but the NSF continues to play a vital role in the development of the Internet. In fact, the activities sponsored by the NSF are laying the foundation for the next generation of high-performance internetworking.

One of the components of the NSF's solicitation (NSF 93-52) was the creation of a high-speed national backbone that would replace the NSFnet T-3 backbone service and continue to serve the needs of the academic and research community after the NSFnet T-3 backbone service was discontinued. The vBNS backbone (which is managed and operated by MCI) is the fruition of the NSF's vision for such a high-speed, high-performance national backbone.

First and foremost, vBNS was intended to interconnect the NSF-supported four super-computing centers (Cornell Theory Center, Pittsburgh SuperComputing Center, the National Center for SuperComputing Applications at the University of Illinois at Urbana-Champaign, and the San Diego SuperComputing Center) and the National Center for Atmospheric Research (NCAR) in Boulder, Colorado. Incidentally, as of this year, as part of the Partnership for Advanced Computational Infrastructure (PACI) program, only two of the four SCCs (San Diego and NCSA) will continue to be funded by NSF.

Other major academic institutions and research networks also connect to the vBNS through the NAPs. vBNS is accessible through each of the four NAPs, provided that institutions that want to connect meet the appropriate connection requirements. NSF working in conjunction with MCI plans to continue to connect more R&E institutions to the vBNS through its Connections Program.

For more information on the Connections Program, surf the vBNS Web site at `http://www.vbns.net`.

The vBNS was initially implemented in 1995 as an ATM/IP network operating over an OC-3 physical layer. Since that time, the vBNS backbone has been upgraded to operate at the OC-12 speed of 622 Mbps. For the physical outline of the vBNS and its connection sites, see Figure 10.13.

The legend of the vBNS map bears some explanation. The OC-12c backbone is an ATM backbone operating at speeds of up to 622 Mbps. The OC-3c is the equivalent of 155 Mbps and the DS-3 of 45 Mbps. When you compare the NSFnet with a 56 Kbps backbone in 1986 to the vBNS in 1997, that's approximately an 11,000% increase in the operational speed in the 11 years that NSF has supported an Internet backbone. This kind of a dramatic increase in the operational speed of the main cyber pipe of the R&E Internet says something about the changing nature of internetworking and communications. Even the stock market hasn't increased at such a phenomenal rate.

FIGURE 10.13 *The new NSF high-performance backbone, the vBN. (Reprinted with the permission of MCI Telecommunications Corporation. Copyright 1997 MCI Telecommunications Corporation. All rights reserved. This material is based upon work supported by the National Science Foundation under grant No. NCR 9321047. Any opinions, findings, and conclusions or recommendations expressed in this publication are those of the author(s) and do not necessarily reflect the views of the National Science Foundation.)*

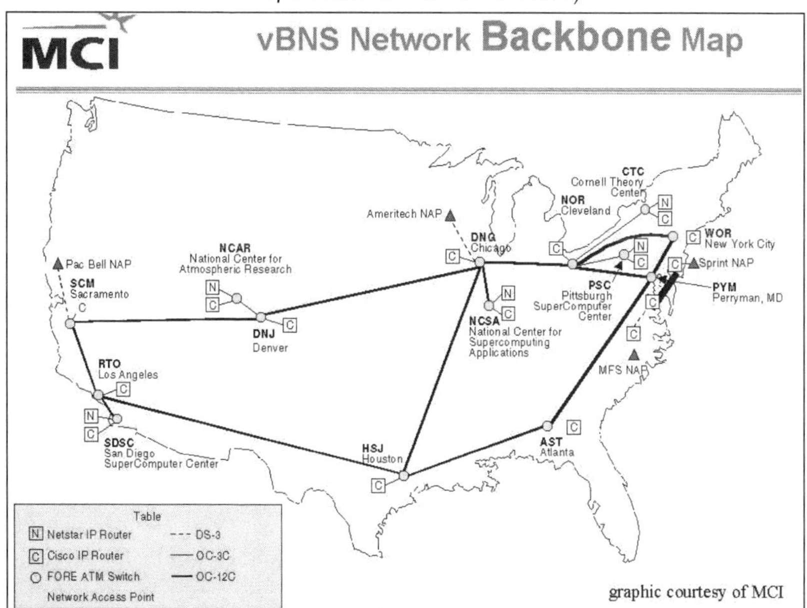

For a logical outline of the vBNS in the context of its BGP peers, see Figure 10.14, which shows the autonomous system numbers assigned to the vBNS, and to the locations and networks (SCCs, NAPs, other R&E or federally sponsored networks) which the vBNS interconnects. For a quick review of autonomous systems and BGP, see Chapter 4.

FIGURE 10.14 *Current vBNS BGP peers (Reprinted with the permission of MCI Telecommunications Corporation. Copyright 1997 MCI Telecommunications Corporation. All rights reserved. This material is based upon work supported by the National Science Foundation under grant No. NCR 9321047. Any opinions, findings, and conclusions or recommendations expressed in this publication are those of the author(s) and do not necessarily reflect the views of the National Science Foundation.)*

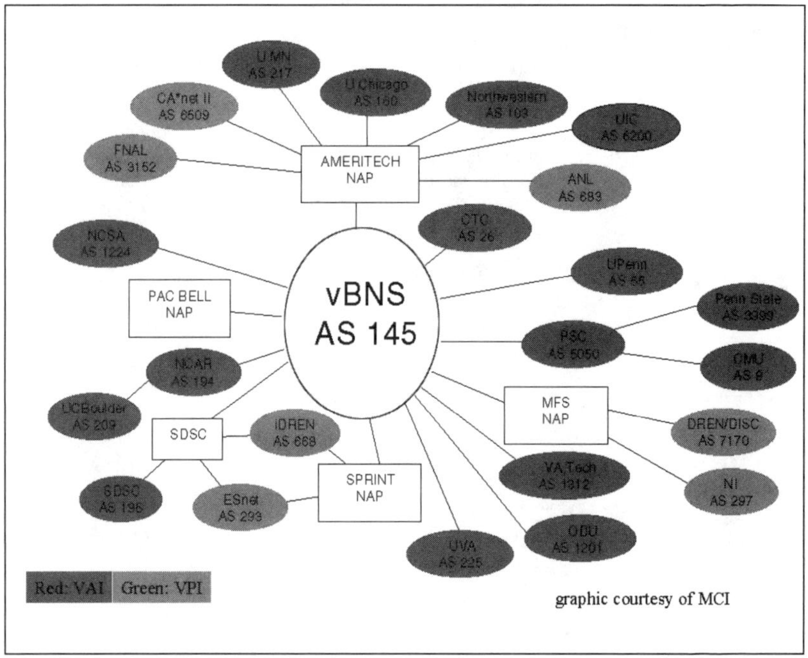

From a historical perspective on the Internet, the vBNS is reinvigorating the research and academic community through its connections program, just like the NSFnet did when it first came online in 1986. The vBNS, which is managed by the MCI/vBNS engineering group, is without a doubt the research frontier of the Internet and of the internetworking field.

The internetworking infrastructure at the SCCs the vBNS interconnects is quite impressive. It includes a high-performance ATM switch, FORE ASX-1000, an Ascend Communications GRF-400 router, and a DEC Alpha traffic monitor. The Fore ASX-1000 is the focal interconnection point. It has two OC-12 interfaces, one to the vBNS and one to the Ascend router. It also has OC-3 interfaces to the DEC Alpha traffic monitor and a local SCC ATM switch. SCC networks interface to the local SCC switch. See Figure 10.15 for a generic vBNS architecture at the SCC sites.

Just to give you some characteristics of the equipment that's deployed at the vBNS connection points, the FORE ASX-1000 provides up to 96 ATM ports with a total switching capacity of 10 Gbps. Some of the 96 ports operate at OC-12 speed of 622 Mbps. Earlier in this chapter, a reference was made to the volume of network traffic being switched through one of the ATM switches at the Chicago NAP. The FORE ASX-1000 has the potential capacity to switch about 40 times that traffic volume. So, the reading of a 2-mile-thick book in an hour — corresponding to the traffic volume in Figure 10.12 — has turned into the reading of an 80-mile-thick book in an hour. How's that for speed reading?

FIGURE 10.15 *Generic vBNS architecture at the SCC sites (Reprinted with the permission of MCI Telecommunications Corporation. Copyright 1997 MCI Telecommunications Corporation. All rights reserved. This material is based upon work supported by the National Science Foundation under grant No. NCR 9321047. Any opinions, findings, and conclusions or recommendations expressed in this publication are those of the author(s) and do not necessarily reflect the views of the National Science Foundation.)*

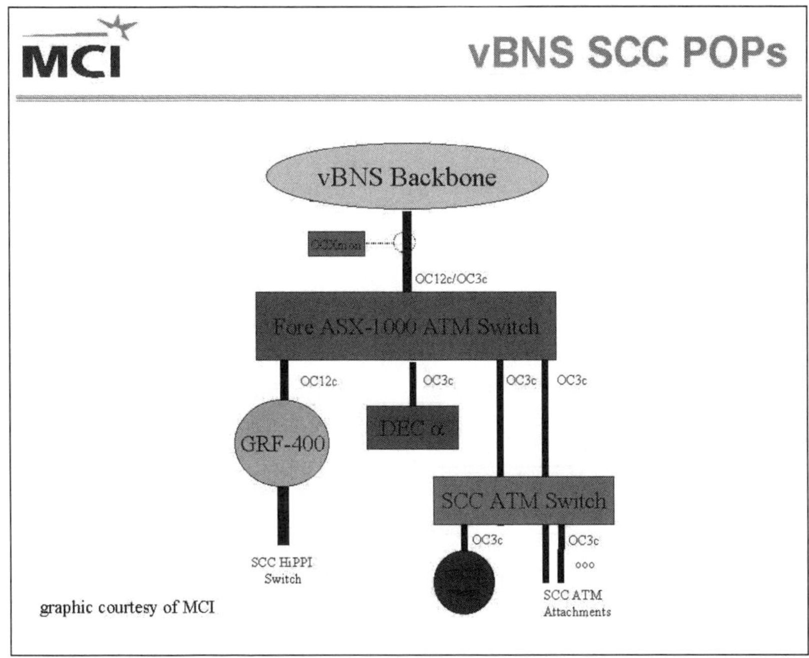

The Ascend GRF-400 router (described in more detail in Chapter 9) is unique in the series of high-performance routers because it offers the OC-12c interface to the backbone in addition to a High-Performance Parallel Interface (HIPPI) for HIPPI-capable hosts. The HIPPI interconnections are extremely high-speed (anywhere from 800 Mbps to 3.2 Gbps) that typically have been deployed between supercomputers. With the network backbone speeds approaching the HIPPI speeds, the HIPPI envelope is being pushed, and some of the high-performance backbone routers now support HIPPI interface processors. A router with a HIPPI interface processor allows HIPPI-capable hosts to be interfaced in a very direct way to the network backbone. Atmospheric modeling and simulation is one application that can take advantage of HIPPI speeds.

The three-letter designations above city names on the vBNS map (Figure 10.13) refer to the MCI Points of Presence (POPs). A few of the MCI POPs from the map are Denver Junction (DNJ), Houston Junction (HSJ), and so on. The setup at the POPs is logically similar to the setup at the SCCs. The Fore ASX-1000 switch is the focal interconnection point, but the AGR-400s are replaced with The Cisco's 7507s. The 7507s are equipped with the interface processors with those funny names (such as AIP, FIP, and EIP), which interface them to the vBNS and to the networks the routers connect to the backbone. The FORE Systems ASX-1000 switch is shown in Figure 10.16.

As the research and academic community becomes more aware of the capabilities and the research potential that the vBNS has to offer, a need will emerge for a new interconnection mechanism. The MCI/vBNS engineering group is now floating a concept of a GIGAPOP.

The idea of a GIGAPOP is to be a logical step down from a NAP. A GIGAPOP would be an interconnection point where multiple vBNS customers, multiple commercial Internet providers, and a vBNS feed would all come together. Effectively, that's what started to happen at the NAPs, which is causing the NAPs to become extremely congested and overcrowded. The big question is, however, who would operate and be responsible for the GIGAPOPs? How the GIGAPOP concept works out remains to be seen. Geography and demographics will likely play a role in their location. Don't bet on a GIGAPOP in Montana any time soon. Also, the operation of GIGAPOPs must be economically feasible, since it's not something that's likely to receive government funding.

If a GIGAPOP is to serve only as an aggregation point for a cluster of universities and research institutions within a close geographical proximity, then its operation and administration may be simple. However, if a GIGAPOP will involve commercial backbone providers and commercial customers in addition to the R&E customers, then its operation and administration may get tricky.

FIGURE 10.16 *FORE Systems high-performance ATM switch (courtesy of FORE Systems, Inc.)*

So, another element in the internetworking evolution is emerging. The concepts of POPs is not new, but typically a POP is operated by a single provider serving its clients. The GIGAPOP concept, on the other hand, is a hybrid between a NAP and a POP. The Internet is definitely a rapidly evolving organism.

Private Interconnects

Private interconnects are a major trend in today's Internet connectivity. A private interconnection is simple. It also makes a lot of sense from a technical and economic point of view. In areas where two major backbone operators want to exchange traffic, they connect two of their routers together. Just like that. They string an appropriate cable between the routers and configure the appropriate router interfaces.

Just imagine a network traffic scenario in the absence of the private interconnects. Two major backbone operators have portions of their backbones running through a state at least a thousand miles from the nearest public exchange such as a NAP. If the customers attached to the two backbones want to exchange network traffic over the Internet, that traffic would have to travel over one backbone all the way to the NAP and then via a second backbone all the way back. It's possible that the companies wanting to talk to each other (but using different providers) are in a very close geographical proximity. So, with a growing commercialization of the Internet and where the Internet is being used to conduct business, a private interconnection makes good economic and technical sense.

From a technical point of view, putting a private interconnect in the proximity of the customers who want to talk to each other does not clog up the backbone further upstream, because the network traffic can now flow more directly between the customers of the two providers. This arrangement has the added benefit of improving the overall network performance since traffic between the customers will now travel shorter distances and the upstream backbone bandwidth will be available to customers who legitimately must send their traffic upstream. The use of the private interconnects also lessens the traffic load at the public exchanges, which are getting overcrowded (more connections) and congested (more traffic).

The concept of private interconnects (or even semi-public interconnects) has the potential of allowing smaller local carriers to link businesses in local areas into mini-regional networks which can then connect to the rest of the Internet via a major national carrier. As the Internet continues to become a major force in commerce and education, even smaller communities will end up hosting local Internet exchanges.

In fact, this is already happening. Just surf the net to `http://www.isi.edu/div7/ra/NAPs/naps_na.html` for a list of active North American Internet exchange points. For an example of a local exchange just click on the Tucson Interconnect (TII).

Commercial Internet Exchange (CIX)

The Commercial Internet Exchange (CIX) was established in 1991 as a nonprofit trade association with its mission to provide a commercial interconnection point for a growing number of commercial Internet providers. The CIX router was the first point for exchanging commercial Internet traffic, and the CIX model became a forerunner of the evolving variety of Internet Exchange (IX) points in use today. Up until the time that the new Internet NAP-based architecture was in place, and the regional networks were connected to the backbones of the major service providers (who, in turn, exchanged traffic at the NAPs), the CIX played a major role in facilitating the exchange of commercial Internet traffic.

CIX started with a single router with the providers connecting to individual ports. This may sound a bit archaic today, but in 1991 it was a state-of-the-art way for commercial Internet providers to come together. Then again, in 1991 a typical high-speed modem operated at 2400 bps, for all intents and purposes the Web did not exist, and the "Internet" was not exactly a household word.

Today, CIX still offers Internet connectivity through a Cisco 7513 router located at the Digital Internet Exchange (DIX) in Palo Alto. The primary mission and purpose of CIX has evolved from being an IX provider to being an active trade organization that provides a forum for ISPs to address issues related to the operation and use of the Internet. These issues are not getting any simpler. They range from issues related to the Internet infrastructure (such as technical standards, coordination between ISPs, and funding) to public policy and legislative issues (such as electronic commerce, taxes, privacy, and content regulation).

Federal Internet Exchange (FIX)

The discussion of Internet backbone interconnections would not be complete without some mention of the Federal Internet Exchanges (FIXs) that have served as the interconnection points for many of the federal agencies networks such as the Energy Sciences Network (ESnet), the Defense Research and Education Network (DREN), the NASA Internet, and more.

There are two FIXs: FIX-East (located at the University of Maryland in College Park, Maryland) and the FIX-West (located at the NASA Ames Research Center in California). Conceptually, a FIX is no different from a NAP, except that it serves a different clientele. The federal networks are quite extensive connecting large numbers of government-operated facilities and schools. Federal networks interconnect at FIXs but they also have feeds into other major interconnection points such as the NAPs.

Interested readers are encouraged to surf the Web at sites such as `http://www.es.net` **or** `http://www.arl.mil` **for more details about the structures of federal networks.**

The Internet2 project

In parallel with vBNS, another major high-performance Internet project that is in the works has become known as *Internet2*. Since not all of the academic institutions that were part of the NSFnet have access to vBNS — and with the commercial and academic traffic competing for the available bandwidth on the commercial Internet backbones — the majority of the academic research community seems to have been squeezed out from the kind of access to the Internet that's needed to support its goals. These goals include world-class research and the enabling of a new generation of applications in support of newly emerging priorities within higher education (such as distance learning and life-long learning).

The Internet2 project has become a collaborative effort between universities and the private sector to develop the next-generation Internet that will serve the academic community just like the original NSFnet. The project was initiated by the representatives from many of the nation's leading universities, and project goals were endorsed at a meeting in Chicago in October, 1996. The Internet2 project goals were also adopted by the White House as part of the Next Generation Internet (NGI) initiative. In his State of the Union address of February 4, 1997, President Bill Clinton pledged "a second generation Internet so that our leading universities and national laboratories can communicate at speeds 1,000 times faster than today." Given that in 11 years since 1986, the speed of the NSF-sponsored backbone has increased by 11,000 times, President Clinton's statement is very realistic.

For more information about Internet2 and the statement of their mission, goals, and priorities surf the web to `http://www.internet2.edu`.

As the commercial Internet continues to grow, there is also no question that the federal government and the academic and research communities are not going to be left behind. The vBNS, Internet2, the NGI, and the National Information Infrastructure (NII) initiative are only some examples of what the R&E community and the federal government are doing. However, the Internet2 project will have its challenges. As it's aimed primarily at the academic world, attracting sufficient capital to move it forward may be its biggest obstacle.

Acceptable Use Policies (AUPs)

Acceptable use policies (AUPs) for the various networks composing the Internet determine how the Internet's infrastructure is used for forwarding traffic and who has access to those networks. Different organizations who own or have owned or subsidized portions of the Internet infrastructure over the course of its evolution may have radically different missions.

For example, the NSF is a government institution whose mission is to promote science, research, and education. NSF fulfills its mission with taxpayers' funds, and, consequently, the portion of Internet subsidized by NSF cannot be used to promote commercial enterprises. The organizations that connect to the NSF-sponsored vBNS are those who meet the NSF's R&E criteria as stated in the NSF's AUPs.

Currently, two categories of institutions may utilize vBNS: the vBNS Authorized Institutions (vAIs) and the vBNS Partner Institutions (vPIs). The vAIs are the four SCCs and NCAR mentioned earlier in this chapter. The vAIs are universities and research institutions connecting to the vBNS through the Connections Program. So, a component of the AUPs for the vBNS is that vAIs may exchange traffic with themselves and vPIs may exchange traffic with vAIs. But vPIs may not use the vBNS to exchange traffic with each other. The partner institutions are not able to use the vBNS as a transit network for their network traffic. Additionally, since NSF recognizes that both authorized institutions and the partner institutions have communications needs that cannot be fulfilled through the use of the vBNS, NSF requires all these institutions to maintain non-vBNS connectivity to the Internet as well.

The national service providers (NSPs) operating the major Internet backbones have an entirely different orientation than NSF for connecting customers to the Internet. They will basically connect anyone to the Internet who pays them. Their policies for forwarding traffic across their networks are different from those of the NSF.

The AUPs for forwarding traffic on military networks will likely be driven by the need for high security (such as encryption, high reliability, as well as a denial of use to unauthorized personnel).

A good portion of any network's AUPs boils down to either granting or denying access to incoming and outgoing traffic that can be enforced through router configuration in the form of BGP filters. Other issues are involved in the AUPs. A component of a network's AUP may be a requirement that authorized network users do not use the network in any way that would disrupt service to other users. This may require that network users not distribute unsolicited advertising or engage in propagation of computer viruses or worms. Unsolicited advertising on the Internet has acquired a name: Stupid Person's AdvertiseMent (SPAM). With the ease of distributing electronic messages to a large number of network users through mailing lists and news groups, spamming can be a serious problem on the Internet. Large volumes of spam cause annoyance to the recipients, clog up mail boxes, and create congestion on the transmission media and in the routers.

To ensure that the AUPs are not violated, they must be translated into appropriate router configuration. However, not all AUPs can be translated into a configuration and enforced through the use of technology. Some AUPs rely on the use of common sense and observing the spirit of the Internet. Overall, the implementation of AUPs is anything but trivial.

Peering Agreements

The established Internet backbone operators typically have a set of policies that must be adhered to before they decide to peer with a newcomer. As an example, Apex Global Internet Services (AGIS) peering policy that was presented at a North American Network Operators Group (NONAG) meeting in late 1996 included the following points:

- must have a DS-3 or greater backbone among routers located at MAE-West, MAE-East, PacBell NAP, AADS NAP, and Sprint NAP
- must not be visible behind Sprint, MCI, UUNet, BBN, PSI, ANS, or NETCOM
- must not be an AGIS customer
- must have a 24x7 Network Operations Center
- must have peering agreements with Sprint, MCI, UUNet, BBNPlanet, ANS, PSI, and NETCOM
- must advertise routes consistently at all exchange points and have a history of doing so

These policy statements are reprinted here courtesy of AGIS and are intended to be used only for purposes of explaining and understanding some of the issues associated with network traffic on the Internet. For current AGIS peering policies or the peering policies of any other major service provider the reader is referred to the providers themselves. So, what do these peering policy statements really mean?

The bottom line behind peering agreements between major ISPs is that the peering ISPs agree to share their backbones with one another. It may not be exactly like a marriage, but perhaps close to it. As the name "peering" indicates, the peering partners are expected to have similar backbone capabilities as reflected in the first policy statement. The AGIS backbone is a DS-3 (45 Mbps) or an OC-3 (155 Mbps) backbone, as shown in Figure 10.17.

The peering partner is also expected to have a national presence, which is also reflected in the first policy statement requesting that peering partner's routers be present at all the major public exchange points. As shown in Figure 10.17, the AGIS backbone spans the continental U.S.

Just think about it. If both peering partners have a national presence but cover different portions of the country, there is a potential benefit to having a peering agreement. The customers of each of the peering ISP will have access to Internet resources served by the other ISP, since each peer accepts the other's peer traffic onto its backbone. It's like the analogy depicted in Figure 10.1, where arriving passengers on one airline make use of another airline to get to their final destinations. However, for a newcomer backbone operator to become a peer with an existing backbone operator, the newcomer is expected to have a similar carrying capacity to what the existing backbone operator has. Otherwise, there might be some serious mismatches in bandwidth. So, if I had a small network in Montana and wanted to peer with AGIS, their suggestion to me probably would be that I could become one of their customers through their access points in Seattle or Salt Lake City.

The next major requirement for a peering partner in this case is to have a Network Operations Center (NOC) manned 24 hours a day, 7 days a week. Carrying national Internet traffic is a serious business and outages can result in significant economic loss. It's not so surprising that a national provider would require its peering partner to maintain a well-staffed and ready-to-respond NOC in case of equipment failures or other problems.

As AGIS is already peering with major providers such as Sprint, MCI, UUnet, BBNPlanet, ANS, PSI, or NETCOM, what it is effectively saying in its statement is that it does not want to peer with the customers of these providers. An autonomous system (AS) that would be visible behind one of those major providers would most likely be a multihomed autonomous system that would be using two providers for Internet access. A multihomed AS would likely belong to a major corporate customer who would not want to permit transit traffic though its AS anyway. If a peer will not allow transit traffic through its network, why bother to peer with it in the first place?

FIGURE 10.17 *AGIS 45-155 Mbps ATM backbone (courtesy of AGIS, Inc.)Bus Topology*

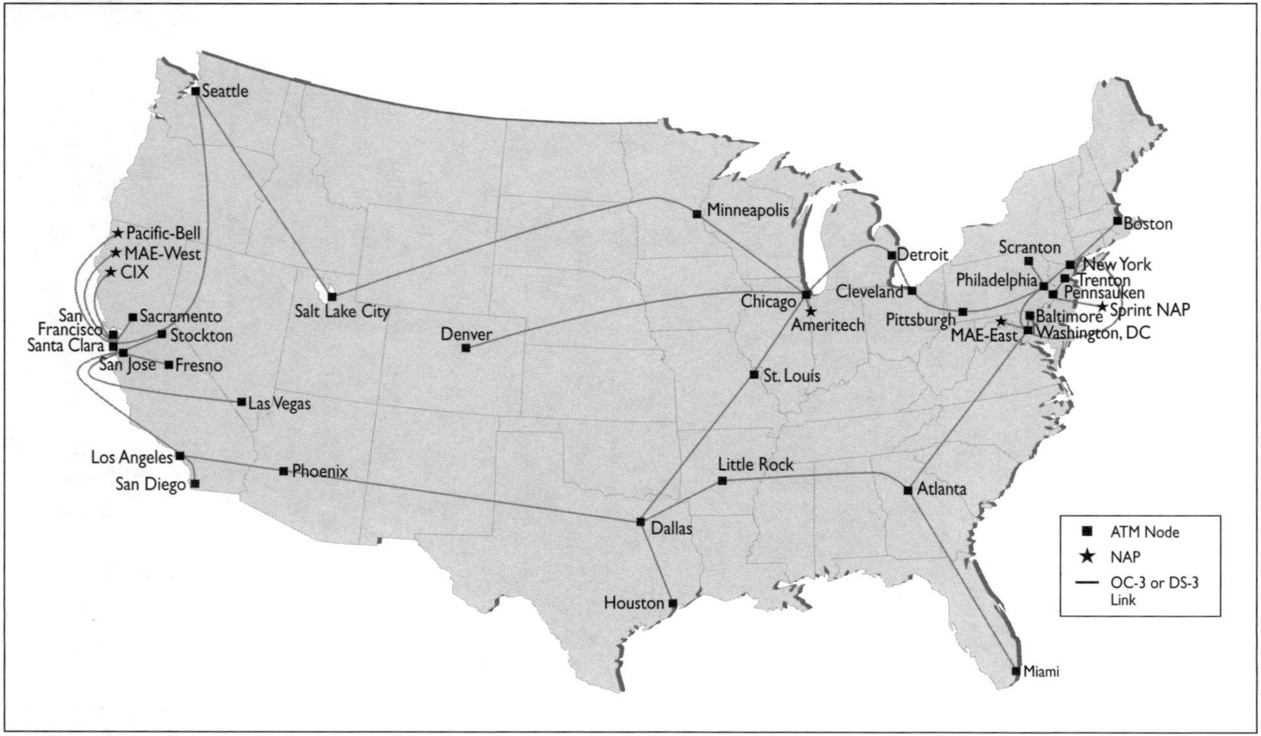

The last major aspect of the sample peering policy is consistency in advertising routing information. The existing peering partner is looking for stability from the newcomer. "No route flapping resulting in extra load on my backbone routers," is what's effectively being stated here. The example peering policies certainly seem reasonable, but, at the same time, it's rather obvious that trying to peer with major providers is like joining a very exclusive club. It takes cash, considerable network expertise, and an extensive telecommunications infrastructure to join this club.

The Near-Death Experiences of the Internet

Much is still unknown about the Internet. Basic facts give a hint about the challenges that the Internet has faced since its inception. In less than 30 years, the Internet has grown from a single network with 4 hosts to more than 40,000 networks and millions of hosts. The exact number of networks and hosts on the Internet will probably never be known — just like it's impossible to know the population of a country down to the last person. Given the explosive growth pattern of the Internet, it's natural to expect that it has gone through some growing pains. These growing pains periodically precipitate a "major crisis" that threatens the Internet's survival. By tracing the major crises that have threatened the existence of the Internet over the years, the near-death experiences of the Internet seem to be related to the following phenomena:

- address exhaustion(s)
- increase on the size of routing tables (or routing table "explosion")
- routing instability

Address exhaustion(s)

Address exhaustion on the Internet is nothing new. The original IMPs of the ARPAnet were designed to handle one network and 64 hosts. After all, ARPA envisioned no more than 19 sites connected to the ARPAnet. That hurdle of the 64-node limit on the ARPAnet was overcome long ago. At another point in the Internet's early history, addressing was limited to 128 networks. That address exhaustion hurdle also seems to have been overcome. More recently, in the decade of the 1990s, the address exhaustion problem stemmed from running out of Class B IP addresses.

Table 3.1 in Chapter 3 presents details about the IP address classes. The column "Maximum # of Net Ids" displays the number of available unique networks for each class. For class B, this number is 16,383. The class B addresses became the most popular addresses during the second and third stages of the Internet evolution. The class B addresses are popular because subnetting a class B address allows for a comfortable number of subnets with a comfortable number of hosts to fit the networking needs of most organizations. Even with the traditional subnetting of applying a single subnet mask to the address space, you can get up to 254 subnets with up to 254 hosts on each subnet from a single class B address. Having a class B address can satisfy the addressing needs of most institutions connecting to the Internet.

Herein lies the problem. There are not enough class B addresses to accommodate all the organizations wanting to connect to the Internet. So, what happened when the InterNIC began to run short on class B addresses? Another crisis related to the running out of addresses could be announced.

With the rapid exhaustion of class B addresses, there was no other option but to start assigning blocks of class C addresses to organizations whose addressing needs could not be satisfied with a single class C address. If you think about it, subnetting a class B address with a subnet mask of 255.255.255.0 effectively creates 254 class C addresses.

Because not everyone requesting a class B address was going to need that many class C addresses after subnetting, why not just take smaller blocks of class C addresses and assign them instead? There is only one problem. The "class C addresses" created by class B subnetting can be masked or hidden behind the single class B address. Routers on the Internet do not have to know about the individual subnets, just about the parent class B address. With a block of actual class C addresses, each class C address requires an entry in the routers routing tables. So, even as one problem was seemingly solved, the earmarks of another near-death experience of the Internet emerged — the routing table explosion.

Routing table explosion

The apparent solution to dealing with the exhaustion of class B addresses created a problem resulting in the dramatic increase in the size of the routing tables. An increase in the size of the routing tables has a direct impact on router performance and the use of network bandwidth. Routers look through their tables to find directions for the packets they receive and they exchange routing updates between themselves. The bigger the routing table, the longer it takes a router to figure out where to forward a packet next, and the more bandwidth it takes to transmit all or a portion of the table to a fellow router.

Imagine what it would be like if you were working in a major information center that has directions to most of the world's cities and even small towns — sounds like an Internet backbone router. Assume that all of these cities and towns are listed alphabetically in a large reference volume (routing table) along with directions on how to get there. Every time that a traveler (an IP packet) goes by requesting directions to some city, you look up that specific city in your large reference volume and tell the person where to go next. However, the directions that you give out are minimal, and they are the same for many travelers. You just tell the travelers to follow a certain road out of your office and then ask for further directions. At most there are only a few dozen roads out of your office — your neighbor routers.

The number of destinations you have in your reference is potentially in the millions — there are potentially more than 2 million class C addresses. The number of travelers asking for directions is also in the millions — that's an understatement for the number of packets processed by backbone routers. You end up spending a great deal of time flipping through the pages of your reference volume looking for your travelers' destinations and giving out very similar and simple directions to most of them. You begin to wonder what can be done to simplify your job.

Because the world is broken down into continents, and within continents into countries, and within countries into regions, wouldn't it be nice if the entries in your large reference included only the continents, countries, and perhaps the major regions, and if the names of the travelers destinations clued you immediately into which continent, country or region they were heading to?

This way, rather than looking for a specific city in a very large reference, you would look for a continent, country, or region in a much smaller reference volume — you can feel the routing tables shrinking. You would give the passing traveler directions on how to get to that continent, country, or region where their cities were located. Your reference volume would be less precise, but you would have much less looking up to do. The directions to your travelers would be identical to those that you would get from the more-precise reference volume. Consequently, you could process your clients (packets) a lot faster. Once they got to the respective continents or countries, someone else (some other router) could give them more specific directions to get to the respective cities.

This analogy outlines what was happening to the backbone routers routing tables when groups of class C addresses were being assigned. In Table 3.1 (see Chapter 3), the number of available class C addresses is more than 2 million. It's enough to last a while, but it's more than enough to overflow the core routers' routing tables very quickly and bring the routers to a standstill.

Routing instability

The NSF recently sponsored a project supported by the NSF Grant NCR-9321060 intended to study the routing information exchanges between the backbone operators at major Internet exchange points. The exchange points included the four NSF NAPs and MAE-West. Researchers from the University of Michigan and Merit who pursued this project came to the conclusion that the level of routing information exchanges between routers at the core of the Internet is significantly higher than would be warranted by topological changes in the Internet or by changes in the routing policies between the providers.

From the discussion of the complexities of the routing protocols in Chapter 4, it follows that the designers of the routing protocol try to do everything possible to make the routing protocols as efficient and as scalable as possible. The implementation of this design criteria ought to translate into a minimal number of routing exchanges when the routers and the underlying transmission media on the Internet are functioning properly. Fewer routing exchanges means that more bandwidth is available for forwarding user traffic. Naturally, the routing protocols ought to be responsive to any topological changes between the autonomous systems (such as router failures or breaks in the transmission media).

Changes to the network topology must be propagated between backbone routers and a map of a new Internet topology must be re-established as quickly as possible so that user traffic can be forwarded correctly. That's called *fast convergence*. The routing protocols also ought to be responsive to any policy changes on the Internet (such as a new transit AS becoming available, or a transit AS discontinuing its service).

However, in the absence of apparent routing policy changes and with a physical infrastructure remaining stable, it's hard to explain what causes a high level of routing updates (mostly route withdrawals) that were observed at the major Internet exchange points during the course of the above-mentioned study. Bugs in router software bore some responsibility for the bogus routing updates. Even after the software bugs were fixed, a certain level of updates remains unexplained. Further research in the area of routing information exchanges between backbone routers is needed. However, just like in medicine, the cause of disease is not always known, but symptoms may be treated. The way to treat bogus route withdrawals is to pretend that they are real and that routes are flapping — which is another contributor to routing instability.

It's altogether possible for some physical links simply to be unstable. What's a router supposed to do when it continues to receive routing updates about a path that continuously disappears and then reappears again? It's a legitimate topology change when a link goes down, and the information about the change ought to be propagated to other routers. But what if some of the links abuse the privilege of being allowed to go down occasionally (they go up and down excessively)? That's called *route flapping*.

Routing protocols are expected to guard against this phenomenon as well. Otherwise, it could bring the entire Internet to its knees. If major links kept oscillating and the backbone routers were busy announcing their transitions from an "up" state to a "down" state and back again, the level of traffic resulting from the routing updates could result in the blocking out of user traffic. So, what's coming to the rescue in this case?

The Rescuers

Just when it seems that the Internet will collapse under the weight of its own phenomenal success, a stroke of genius on someone's part comes to the rescue and breathes new life into it.

Address exhaustion rescuers

There are several rescuers in this category. They include the following:

- Address classes
- Address translation
- IPv6 addressing

Address classes

The class B addresses may be exhausted (assigned to networks) but there are still plenty of class C addresses. Table 3.1 (see Chapter 3) shows more than 2 million class C addresses that can be used on the Internet. Yes, there is a "reserved" range that has been carved out of that address space (and all of the examples in the book use the addresses from the reserved range), but the reserved range accounts for only 256 out of the more than 2 million. So, the address exhaustion resulting from the exhaustion of class B addresses was averted by using smaller (but more numerous) class C addresses.

Address translation

Another mechanism that prevents address exhaustion is the concept of *address translation*. With address translation, organizations use a "private" address from one of the reserved ranges, which is then translated into a valid

Internet address. The basic idea is that even if a large organization is connected to the Internet, not everyone within the organization will be using the Internet at the same time. This enables an unregistered (from the reserved range) class B or even a class A address to meet internal organizational needs, while enabling the organization to represent itself to the rest of the world with a smaller class C address.

Those from inside the organization getting out on the Internet will have their private IP address mapped to valid IP addresses from the smaller registered address space. This translation is typically done through a *firewall*, be it a packet-screening router, a circuit-level gateway, or an application-level gateway. In today's commercial Internet environment, no self-respecting organization will connect to the Internet and allow access to all its computing resources without the insurance policy of a firewall. That would be like heading for the Western frontier of the last century without a horse and a gun.

Successful address translation hinges on making a reasonable estimate of the number of simultaneous Internet users within the organization. The obvious disadvantage of address translation is that if the number of users wanting to gain access to the Internet simultaneously exceeds the number of available IP address within the registered address space, some of those users must wait. Address translation is deployed in scenarios where an organization has a direct connection to the Internet through a router, as opposed to having individual users with modems dial in through a local service provider.

IPv6

Furthermore, a new IP addressing scheme has been specified: IPv6. It's really hard to imagine the number of IP addresses that are available through this addressing scheme. If you can imagine a number with 38 zeros behind it, then you have imagined how many IPv6 addresses will be available. We should never run out, right? That's probably what the designers of IPv4 also thought some 20 years ago. IPv6 can operate with IPv4 on the same routers. Experiments with an IPv6 are already in full swing, including an IPv6 backbone sharing the same physical media that's used for IPv4 Internet traffic.

Classless Interdomain Routing (CIDR)

Classless Interdomain Routing (CIDR) is the rescuer that saved the Internet by saving the Internet backbone routers from choking while chewing on their swelling routing tables. CIDR support is a key feature of BGP-4 deployed on the backbone routers. Prior to BGP's support of CIDR, the assignment of blocks of class C network addresses to organizations connecting to the

Internet via BGP resulted in each of the class C networks being present in the backbone routers' routing tables. This created the "routing table explosion." From a historical perspective, the assignment of the blocks of class C addresses started during the days of the NSFnet and the regional networks before the commercialization of the Internet was in full swing.

BGP-4 is the first version of BGP to support CIDR by allowing groups of contiguous class C addresses to be aggregated and then advertised as a single route. The aggregation of multiple class C addresses into a single network "prefix" was first referenced in the discussion of BGP in Chapter 4. It depends on finding the common portion of a group of class C addresses and then representing that group with a single common prefix and the length of that prefix.

CIDR aggregation is called *supernetting* as opposed to *subnetting*. The mask moves to the left instead of to the right, creating dotted decimal notations whose meanings depend on the length of the CIDR prefix. For example, 192.168.0.0 by itself represents a single class C address. However, CIDR notations of 192.168.0.0/18 or 192.168.0.0/19 represent groups of 64 and 32 class C addresses, respectively.

Route flap dampening

Route flap dampening is a technique that's used to guard against propagating routing information about unstable routes. The best way to relate to route flap dampening is to think about accumulating points for driving traffic violations. If you drive and continue to receive traffic citations for bad driving habits, when you accumulate a certain number of points, your driver's license may be pulled and you will not be allowed to drive. It's the same with route flap dampening. A configurable *suppress limit* value represents the maximum number of points that a flapping route is allowed to accumulate before its wings are clipped. A *penalty value* is also configurable. Every time a route flaps, it is assigned the penalty value. That's equivalent to the points you get for each violation. When a route accumulates a penalty that's equal to the suppress limit, it's curtains. The route is suppressed and no longer advertised.

There are refinements to this process that allow a flapping route to reform itself. There is another configurable metric known as *half time* (sounds like radioactive decay stuff). Half time means that the route's total accumulated penalty is reduced by half during that time. If a route misbehaves by flapping and gets suppressed, but later decides that it's time to behave again, over multiple half times, the route's penalty is reduced to a point where it's below the *reuse limit*, and the route may be advertised again.

Doesn't this remind you of being grounded in your younger years? Anyway, route flap dampening is a serious concept and one of the rescuers of the modern Internet. Without route dampening, a few misbehaved routes could cause a great deal of havoc by creating so much routing update traffic that there might be little room left in the cyber pipes for your traffic to flow.

The Providers

The Internet access providers fall into the following four general categories:

- *Local ISPs* serve small communities.
- *Regional ISPs* aggregate local ISP's traffic.
- *Major or national ISPs* are the major backbone operators.
- *Extended ISPs* provide additional services.

Local ISPs

At the lowest end of the Internet access-provider spectrum are the local ISPs. A typical local ISP may have a single router, a modem bank, a terminal server, a CSU/DSU, and a connection by way of a 56K line or a T1 line to a router upstream. A local ISP may have dial-up customers only, or it may have a few dedicated customers using a portion of the available outgoing bandwidth to an upstream router. A typical local ISP setup is shown if Figure 10.18.

In Figure 10.17, the router, terminal server, and the ISP's administrative server form a single network. The dial-in customers whose typical equipment is a personal computer with a modem dial a main number assigned to the telephone lines coming into the ISP's modem bank. Once a session is established between the modems, the terminal server multiplexes the modem signals from the dial-in sessions and passes them on to the ISP's server for authentication. After the dial-in customers are authenticated — and if everything is configured properly in the customers' Web browsers — the dial-in customers will display the ISP's "home page" on their screens. From here, the sky is the limit. Actually, it's the capacity of the dial-in link that's the limit. A typical dial-in connection will operate at 28,800 bps, which is adequate for browsing and small downloads, but not for downloads on the order of hundreds of megabytes.

The representative equipment at a local ISP's site could be a router like those referenced in Chapter 5 or Chapter 9, a Multi-Tech modem bank as shown in Figure 10.19 and Livingstone Enterprises terminal server as shown in Figure 10.20.

FIGURE 10.18 *A typical local ISP's setup*

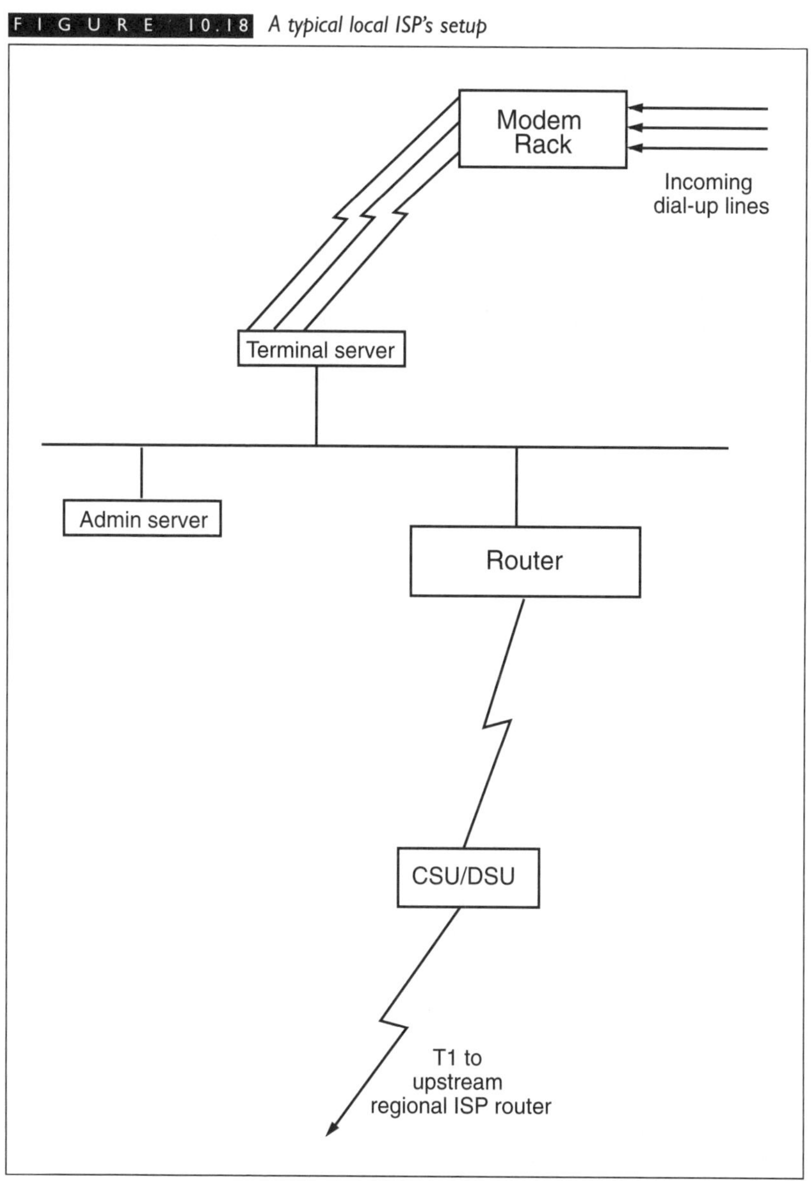

FIGURE 10.19 *Multi-Tech modem bank: the MultiModemManager (courtesy of Multi-Tech Systems Corporation)*

FIGURE 10.20 *Livingstone Enterprises PortMaster 25 terminal server (courtesy of Livingstone Enterprises Corporation)*

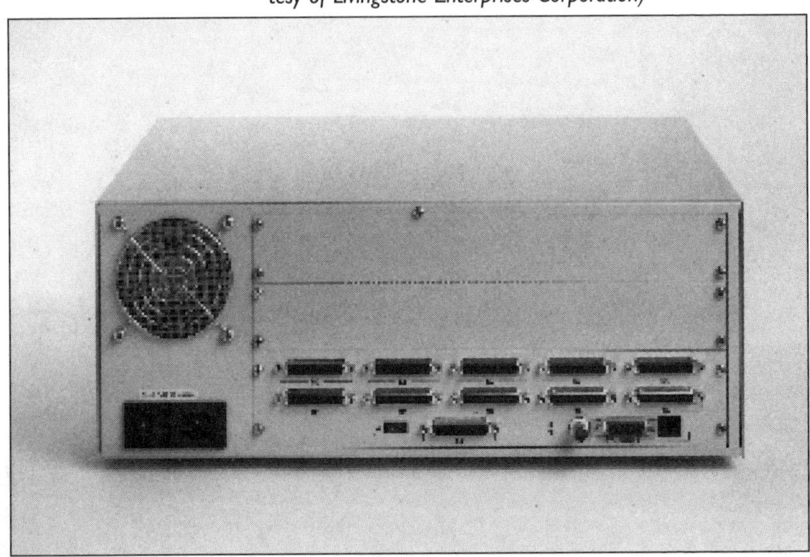

The local ISP's router configuration can be very simple. In fact, it can be so simple that there is no need to run any routing protocols on it. A default route pointing to the interface connecting to the upstream router is all that's needed in the simplest of cases. The upstream router to which the local ISPs router connects typically belongs to a regional provider or is located at a POP of a major national ISP.

Regional ISPs

Regional ISPs are not much different from the local ISPs. It's a matter of scale. Their routers will be more powerful with more media interfaces, as the regional ISPs typically aggregate traffic from several local ISPs. Regional ISP's setup may also include several smaller routers for customers connecting directly to the ISP's network. Figure 10.21 shows a typical regional ISP setup. Regional ISPs may have dial-up customers set up the same way as the local ISPs.

FIGURE 10.21 *Typical regional ISP's setup*

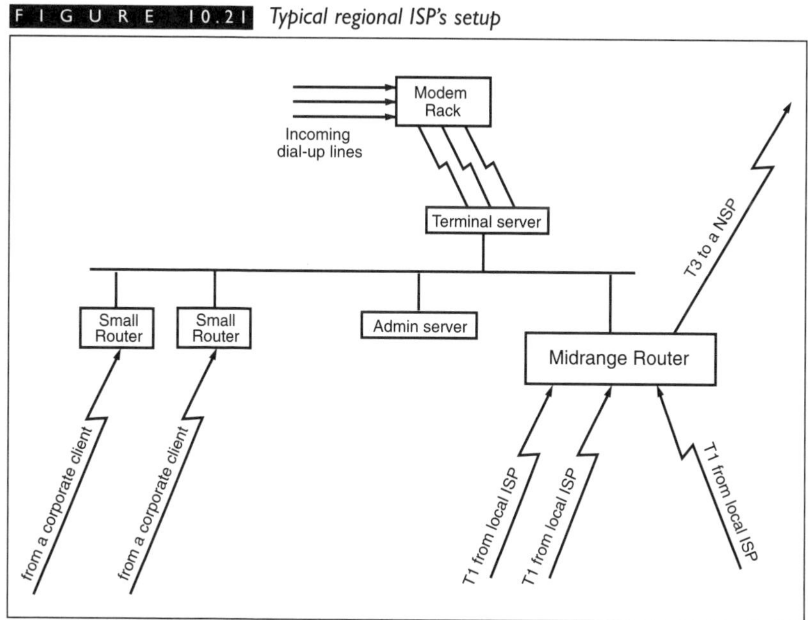

In Figure 10.21, the hypothetical regional ISP accepts traffic from several local ISPs, provides dial-in access to individual customers through a setup similar to a local ISP's dial-in setup, and provides direct access to a few clients who require dedicated Internet access at speeds greater than the dial-in speeds. The regional ISP now must do something with all of the traffic that it aggregated from all of its tributaries. This traffic must now be forwarded to a router located at the POP of the national or carrier-class ISP. A typical example of a regional ISP would be a local telephone carrier.

The router setup at a regional ISP is more involved than at the local ISP, but still does not need to be complex. The main router interfacing the regional ISP to a POP router would have to advertise the reachability of the client and the local ISP's networks, but even at the level of a regional ISP, all the outgoing traffic could be aggregated into a single default static route. Most likely, a regional ISP would be part of an AS assigned to an NSP operating the POP, and would not have to run the BGP. In this business, however, there is no "one size fits all" formula.

Internet backbone owners

The Internet backbone owners are known by many names: carrier class ISPs, national ISPs, major ISPs, Internet backbone operators, and perhaps some other names. However they are labeled, these are the ISPs who must work together very closely to make your Internet experience a meaningful one. These ISPs aggregate traffic from the regional ISPs, as well as from the major corporate sites requiring direct access to the Internet backbones. If these ISPs did not cooperate on accepting and passing one another's traffic through their networks, the Internet would not be the Internet. Instead, it would be a group of huge networks, which could not talk to one another. The backbone maps shown in Chapter 2 and in this chapter are examples of the span of the communications infrastructure operated by the national ISPs.

The national ISPs come together (and cooperate) at the peering locations discussed in the previous sections — the NAPs, the MAEs, the FIXs, the CIX, the private interconnects, and so on. By the time this book is in your hands, the list of the different types of Internet interconnect points may be longer. National ISPs will have one or more AS numbers assigned to them. Their backbone routers will have to run BGP because those routers hold all the reachable destinations on the Internet. The router configuration issues of the carrier-class ISPs are a function of their routing policies and are discussed later in this chapter.

Extended ISPs

Extended ISPs are those who provide additional services other than simply access to the Internet. Examples of extended ISPs are companies such as America Online (AOL) or CompuServe. They started out as huge electronic bulletin boards providing discussion forums, travel, sports, and other information (not unlike large bulletin boards you can still see in some grocery stores). In the "pre-Web" days, AOL and CompuServe also provided a mechanism for many companies to post technical information and updates about their products. It used to be common to go to a CompuServe Forum for "such and such" vendor and download a patch for their often buggy software.

However, market forces pushed AOL and CompuServe into providing access to the Internet. AOL's acquisition of ANS is a good indication that remaining as a huge electronic board provider only could have had serious consequences for AOL's future. Recently, AOL has also acquired CompuServe. AOL and CompuServe are not the Internet, however. Remember, the Internet is an interconnection of autonomous systems, thousands of them.

Virtual Private Networks (VPNs)

A *virtual private network* is a network that offers companies with geographically dispersed locations the benefits of connecting all their locations together into single transparent network. A VPN is not the Internet. A VPN is "your" network which you may or may not choose to connect to the Internet. The Internet allows you to access resources on other networks. A VPN links your resources together into a single network.

A typical VPN would be composed of local area networks (LANs), which are owned and maintained by the customer company, and transit connections between the LANs, which are owned and maintained by the VPN provider. VPNs can either be dedicated, dial-up, or both. With dedicated VPNs, all connections linking the geographically dispersed locations are up continuously. In the case of dial-up VPNs, the connections between the locations become active for the duration of communication between the devices at those locations.

A VPN is not limited to linking the resources of a single company. A VPN may link an organization with its business partners, customers, or employees. The nature of a VPN depends on an organization's need and a business plan.

The difference between a VPN provider and an ISP is that a VPN provider takes responsibility for your traffic from its point of origin to its final destination. This responsibility translates into traffic security, network access tracking (who gets on), billing (for how long), customer support, and reliable delivery. Security is a vital issue in VPNs because the same infrastructure is used by the VPN providers to create virtual networks for many customers.

The function of an ISP is to get on the Internet. If some of the Internet destinations or resources you want to reach are not available, it's not necessarily the ISP's responsibility to make them available to you. The Internet can be compared to a jungle. Your ISP will get you to the edge of it, but to get through it and reach your final destination, you will rely on many other providers. You are not a direct customer of those other providers. This stands in contrast to a VPN, where a VPN provider assumes responsibility for your traffic from beginning to end.

A typical VPN provider will allow Internet access to its customers as an additional feature of its service. Some of the major ISPs also provide a VPN service using a component of their Internet infrastructure for that service. A VPN is, effectively, your own dedicated, secure, private network. An effective VPN provider must have a significant investment in the underlying communications infrastructure spanning a wide geographical area. So, a VPN from a reliable provider offers the benefit of secure and dedicated private network without the associated costs of ownership and maintaining the underlying networking infrastructure.

An example of a company that offers VPN service is Concentric Network Corporation. Concentric Systems operates a dedicated DS-3 ATM backbone between its super POPs with over 250 dial-up locations in the U.S. and Canada. The Concentric network map is shown in Figure 10.22.

FIGURE 10.22 *Concentric Network Corporation DS-3 ATM backbone (Diagram reprinted with permission of Concentric Network Corporation. Copyright 1997. Concentric Network Corporation and the Concentric logo are trademarks of Concentric Network Corporation.)*

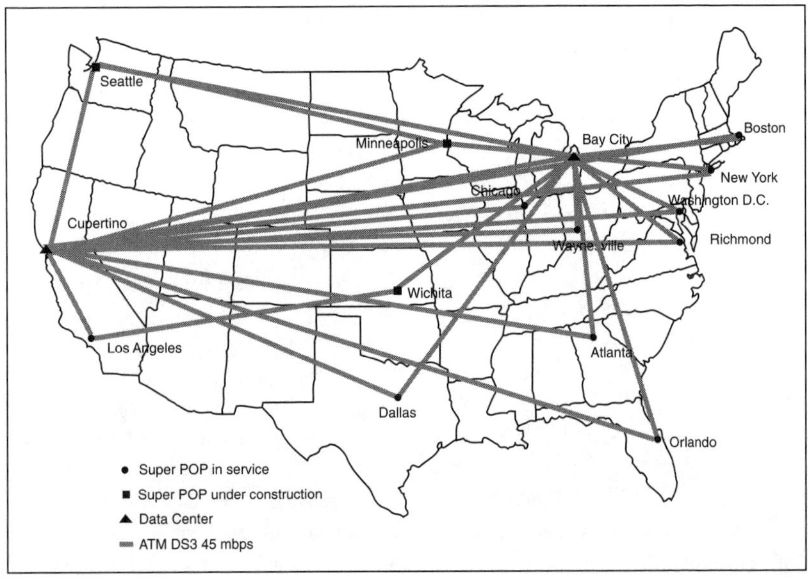

Many VPNs can be carved out of the available bandwidth on the Concentric's backbone, just as many Internet customers use the ISP's backbones. In fact, doesn't this map remind you somewhat of the maps shown in Chapter 2 and even the vBNS map (Figure 10.13) and the AGIS map (Figure 10.17) in this chapter? The question that may come to mind is, where does one type of service end and the other begin? What if your company had a VPN and wanted to host several Web sites on that VPN? Ponder this question, because by the time this book goes to press, the answer may change. It seems that the Internet and the field of internetworking is almost as unpredictable as the Montana weather. If you don't like it, just wait ten minutes and it will change. Or, to sum it up in the words of the Assistant Director of the Michigan Net, Jeff Ogdan (who's been with the Merit corporation for many years), "The Internet has many players. They are doing many different things. And it's sort of chaotic. And it pretty much works."

Backbone Router Configurations

This chapter is about Internet routing, especially in the Internet's core. The preceding sections have outlined a glimpse of the Internet's core as it was in the past (the NSFnet backbone), as it is today (major backbone interconnections at public and private exchanges), and as it transforms itself to become something in the future that no one can necessarily foresee. Router configurations on the Internet's periphery (local ISP's configurations) are simple compared to the core router configurations. Issues relating to peering agreements, AUPs, traffic aggregation, multihoming, new customers, and new providers coming online must all be taken into account and translated into correct configurations when configuring the Internet's core routers. So, how does routing even take place in the Internet's core where the Internet's core is constantly transforming itself? It's not easy. Occasional losses of Internet connectivity do occur as a result of misconfigured routers.

The bringing up of a BGP routing process and defining of BGP neighbors were discussed in Chapter 5. It's not enough to bring up the BGP process and define the BGP neighbors in the backbone routers. That's only the first step. More complex components of BGP configuration are needed to implement routing in the Internet's core. For example, at one of the NONAG's meetings, AGIS presented the following routing policies, which would have to be translated into router configurations in AGIS routers:

- will filter TWD at /24
- will filter 206+ at /19

- will filter everything else at /16
- will apply the next-hop-self to all exchange point peering sessions
- will expect peers to do likewise and will route map if necessary

Again, what does this all mean?

First of all, AGIS *never implemented* all these policies. Even though some of them are dated, some of them are still valid and they serve as an excellent example for a discussion. Incidentally, this book is worth its price just for the explanation of TWD, which stands for Toxic Waste Dump.

CIDR relies on careful assignment of blocks of class C addresses to major geographical regions (such as the world continents). See RFC 1466 (RFC 1466, Appendix A) for the suggested assignment of class C address ranges to the continents. Organizations seeking and providing Internet connectivity within a certain region get continuous blocks of class C addresses from a pre-assigned range. These organizations — some are commercial customers, but the rest are mostly ISPs — when advertising their reachability can aggregate their address ranges into a single CIDR prefix matching their CIDR blocks. This, in turn, would allow the major ISPs serving those regions to further aggregate the longer CIDR prefixes from those organization into an even shorter CIDR prefix. The net result: less routes in the backbone routers tables. It sounds pretty ideal, but it's not the reality of what often happens on the Internet.

So, what happens when addresses from a certain range are scattered all over the world (which is what was happening with the 192.x.x.0 range prior to CIDR)? Customers who have one or two of these addresses don't have a choice but to advertise them without aggregation, meaning with a prefix length of 24. The implication is that individual class C addresses from that range will end up in the backbone routers routing tables. Because of the widely dispersed nature of the 192.*x*.*x*.0–193.*x*.*x*.0 range of addresses, they have been affectionately referred to as the Toxic Waste Dump (polluters of the backbone routers' routing tables).

If a major provider decided to filter the TWD range on a shorter prefix, this provider would effectively refuse to recognize the existence of some of the networks in that range, making Internet connectivity for those networks very challenging. However, filtering on /24 has the potential implication of overcrowding the routing tables, and those issues have already been discussed.

But advances in technology often come to a rescue. Filtering on /19 and /16 as stated in the AGIS routing policies was intended to lessen the number of entries on the routing tables of backbone routers. But as the backbone routers can now hold a much larger number of routing table entries, the need to filter on /19 and /16 disappears. The /19 and /16 element of the AGIS policy *was never implemented*, but it still serves as a good example for a discussion of the evolving nature of the Internet and Internet technology. AGIS filters all routes on /24 resulting in approximately 46,000 routes in their tables, far below the capacity of 150,000 of some of the backbone routers.

The additional benefit of filtering on /24 is that many large commercial customers ensure redundancy by multihoming their sites with different providers. Multihoming implies that a customer will have several class C addresses and will want to be reachable through each one. Effectively, each class C address from this customer will end up in the backbone routers routing tables (with no aggregation) if multihoming is to serve its purpose. From a technical point of view, multihoming is no different than TWD. However, with the increased capacity and processing speed of routing tables in the modern backbone routers, multihoming can be easily accommodated. Multihoming is a big trend in today's Internet.

The last element of AGIS routing policy has to do with the enforcement of the "next-hop-self." Assume a scenario where AGIS does not want to peer with provider *X* at an exchange because provider *X* does not meet the AGIS peering policy (discussed earlier in this chapter). Provider *X* has a presence at the exchange point and it also offers transit service to provider *Y*, who peers with AGIS. The AGIS's peer (provider *Y*) could theoretically advertise the next-hop as the address of the provider *X* with whom AGIS did not want to peer in the first place. This would create a situation where provider *X* could be charging AGIS customers for transit services but not really offering any transit service, because AGIS does not peer with it in the first place. It's an indirect way of forcing a provider to peer with someone without any benefit to that provider. It may sound convoluted, but that's the reality of routing policies at the exchange points.

Route maps are a mechanism for controlling and modifying routing information which includes the values of the BGP attributes. The route maps also define conditions for distribution of routing updates between BGP peers through the use of access lists. The key concept behind a route map is to *permit* or *deny* a certain set of conditions, which are listed in a *route-map tag*. A route-map tag represents a list of configuration statements beginning with key words like *match* or *set*. These words, in turn, are associated with values of BGP attributes and other router configuration parameters. When the *match* conditions inside of a route-map tag have been met, the *set* conditions that follow the *match* conditions take effect. Using route maps in router configuration is not unlike programming with subroutines with *case* or multiple *if* statements.

An example of a simple route map using Cisco's syntax would be

```
route-map xxxx permit yy
```

The *route-map* is a keyword command. The *xxxx* represents the name of the route map tag. *Permit* is a key word (could be replaced with *deny*). And *yy* is a sequence number. In a router configuration, there can be a whole series of route-map commands identified by successive sequence numbers. The name of the route name tag *xxxx* would stay the same, but the sequence number *yy* would vary from one route-map command to another. Route maps are frequently used with access lists, which facilitate more extensive matching conditions. Access lists have multiple uses and are not limited to route maps.

What could follow the *route-map* configuration line from the preceding example might look like this:

```
match IP address 1
set metric zzz
set next-hop x.x.x.x
!
access-list 1 permit 192.168.31.0 0.0.224.255
```

The 1 in the *match* statement refers to the access list number. Generically, if the *match* conditions following the route-map command line with the lowest sequence number are not met, then processing moves on to the next route-map command line identified with the next higher sequence number. If a match is found in this next group of *match* conditions, then the *set* conditions that follow are applied and processing breaks out of the route-map sequence.

If you think about it, if there are multiple route map command lines each followed by a group of *match* and *set* statements, then the last instance of the route map ought to have either no *match* conditions or *match* conditions that can be met by all updates. Otherwise, if none of the *match* conditions in all of the route-map instances are met, then the updates which would otherwise be subject to the route-map *set* conditions will be dropped.

In the preceding example, if a route matches the IP address condition specified in the access list, then the metric for that route would be set to *zzz* and the next-hop value for that route would be set to *x.x.x.x*. The metric value of *zzz* and the next-hop value *x.x.x.x* correspond to the values of the multi-exit-discriminator (MED) and the next-hop attributes in the BGP route update message.

Route maps are a powerful tool for controlling the flow of routing updates. However, to apply route-map conditions and to control the distribution of route updates, the routing issues need to be understood. The syntax details of the route map *set* and *match* conditions can be found in the manuals of respective router vendors. Route maps are not the only tool for controlling the flow of updates. Filtering on the BGP attributes like the AS_path or community attributes is another potent tool in enforcing the routing policies in the Internet's core.

The conclusion is that, when it comes it Internet routing, the router configurations range from almost trivial in the case of local ISPs, to very complex in the case of NSPs. The actual configurations for NSPs are very strictly guarded.

CHAPTER 11

Switches: The Latest Rage

Switches are faster than routers because they process less information. Operating at Layer 2 of the OSI Reference Model (see Chapter 3), switches deal with less overhead to make forwarding decisions. However, switches have a problem. Since they use Data-Link Layer addresses for forwarding decisions, they create flat, homogenous networks of limited physical size. Switches do not scale in large internetworks.

Routers are "store-and-forward" devices operating at Layer 3 of the OSI Reference Model (see Chapter 3). Routers store packets while determining where to forward them. Routers accept the incoming packets, strip their Data-Link Layer overhead, look at each packet's Network Layer destination address, consult the routing table, and then make a next-hop forwarding decision. Routers may be less efficient in their decision-making process, but they create large scalable networks.

The Internet is a perfect example of a router-based network. However, routers are not without their faults. When overloaded with packets, they are prone to exhaustion and run out of stream. With the increasingly large volumes of traffic flowing across the Internet exchange points, the traditional hop-by-hop routing process becomes inefficient and begins to break down. A new approach to packet forwarding is needed.

New Developments

Imagine that, for whatever reason, you find yourself in a situation where you constantly relay messages between several groups of very talkative, screaming people — just like a backbone router. Relaying messages between boisterous characters is no fun at all. Yet, in effect, that's what routers do all the time. Each message you relay is preceded with, "This message is for so-and-so and it pertains to such-and-such." After hearing this introduction over and over again, you realize that most of the conversations are between the same "so-and-sos" and they pertain to the same "such-and-such." You get a brilliant idea. I'll get out of the way! And I'll set up an imaginary air tunnel between all of the "so-and-so's" and let them continue their conversations about "such-and-such" without me in the middle of it!

Well, it's not that easy for a router to totally get out of the way. However, it can step back somewhat, or tune out a bit. Have you ever met people who are doing things but are not quite there, not quite conscious of what they are doing — somewhat on an automatic pilot — doing things almost in a subconscious way? In a way that's what routers do when they stop routing and start switching. Since switching is at Layer 2, which is below Layer 3, a switching router might as well be operating at the subconscious (below the conscious) level.

These router "tune outs" seem to be the driving force behind several new techniques aimed at the integration of switching and routing to get the best of both worlds — the speed of switches and the scalability of routers. Three of these techniques are described in this chapter. Their implementation details may differ, but the fundamental idea is the same: eliminate the overhead associated with traditional routing and take advantage of the speeds of the underlying ATM switch fabric.

Cisco's Tag Switching

Before proceeding with the discussion of "tag switching," a simple definition of a tag might be in order. Webster's Dictionary has many definitions of a tag, but one of them is that a tag is a "label." So, when something is tagged, it is effectively labeled. You have probably guessed that since this book deals with routing, and what's being routed is packets, tag switching has something to do with tagging (or labeling) packets and then changing (or switching) those tags on the packets as they move through an internetwork.

Tag-switching overview

Cisco's tag switching is primarily aimed at the core of the Internet — the national service provider networks — where the traffic volumes are highest. Most of the major service providers operate ATM backbones, and tag switching is initially being developed to work with high-performance backbone routers and ATM switches. Tag switching is a concept, however, and a technology that is not limited to the Internet's core, or to any particular Data-Link Layer technology.

The motivation for developing tag switching is no different from the motivation for the development of more scalable and more robust routing protocols: improved network performance and better network scalability. The most basic idea behind tag switching is for routers and ATM switches to move packets through the core of the Internet faster then they are currently able to do. Traditional routing techniques and the existing IP routing/ATM integration techniques, such as the classical IP over ATM specified in RFC 1577 (see RFC 1577, Appendix A), do not scale well in the Internet's core.

The first devices where tag switching is being implemented are Cisco's 7500 series high-performance backbone routers (see Chapter 10) and Cisco's LS1010 ATM switches. The difference between a technique such as tag switching and further optimization of the routing protocols is that tag switching aims at optimizing the interface between Layer 2 and Layer 3. When the interactions between the Data-Link Layer (Layer 2) and Network Layer (Layer 3) in switches and routers are optimized, the performance of an entire network is improved.

Tag-switching concepts

Cisco's tag switching incorporates the following concepts:

1. Tag switching is a software solution and it's a component of Cisco's IOS.
2. Tag switching functions co-exist with the traditional routing functions and routing protocols.
3. Tags or labels are derived through several algorithms from the information in the routing tables and from the contents of the packet headers.
4. Tags have purely local significance and change at each hop of a packet's journey through the tag-switched internetwork.
5. Tags are assigned to packets as they enter a tag-switched network and stripped from packets as they leave a tag-switched network.
6. Tags are switched, changed, or swapped at each hop as packets traverse the core of a tag-switched network.
7. A tag-switched network can consist of as few as two devices participating in tag switching, or as many as network administrators choose to deploy.
8. Tags are stored in a tag database, or a tag table referred to as the Tag Information Base (TIB).
9. Each router/ATM switch participating in tag switching has its own TIB.
10. Tags assume different values as a function of the Data-Link Layer technology.
11. Tags are distributed between the routers and switches participating in tag switching by way of the Tag Distribution Protocol (TDP).

These concepts are expanded upon in the next few sections.

Software solution (Concepts 1 and 2)

Since Cisco's IOS is flash-upgradable, no new hardware is required to implement tag switching on existing IOS-based networks. This represents an evolutionary approach to upgrading the current network infrastructure to deal with any increasing pressures on the network performance. IOS-compatible routers and switches that are already deployed in the field can be upgraded to tag switching through an IOS upgrade. For any major ISP with IOS-compatible hardware this represents investment protection. Also, since tag-switching functions coexist with the routing protocols (such as OSPF, IS-IS, or BGP), the transition to tag switching can be gradual without disrupting current network operations.

Tag-assignment algorithms (Concept 3)

Tag switching can be broken into two major components: control and forwarding. The algorithms for assigning tags and the distribution of tags between tag-switching devices are part of the control component of tag switching. The process of making forwarding decisions based on tag values represents the "forwarding" component.

The following categories of algorithms for assigning tags to packets have been proposed:

- topology-driven or destination-based allocation
- allocation based on packet header contents
- multicast-supporting allocation
- routing hierarchy-based allocation

Topology-driven or destination-based tag allocation is also referred to as *control-based allocation*. It's control-based because tags are assigned based on routing table destinations, which are independent of the network traffic itself. Routing tables exist prior to any user packets flowing through the network. It's the routing tables that determine or control what path a packet will take through an internetwork. This topology-driven tag allocation approach seems to be the simplest, requiring no administrative input. The IP destinations from the routing tables are translated into tags, and that's it.

The obvious question that might be asked here is: What's the value of this approach and what would be the difference between a routing table and a TIB? The answer is that tag lookups are hardware-based and are much faster than routing table lookups because tags are short, fixed in sized, and indexed for fast lookups. Also, it's possible for a single tag to be assigned to a group of routes, which reduces the number of entries in the TIB as compared to the number of routing table entries.

Algorithms for assigning and managing tags can combine the control-based information with values from the packet headers to create a powerful mechanism for network traffic engineering. Information from the packet headers that can be associated with tags includes the source and destination addresses, the type of service (TOS), or the application type (TCP or UDP port numbers). This tag assignment granularity effectively allows network administrators to control the path that network traffic takes through a tag-switched network.

Suppose that a network administrator determines a certain link is underutilized in a destination-based tag-switched network. By assigning tags based on packet header contents, network traffic can be steered through the underutilized link (along a predetermined path) based on the traffic's origin, destination, or type. That's considered *traffic engineering*. Only remedial forms of control over traffic flow are now possible in the connectionless IP world. It's done through metric assignment to router links resulting in load balancing. Link metrics can also be used to favor one link over another. Link-metrics manipulation, however, hardly compares to the granularity of tag switching. When traffic paths can be predetermined based on any combination of its source, destination, or type, the possibilities for traffic-flow management seem almost endless.

Tag switching also supports an algorithm for allocating tags to multicast traffic. With multicasting continuing to assume a greater role in today's Internet, a brief review might be appropriate. When a traffic source such as a Web server sends traffic to a multicast address (224.0.0.1 through 239.255.255.255), any host listening to that address receives that traffic. The server makes only one transmission, no matter how many listeners there are. However, by its very nature multicasting is not applicable to all Internet communications.

Multicast traffic is like watching a movie. The movie rolls and everyone in a theater sees the same thing. It's a one-time deal unless a movie is replayed. So, multicasting lends itself to transmission of real-time events or to having servers transmit the same thing over and over — just like playing a movie over again. Since there are many movie theaters in any major city, there can be many different groups of people watching different movies. You get the picture? All the hosts configured to listen to a particular multicast address form a multicast group (they are watching the same movie).

Assume a scenario where a server is attached to a router that has a dozen point-to-point links to other routers. Networks at the end of the point-to-point links have hosts participating in a multicast group. If this server were to be accessed by each host requesting the same information, this server would be transmitting the same data a dozen times. With multicasting, a single stream of data from the server reaches all the participating hosts, but they have to be listening at the same time.

The multicast traffic path in an internetwork effectively resembles a tree composed of a trunk, branches, and leaves. The tree trunk and the branches are networks. Hosts are the leaves participating in a multicasting group. Routers connect the tree trunk and the branches together. Routers, which are part of the multicast tree, must be configured to forward multicast traffic. Tag allocation for multicast traffic relies on the binding of tags to a multicast address and to routers' physical interfaces over which the multicast traffic must flow to read a multicast group participant.

The last approach to allocating tags has to do with an interaction between an interior gateway protocol (such as OSPF or IS-IS) and BGP. Assume that a transit provider network (an AS) is using BGP to communicate with external neighbors and uses OSPF or IS-IS internally. The ASBRs on the edges of the AS maintain internal BGP sessions, but do not share direct connectivity. Tag switching in this scenario effectively eliminates the need for the redistribution of BGP routes in OSPF. The internal OSPF routers would carry routes that only pertain to their internal network, rather than importing all the BGP routes that would normally be needed to support the transit traffic. However, the ABSRs would be required to place two tags in a packet, one for transit through the internal network, and one for use by a peer ASBR as the packet leaves the transit network.

It must be understood that tag switching is not an open standard yet, and that no claims are made here as to how the final tag-switching implementations will pan out. The concept of tag switching has a great deal of potential. It's also gaining wider acceptance and multiple vendor support. An informational category RFC 2105 (see RFC 2105, Appendix A) provides an overview of the proposed Cisco's tag-switching architecture. A formal IETF Multiprotocol Label Switching (MPLS) working group has been chartered to develop a set of common standards for multilayer switching, which encompasses tag switching. The MPLS working group was founded as a result of Cisco's efforts and Cisco continues to be a major contributor to its deliberations.

Tag-switched topology (Concepts 4 through 7)

In a traditional routed internetwork, every packet that arrives at a router is first stripped of its Data-Link Layer overhead. Next, the router examines the packet's Network Layer header to determine the packet's destination. The router then makes a lookup in its routing table to determine where to send the packet next (the packet's next hop). After the router has determined the packet's next hop, the router encapsulates the packet into a Data-Link Layer frame corresponding to the outgoing physical interface. After all this — and perhaps with some ARPing on a broadcast network — the packet is sent on its way. This overhead-intensive processing is simplified in a tag-switched topology.

Since tag switching co-exists with the existing routing/switching functions of routers and ATM switches, the topology of a tag-switched implementation will include three broad areas, as shown in Figure 11.1.

FIGURE 11.1 *Typical tag-switching topology*

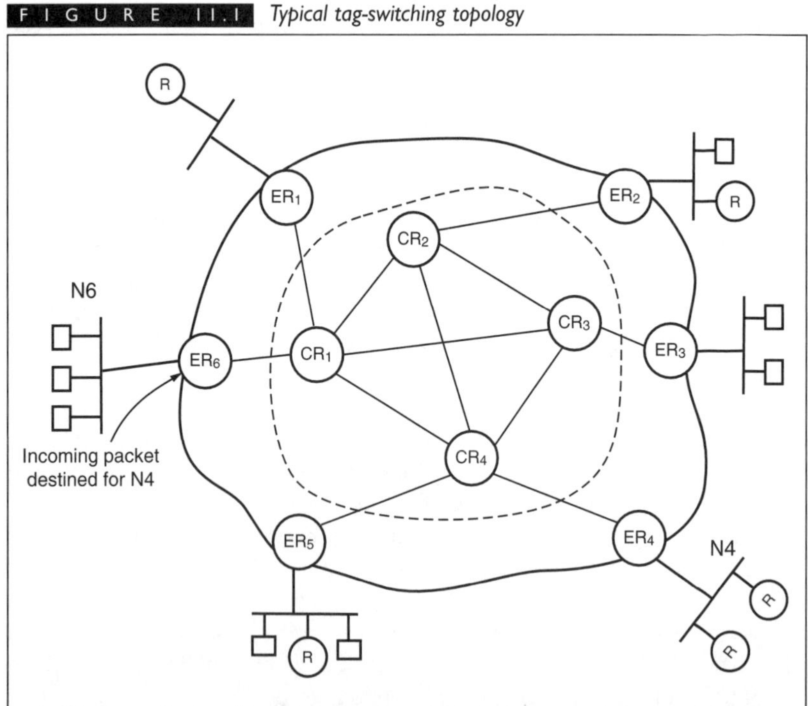

In Figure 11.1, the topology includes the tag-switching core devices, the tag-switching edge devices, and the remaining networks with devices not participating in tag switching. The devices labeled CR1, CR2, CR3, and CR4 are the *core devices*. They can either be routers with ATM interface processors (Cisco's 7500s) or ATM switches supporting routing protocols (Cisco's LS1010s). The devices labeled ER1 through ER6 are the *edge routers*. They interface to the core devices and to networks with devices not participating in tag switching. The nonparticipants are labeled with letters R and N.

In the topology in Figure 11.1 a packet from N6 is destined for N4. It enters the tag-switched network through the edge router E6. When E6 looks at the incoming packet, it detects that the packet is untagged. Since tags represent the router/switch links inside of a tag-switched network, the core devices inside the dotted circle in Figure 11.1 will have tags for all their links. The edge devices will only have tags for their links to the core devices. So, E6 will have a tag for its link to C1, but not for its link to N6.

Upon receipt of a packet from N6, E6 determines where to forward it through the traditional routing processing. Thus far, nothing special has happened. However, since E6 has a tag for its link to C1, E6 applies this tag to the incoming packet before forwarding it to C1. Herein lies the big difference between the traditional routing and the routing in edge routers. When a packet leaves an edge router, it will be tagged.

When C1 receives this packet from E6, it will recognize that this is now a tagged packet. Since C1 is in the core, it has tags for all its links. Instead of the normal routing processing, C1 just examines the packet's tag — which it perceives as an incoming tag — and then determines what outgoing tag corresponds to it.

The incoming and outgoing tags are associated with each other in the TIB through the IP addresses of destination networks. The process of determining the outgoing tag is fast and optimized. Once C1 determines the outgoing tag corresponding to the packet's incoming tag, it replaces (swaps) the tags and sends the packet on to the next device. The same process continues through the remainder of the packet's journey until another edge router is reached (ER4 in Figure 11.1). What needs a bit of clarification, perhaps, is that outgoing tags applied to a packet by one device become incoming tags when the same packet is received by the next tag-switching device.

The packet from Figure 11.1 will transit the core of the tag-switched network, relying on the switching (swapping or changing) of tags as opposed to the traditional routing. The edge router E4 will strip the packet's tag when it exits the tag-switched core, and the packet's remaining journey will be subject to normal routing processing.

The TIB: where the tags are stored (Concepts 8 and 9)

Fields in a sample TIB entry include the incoming tag, the destination IP network, the outgoing physical interface, and the outgoing tag. Cisco's destination-driven tag allocation uses the existing forwarding information base (FIB) table to store tags. The FIB entries already associate a destination network with an outgoing physical interface. FIB entries turn into TIB entries after they are padded with an incoming and outgoing tag. So, does the FIB turn into a TIB? Actually, the FIB turns into a tagged FIB (or T-FIB), and it assumes the role of both: the FIB and the TIB.

How packets are tagged (Concepts 10 and 11)

Tags can be associated with packets in different ways depending on the underlying Data-Link Layer technology and the nature of the packet itself. Because tag switching is aimed initially at service provider networks, the current emphasis is on making tag switching work with ATM switches. With ATM, the tags are placed in the VPI/VCI field in the ATM cell header. Tag values are distributed between switches via the Tag Distribution Protocol (TDP).

In Chapter 8, an ATM switch is compared to a "cross-connect" that either maintains PVCs or sets up SVCs as needed. One of the advantages of using tags with ATM is that the need for PVCs and SVCs is eliminated. The ATM PVCs are set up by network administrators supplying the values of VPI/VCIs to the switch interfaces through switch-management software. With PVCs, the circuits are up all the time and the ATM network is normally fully meshed, which consumes bandwidth and CPU resources. With SVCs, it takes time to set up the ATM circuits. When the number of interacting ATM hosts begins to increase, the amount of time spent setting up SVCs also increases.

With tag switching the values of the circuit identifiers in the form of VPI/VCIs are distributed by way of the TDP. This eliminates the overhead associated with call setup time of SVCs and the maintaining of the mesh of PVCs. TDP enables ATM to act as though it were connectionless (as opposed to connection-oriented) technology. Since IP is a connectionless protocol, tag switching seems to provide a clean integration between IP and ATM. The key, however, to ATM switches participating in tag switching is that they must be running routing protocols.

Tag switching is not limited to any Data-Link Layer technology, but packet tagging will vary as a function of the Data-Link Layer. With ATM, tag switching takes advantage of the existing fields in the ATM cell. With the new version of IP (which relies on the use of extension headers), the tags will be carried in the flow header. When the Layer 2 fabric is a traditional LAN technology such as Ethernet, Token Ring, or FDDI, and the packet structure cannot accommodate the tags, the tag can be inserted between the Data-Link Layer header and the packet header.

Tag-switching benefits

A key benefit of tag switching is the very high level of granularity that it affords in managing network traffic. The various mechanisms for allocating tags and the decoupling of tag allocation from tag forwarding are a definite plus. Providing an evolutionary path to upgrading network performance through a software upgrade is also a plus from an implementation point of view.

Tag switching is also intended to be independent of the underlying Data-Link Layer technology and the routable protocols. In the future, tag switching is intended to work with Network Layer protocols other than IP. And when tag switching becomes part of a fully open standard it will definitely be a great plus.

Any minuses to tag switching will show up under stress. I also would like to see how tag switching will handle ATM QoS for aggregate routes. I will reserve my comments on any potential defects of tag switching until it has been implemented and operational for a while.

Ipsilon's IP Switching

Ipsilon's IP switching implementation provides another mechanism to integrate IP and ATM. Many major Internet backbone operators rely on ATM as the Physical/Data-Link (Layers 1 and 2 of the OSI Reference Model) infrastructure of choice to move Internet traffic (see the backbone maps in Chapter 2 and Chapter 10). The ATM switching fabric offers high bandwidth and the ability to classify the increasing volumes of Internet traffic. ATM is connection-oriented; IP is connectionless. How do these two worlds of almost diametrically opposed philosophies (connection-oriented and connectionless) come together through IP switching?

The business perspective

What's Ipsilon trying to do with IP switching? Today's Internet is facing an ongoing challenge to its successful survival, resulting, ironically enough, from its phenomenal success and growth rate thus far. With the Internet's commercialization, it's become subject to the same market forces and competition as other commercial enterprises. Major Internet backbone operators and local

ISPs alike must be profitable to stay in business. To keep existing customers and attract new ones, ISPs must sustain exceptional levels of customer service, which translates into having the ability to meet serious technical challenges. Improving network performance (upgrading the existing infrastructure) while keeping the networks stable (minimal down time) and providing new creative services are only some of the technical challenges that ISPs must face successfully to meet their business plans. Ipsilon's IP switching solution helps ISPs address these challenges.

The specs

Ipsilon's IP switching solution implements two publicly available software specifications: the Ipsilon's Flow Management Protocol (IFMP) described in RFC 1953 (see RFC 1953, Appendix A) and the General Switch Management Protocol (GSMP) described in RFC 1987 (see RFC 1987, Appendix A). Additionally, RFC 1954 (see RFC 1954, Appendix A) provides information on ATM encapsulation of flow-labeled IPv4 datagrams. As of press time, these three RFCs have informational status and are not considered to be open, IETF-approved Internet standards. However, the generic source code for IFMP and GSMP can be licensed from Ipsilon free of charge, pending the acceptance of conditions stated in the license agreement.

The "flows"

Ipsilon's IP switching implementation relies on classifying network traffic into "flows" and then applying accelerated processing to the flows. Effectively, a *flow* is a conversation between two devices communicating over the network. A *conversation* between network devices can be short or prolonged and can cover many different subjects. The simplest way to think of a flow is to consider it as a prolonged network conversation on a particular subject. Very short network conversations typically do not qualify as flows.

TCP/IP applications that lend themselves to having long conversations qualifying as flows include Web downloads, FTP file transfers, or audio/video distributions. These applications tend to create large numbers of packets with the same source and destination addresses and the same TCP or UDP port numbers. Other TCP/IP applications, such as e-mail, Domain Name System (DNS), or Simple Network Management Protocol (SNMP) tend to create shorter conversations that typically do not qualify as flows. There are exceptions, of course. A Web download can be very short and an e-mail message very long.

What's important to understand is that network managers have total control over the number of packets and the parameters used to define a flow. A flow can be defined based on IP addresses (source, destination, or both), application types (port numbers), subnet numbers, CIDR blocks, or a combination of these variables. Flows are defined through Ipsilon's browser-based network-management software, the Voyager. So, by now you are probably saying, "So what? Tell me what the purpose of defining a flow is in the first place, what happens after the flows are defined, and where the flows are defined." To do so, a look at the IP switch-system hardware components is necessary.

The hardware components

The key component of the IP switching technology is the IP switch processor. The switch processor has a dual role: a controller and a gateway. In its capacity as a controller, the switch processor implements the communication protocols IFMP and GSPM, the flow classification software, and the standard routing protocols (such as OSPF and BGP). The controller component of the switch processor can be thought of as an equivalent of the Route Switch Processor (RSP) in Cisco's 7500 series, or the IP switch/control board in the Ascend's GRF series. In its capacity as a gateway, the switch processor supports Ethernet and FDDI interfaces to connect existing IP networks into an ATM-based IP-switched network.

The IP switch processor is interfaced to an ATM switch, which can be Ipsilon's or any other vendor's ATM switch. The only requirement here is that the ATM switch implement GSMP to communicate with the IP switch processor. The last hardware component of the Ipsilon's IP switch system is a device, such as a FAS200 or a FAS1200, offering up to 24 10/100 Mbps Ethernet interfaces into the switch system. The FAS, like the IP switch processor, is also interfaced to the ATM switch.

A complete example of Ipsilon's IP switching solution including the IP switch processor, the ATM switch, and the FAS1200 is shown in Figure 11.2.

FIGURE 11.2 *Ipsilon's IP switch hardware: the IP switch controller, ATM 1600 switch, and the FAS1200 (courtesy of Ipsilon Corporation)*

Flow detection and operation

The flow qualification parameters are defined in the switch processor (the controller component) which decides whether the incoming packets ought to be routed or switched. The stages of detecting a "flow" and then changing the forwarding of packets from routing to switching are shown in Figure 11.3.

FIGURE 11.3 *Operation of Ipsilon's IP switch controller (courtesy of Ipsilon Corporation)*

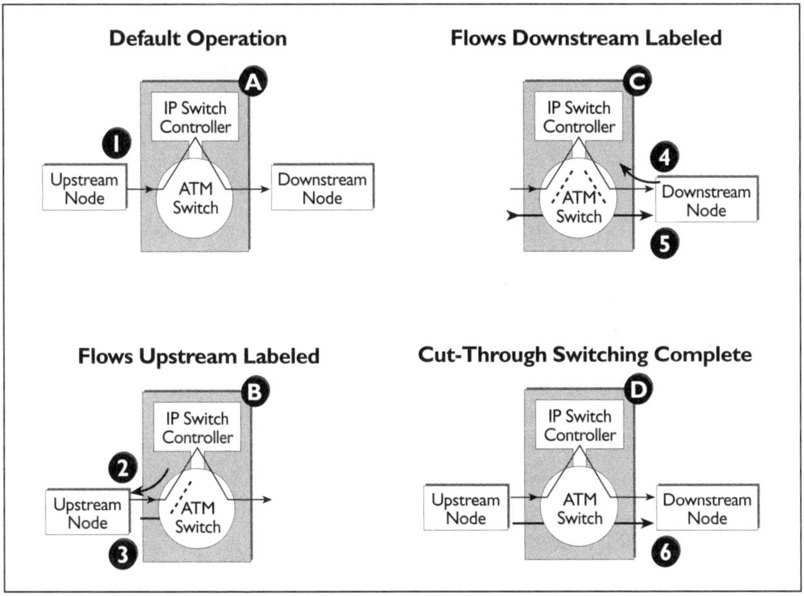

The upstream node in Figure 11.3 can be a router (connecting other networks to the ATM switching fabric), a single host, or the gateway component of the switch processor. The upstream node implements IFMP and is equipped with an ATM card that connects to the ATM switch. Upon startup, it sets up a default forwarding virtual channel to the switch. The downstream node and the IP switch controller interface to the ATM switch in a similar fashion. When network traffic from the upstream node arrives at the ATM switch, the switch first forwards it to the controller for routing and flow analysis (Step 1 in Figure 11.3). This traffic could be destined for transit across an entire ATM fabric (such as an ATM backbone), but in the example its next hop is the downstream node.

The IP switch controller performs the normal routing functions on the arriving traffic and forwards it to the downstream node. It also detects if the traffic from the upstream node may qualify as a flow. If the IP switch controller qualifies the traffic as a flow, it uses IFMP to inform the upstream node that any remaining traffic meeting the same characteristics should have a flow label applied to it. The flow label takes the form of a new virtual ATM channel to be set up between the upstream node and the ATM switch. The "flow labeled" traffic is now forwarded by the upstream node to the switch on this new virtual ATM channel (Step 2 and Step 3 in Figure 11.3).

Even as the IP switch controller is determining a flow between itself and the upstream node, it's going through a similar process with the downstream node. The downstream node sets up a new outgoing virtual channel for the same flow between itself and the ATM switch (Step 4 and Step 5 in Figure 11.3). Now that the switch controller has identified a flow with an input channel from the upstream node and an output channel to the downstream node, there is no longer a need for it to perform the normal routing/forwarding functions.

The switch controller uses GSMP to inform the ATM switch to mate two channels together (Step 6 in Figure 11.3). The flow has now been completely established and the packets (broken into ATM cells) are forwarded from the upstream node to the downstream node without reassembly and bypassing the overhead of the normal routing functions. The IP switch controller can "tune out" a bit, or take a back seat for a while. However, flows, unlike diamonds, are not forever!

If ATM channels are set up based on flows, they must be torn down when the flows disappear. After all, conversations come and go. The tearing down of an ATM flow channel takes place when a flow fizzles out. For example, a typical criteria to set up a flow could be 10 packets within a 20-second period. A criteria to tear down a flow could be the absence of packets on the flow channel in a 20-second interval.

It has taken some time to describe the flow setup process. And it's taking you some time to read about it. But don't be fooled by time. Flow determination and setup is much faster than it takes to describe it or to read about it. Otherwise, it wouldn't work.

Performance and migration strategies

An implementation example of IP switching based on flows is shown in the logical diagram in Figure 11.4.

In Figure 11.4 two redundant FDDI backbones are separated via an ATM-switched WAN. The IP switches incorporate a GSMP-compliant ATM switch and the IP switch processor configured as a switch controller. The IP gateways represent devices aggregating legacy LAN traffic (Ethernet, FDDI). Physically, the IP gateways could be part of the IP switch processors, which support both FDDI and Ethernet interfaces.

FIGURE 11.4 *Implementation example of IP switching (courtesy of Ipsilon Corporation)*

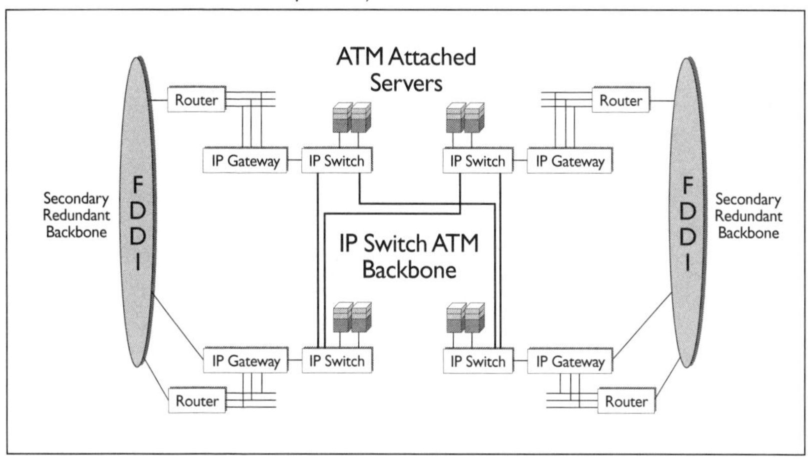

As traffic flows between the backbones, or between the backbones and the ATM-attached servers it's either switched or routed. The switch processors perform flow classifications. Traffic qualifying as flows will be switched; other traffic will be routed.

Large volumes of traffic flowing between the ATM servers and the FDDI-attached users will be switched, offering a boost in network performance. Yet, the routed (connectionless) nature of the entire internetwork is preserved with no need for PVCs between the ATM switches. A key benefit of connectionless networking is the automatic rerouting of traffic around router failures without reconfiguration.

This graceful co-existence of IP switching with routed-based networks also lends itself to gradual migration strategies. High-performance work groups can be phased into the existing router-based infrastructure to take advantage of IP switching speeds over ATM. What happens, though, when more and more users qualify to become part of the high-performance workgroups? Figure 11.4 exemplifies a scenario where, eventually, the FDDI backbones could be retired or relegated to handle only local traffic as the internetwork makes a transition to a fully switched environment. While the IP-switching equipment is going in to support the future, it blends well with the existing infrastructure supporting current business needs.

Web hosting or colocation

One of the fast-emerging services that major ISPs offer their corporate customers is Web hosting or colocation. Many corporate customers with dedicated Internet connections for their employees also use the same connections to provide their clients with access to their external Web sites. However, a typical corporate Internet connection has a fixed bandwidth (fractional T1, full T1, or higher).

What happens when a Web site becomes very popular? What tools does the average corporation have to monitor an increased bandwidth usage at its Web site? When and how does the Webmaster make a decision that the current connection bandwidth is no longer sufficient? Should this decision be based on the number of site hits, feedback from clients not able to get through, or complaints from employees not able to get out? Even when a decision is made to purchase an incremental bandwidth increase from a local telco provider, there is a lag time because of internal bureaucracies and telco's backlogs that can seriously impact the corporate image and bottom line.

When you consider the problems that corporations face with this model of providing Web access, Web hosting or colocation offers a refreshing solution. With Web hosting, corporate Web servers are set up at the ISP's site. This is different from using the ISP's server to put up a Web site, which has a limit on the disk space. Here, it is a case of physically moving a Web server hardware to an ISP's site.

What are the advantages of the Web hosting approach to providing Web access? Major ISPs are connected to the Internet through high-speed backbone routers. If your corporate server is set up on an ISP's network interfaced via a high-speed interface to a backbone router, there will be no shortage of bandwidth for your Web traffic. However, the ISP may have a problem with monitoring just how much bandwidth you are using. This is where Ipsilon's IP switching solution with bandwidth management (or *bandwidth rate shaping*) based on flows really shines.

Suppose an ISP has numerous corporate clients who want to co-locate their Web servers at its site. All the clients have different bandwidth requirements. How will the ISP manage this situation? What pricing model is the ISP going to use to differentiate between clients who need 64 Kbps and those who need 1.5 Mbps or more? The IP switch solves this problem. This sample scenario is shown in Figure 11.5.

FIGURE 11.5 *Web server hosting or colocation using Ipsilon's IP switching*

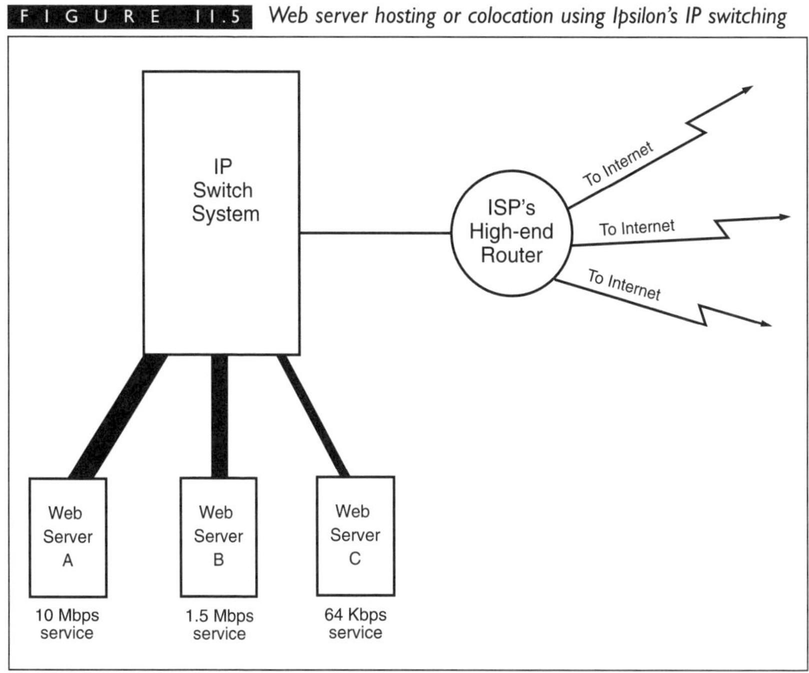

The ISP's backbone router is interfaced to the IP switch system. The IP switch systems in Figure 11.5 consists of the switch processor, Ipsilon's ATM 1600 (or any other GSMP-compliant ATM switch), and a FAS200 or a FAS1200 providing Ethernet access. To help with this visualization, substitute Figure 11.2 into the IP switch system box in Figure 11.5. Corporate Web servers plug into the 10/100 Ethernet ports on the FAS, as shown logically in Figure 11.5. After the initial per-port allocation bandwidth is defined, the switch processor software monitors each FAS port for bandwidth usage.

Because the FAS-Web servers connections can be 100 Mbps Ethernet, there is no shortage of bandwidth there. The bandwidth usage that's monitored and allocated is for each Web server's traffic (to and from) passing through the switch. The detection by the switch processor that the current bandwidth allocation limit is being reached on any one port translates into several options for action. Those actions will depend on the contract between the Web server owners and the ISP.

The switch processor can automatically allocate more bandwidth to a FAS port, provided the Web server owner has contracted for such on-demand allocation. With no on-demand allocation, the ISP can inform a Web server owner that the current allocation limit is being reached, and that it's time to renegotiate a contract for a higher bandwidth. The last option may be for the ISP and the client to know that the allocation limit is being routinely reached and do nothing about it (most likely because of funding problems on the client's part).

The bandwidth allocation and monitoring capabilities of the switch processor offer ISPs a powerful tool to monitor, allocate, and correctly charge their customers for what they really need and use. The varying thickness of lines connecting the Web servers to the FAS in Figure 11.5 conveys the concept of varying bandwidth allocations for the different servers.

Does that sound simple enough? Yes. Is this an elegant and effective solution for major ISPs looking at hosting services? Yes.

The controversy?

There is some controversy regarding the applicability of the Ipsilon's flow-based IP switching to the core of the Internet, since the traffic in the Internet's core seems to be very diverse. The best way to eliminate controversy is by looking at the facts.

Most backbone network administrators have the tools to analyze traffic patterns across their backbones. Applying the flow-selection criteria to the backbone traffic will determine if the Ipsilon's IP switching solution is applicable. If the traffic pattern analysis reflects a large number of potential flows, then Ipsilon's approach is applicable to improving backbone network performance. Otherwise, a different approach is needed. As seen in the preceding examples, however, the IP switching technology has multiple applications and is not necessarily aimed only at the core of the Internet.

The key to successful deployment of IP switching is to understand the technology and business issues that are being addressed. Ultimately, market forces will decide the future of each technology, but IP switching is here to stay for a while. And it's gaining support from other vendors. DEC, for one, has implemented Ipsilon's IP switching in its GIGAswitch/IP solution package.

ATM Forum's MPOA

The ATM Forum's Multiprotocol Over ATM (MPOA) standard is another mechanism for merging the scalability of Layer 3 routing with the speed and

QoS capabilities of ATM switching. MPOA relies on other standards and drafts already proposed by the ATM Forum, as well as by other standards bodies, including LAN Emulation (LANE), the IETF's classical IP over ATM encapsulation scheme as defined in RFCs 1483 and 1577 (see RFC 1483, 1577, Appendix A), and an IETF draft proposal for the Next Hop Routing Protocol (NHRP).

If all the end-user applications were written to interface directly with ATM, and if most of the user networks were ATM-based, there would be no need for MPOA. However, the reality of the installed equipment and user applications is different. Most applications interface to the higher-layer protocols (such as TCP/IP), and there are plenty of Ethernet, Token Ring, and FDDI LANs out there. There are also ATM hosts to which the traditional LAN-attached users want access.

MPOA and the associated standards merge the worlds of ATM and IP-based networks and applications. Conceptually, MPOA, IP switching, and tag switching attempt to accomplish similar objectives: merge the performance of Layer 2 with the scalability of Layer 3. The implementation details of all of these techniques are quite different, but not without some conceptual similarities. The hardware components of MPOA architecture — the edge devices and route servers — conceptually resemble the edge routers and core devices of tag switching, or the upstream/downstream nodes and the switch processors of IP switching.

The edge devices

The edge devices aggregate legacy LAN traffic from hosts attached to legacy LANs. Edge devices are not routers. They do not run any routing protocols such as OSPF or BGP. Typically, an edge device is an Ethernet or a Token Ring switch with an ATM interface and the MPOA client software running on it. The MPOA edge devices have also been referred to as multilayer switches. Because MPOA relies on LANE — which is an earlier ATM Forum standard for IP/ATM integration — the edge devices are also LANE clients (LECs) running the LANE software. Through LAN Emulation, an edge device maintains a default ATM circuit to an MPOA server or MPS. How's that for a few more acronyms?

Assume a ground zero scenario where an edge device receives traffic from legacy hosts. That traffic is destined either for an ATM-connected host or another legacy host interfaced to a second edge device across the ATM internetwork. Because an edge device has no routing intelligence, it forwards this traffic over the default ATM interface to an MPS. The MPS acts as a default router for the edge devices. But edge devices have some extra intelligence provided to them by the MPOA client software.

The MPOA client software allows an edge device to monitor the nature of the traffic it receives from legacy hosts. If an edge device detects that there is sufficient volume of traffic for any one destination, it will want to open an SVC to that destination. The idea is to bypass the default router or the MPS. The only remaining mystery is how the edge device is going to get the ATM address corresponding to the IP address of the destination. You may have guessed already that before the MPS can be bypassed, it must supply the edge device with the address mapping.

The MPOA servers

The MPOA servers are the second major component of the MPOA architecture. Devices that function as MPOA servers wear two distinct hats. An MPS is usually a router with an ATM interface implementing the server component of MPOA software. Cisco's 7513 unit qualifies as an MPS. In its role as a router, the MPS implements routing protocols (such as OSPF and BGP) and maintains the awareness of the network topology as explained in Chapter 4. In its MPOA support role, an MPS also maintains the bindings between the IP and ATM addresses for devices attached to the ATM fabric.

To non-MPOA routers that maintain connectivity with an MPOA-based internetwork, the MPOA servers appear as other ordinary routers (wearing their router hats). So, the moral here is that the plain routers see only what they've been empowered to see — other routers. The MPOA capabilities of their MPS neighbors are transparent to them.

When an edge device detects that it has a steady flow of packets destined for a certain IP destination, it can request the MPS to supply it with the binding between the IP and the ATM address of the destination. The ATM address of the destination returned by the MPS may be that of an ATM-attached host or another edge device. If the returned ATM address is for another edge device, it indicates that the traffic is ultimately destined for a legacy host interfaced to it.

With an ATM address of the destination "in hand," the edge device now sets up an ATM SVC across the ATM fabric. Any remaining traffic for that destination now flows across this newly set up virtual circuit. So, the network traffic that would otherwise have to be routed with all its associated overhead now flows across an ATM SVC between two edge devices or between an edge device and an ATM-attached host.

What's the difference?

By now, you are probably asking about the difference between MPOA and Ipsilon's IP switching. There are actually quite a few. Whether these differences are perceived as advantages or disadvantages depends on whom you are talking to. Discussions regarding the advantages and disadvantages of each approach tend to be very heated.

The MPOA's SVCs are end-to-end and can span the multiple ATM switches between the communicating devices. With IP switching, each IP switch controller is responsible for creating a portion of the ATM virtual channel between the end nodes.

With IP switching, the switch processor is needed for every ATM switch. With MPOA, additional hardware is needed for the MPOA server(s). This implies that the core of an MPOA-based internetwork can use standard ATM switches as long as the edge devices and at least one MPS are MPOA-enabled. In an IP switching core, an IP switch processor must interface to each ATM switch.

MPOA relies on the use of servers for address resolution. IP switching does not.

For redundancy and scalability MPOA supports multiple MPSes. IP switching preserves the connectionless nature of IP in the ATM environment by not setting up end-to-end SVCs.

MPOA uses standard ATM UNI signaling. IP switching doesn't need it. IP switching code is smaller and simpler. The MPOA code is larger and more complex.

How about some similarities? The MPSes communicate via NHRP. IP switching devices communicate via IFMP. Both MPOA and IP switching switch some traffic and route others. They both look for long-duration flows and setup circuits. So, why is there so much fervor surrounding their differences? Because when you get right down to it, the implementation differences reflect drastically different philosophies between the proponents of the two switching approaches.

Competition or Complementariness

Another whole chapter could be written on the implications of the differences between MPOA and IP switching, and another one on comparing them to Cisco's tag switching. The bottom line is that Ipsilon's IP switching, Cisco's tag switching, and MPOA all have their strengths and their weaknesses. They are all new emerging technologies with the final chapter on each yet to be written. Their success will depend not only on their technical merits, but also to what extent their proponents will educate the Internet community about their practical applications. These technologies are overlapping, but also complementary.

If I were looking at router performance issues at the core of the Internet, I would pick Cisco's tag switching as the pack leader. For Web hosting applications or performance improvements on the enterprise, I'm an Ipsilon fan. And if I were to choose the most standardized approach taking the fullest advantage of ATM's QoS capabilities, my vote would be for MPOA.

There are other approaches in the area of integrating the scalability of Layer 3 routing with the performance and QoS capability of Layer 2 ATM switching. Most notable are IBM's Aggregate Route-based IP Switching (ARIS) and Cascade's IP Navigator. So, out of all of this initial and still somewhat proprietary creative chaos, there is hope on the horizon for future open standards. Keep your eye on the activities of the IETF MPLS working group.

Can Switches Replace Routers?

Not likely. At least not yet. And not in the entire Internet. In all new approaches discussed thus far, one thing stands out: Switches need routers and routers need switches. A futuristic vision of switch/router devices is this: They will have processing power and memory to keep track of the entire Internet topology with no degradation in their performance. They will be able to set up a circuit between themselves and multiple other devices on the Internet with zero latency. They will use a minimal amount of power and take up very little space. They will not only be self-installing, but also self-configuring. They will not need physical media to communicate. They will be telepathically upgradable. And they will never fail. Doesn't this make you feel like you are in a network administrator's heaven?

AFTERWORD

What the Future Holds

I've heard it said that books are not written, they are abandoned. I couldn't agree more. There is always more to say. Yet, out of necessity (publisher's deadlines) and practicality (book size), this book is being abandoned by me to the fast-blowing sands of advancing technology and to the perceptive eyes of its readers. Its contents now frozen in time will gradually gather silicon dust until once again polished and revived in the second edition. However, this abandonment would not be complete without sharing my vision of the Internet's future.

Predicting the future is nothing new. Future world events have been prophesied for centuries. Today, political and stock market pundits speculate endlessly about the future election results and stock prices. The future of internetworking and the Internet is no different. The press is full of dire predictions regarding the demise of the Internet. Here are some of my thoughts on the subject.

Surf the net to `http://www.merit.edu/impa/press/` **and read for yourself what's being said by the popular media.**

With my physics background, it's easy to slip into the classical mechanics model and invoke Newton's first law of motion that an object will continue in its course unless acted upon by a force. If an object is known and the forces acting on it are known, its future position can be predicted or, better yet, calculated. The Internet, however, is not an object that fits into the classical mechanics model. It's doubtful that any one person understands all the forces acting upon it. So classical mechanics can't be applied here. I doubt if quantum mechanics would be any more successful if applied to predicting the future of the Internet. So, how does one go about predicting the future of the Internet without the aid of the pillars of modern science?

Without getting too philosophical, I see the future survival of the Internet tied to the survival of its spirit. Technical issues such as running out of address space, the increasing size of routing tables, and router bugs causing routing instability will likely continue to be with us as long as the Internet is with us. New ideas, new paradigms will resolve these issues. They will not cause the Internet to disintegrate.

Also, isolated incidents of router failure or construction backhoes snapping a fiber backbone here and there will not cause the Internet to collapse. In some ways, the Internet is no different than our transportation network, electrical power grid, or the telephone network. Each of these networks has certain focal points of vulnerability. The vulnerabilities that plague these systems can also be applied to the Internet.

The real issue that will decide the future of the Internet is: Will we remember the spirit and the vision that went into laying its foundations and building it into the most advanced communication network on the planet?

The early Internet was based on the spirit of trust and cooperation. The open nature and poor security of the TCP/IP protocols reflect this. As the Internet grew, the force of competition entered in to make its operation economically feasible. The commercialization of the Internet offers unprecedented access to information by millions of people. But at what price? Many of the social ills of our time have begun to migrate to the commercial for-profit environment of the Internet.

So, my prediction is this. If the Internet is used to elevate the highest ideals and values of our society, the Internet will survive in spite of any technical obstacles that it may face. If the Internet users are educated on the early history of the Internet and remember the spirit and vision of its founders, then the Internet will survive. If the Internet is used to promote freedom with responsibility, then the Internet will survive.

I don't find those who spread Internet viruses amusing. Neither do I find amusing those who use the Net to invade the privacy of others. Those who engage in these activities clearly do not carry the spirit of the Internet founders. To me, the Net has a spirit. It's the sum total of the highest ideals and aspirations of thousands of people who've made the Net possible. It's their joy, their sweat, their vision, their sacrifices all put together. The spirit of the Net should not be violated. If it is, we may all end up with a computer network that spans the globe and reaches into every home — but it won't be the Internet. Without its spirit, the Internet will become a mechanical tool used, perhaps, to get a quick fix.

The Internet should not be used to exploit and degrade — especially the younger generation. Those who hide behind their First Amendment rights and use the Internet to propagate material with no educational or moral value only risk bringing about increased government regulation. When that happens, the spirit of the Internet will gradually begin to die.

So, as the Internet's infrastructure strives to rendezvous with the future, the question is: Will the true spirit of the Internet survive along with it? That's where you — the Internet users — come in.

And that's my cyber bottom line.

APPENDIX A

RFC References

Each Request for Comments (RFC) listed in Table A.1 has been referenced in the book. Information provided here includes the RFC number, title, author(s), the IETF working group responsible for the RFC, date published (month and year), RFC status (and category), and comments (including which RFCs are obsoleted and/or updated, by which RFCs it is obsoleted and/or updated). Often, status is the same as category. Some RFCs have not been assigned to categories but have been assigned a status. Between the RFC status and category it's possible to figure out the level of current thinking by the Internet community about an RFC and the standardization level of protocols that are covered by it.

TABLE A.1 *Request for Comments*

RFC	TITLE	AUTHOR(S)	IETF WORKING GROUP	DATE	STATUS/ CATEGORY	COMMENTS
791	"Internet Protocol"	J. Postel		September 1981	***Status:*** Standard	Obsoletes RFC 760
792	"Internet Control Message Protocol"	J. Postel	Network Working Group	September 1981	***Status:*** Standard	Obsoletes RFC 0777 0760. Updated by RFC 0950
793	"Transmission Control Protocol"	J. Postel		September 1981	***Status:*** Standard	
826	"Ethernet Address Resolution Protocol: Or Converting Network Protocol Addresses to 48-Bit Ethernet Address for Transmission on Ethernet Hardware"	D.C. Plummer		November 1982	***Status:*** Standard	
950	"Internet Standard Subnetting Procedure"	J.C. Mogul, J. Postel	Network Working Group	August 1985	***Status:*** Standard	Updates RFC 792

(continued)

TABLE A.1 *Request for Comments (continued)*

RFC	TITLE	AUTHOR(S)	IETF WORKING GROUP	DATE	STATUS/ CATEGORY	COMMENTS
1000	"Request For Comments Reference Guide"	J.K. Reynolds, J. Postel		August 1987	***Status:*** Unknown	Obsoletes: RFCs 84, 100, 160, 170, 200, 598, 699, 800, 899, 999
1058	"Routing Information Protocol"	C.L. Hedrick		June 1988	***Status:*** Historic	
1163	"Border Gateway Protocol (BGP)"	K. Lougheed, Y. Rekhter	Network Working Group	June 1990	***Status:*** Historic	Obsoletes RFC 1105. Obsoleted by RFC 1267
1256	"ICMP Router Discovery Messages"	S. Deering	Network Working Group	September 1991	***Status:*** Proposed Standard	
1267	"Border Gateway Protocol 3 (BGP-3)"	K. Lougheed, Y. Rekhter		October 1991	***Status:*** Historic	Obsoletes RFC 1163
1388	"RIP Version 2 Carrying Additional Information"	G. Malkin	Network Working Group	January 1993	***Status:*** Proposed Standard	
1466	"Guidelines for Management of IP Address Space"	E. Gerich	Network Working Group	May 1993	***Status:*** Informational	Obsoletes RFC 1366

RFC	TITLE	AUTHOR(S)	IETF WORKING GROUP	DATE	STATUS/ CATEGORY	COMMENTS
1577	"Classical IP and ARP over ATM"	M. Laubach	Network Working Group	January 1994	***Status:*** Proposed Standard; ***Category:*** Standards Track	
1583	"OSPF Version 2"	J. Moy	Network Working Group	March 1994	***Status:*** Draft Standard; ***Category:*** Standards Track	Obsoletes RFC 1247. Obsoleted by RFC 2178
1483	"Multiprotocol Encapsulation over ATM Adaptation Layer 5"	Juha Heinanen	Network Working Group	July 1993	***Status:*** Proposed Standard	
1661	"The Point-to-Point Protocol (PPP)"	W. Simpson, Editor	Network Working Group	July 1994	***Status:*** Standard; ***Category:*** Standards Track	Obsoletes RFC 1548. Updated by RFC 2153

(continued)

TABLE A.1 *Request for Comments (continued)*

RFC	TITLE	AUTHOR(S)	IETF WORKING GROUP	DATE	STATUS/ CATEGORY	COMMENTS
1700	"Assigned Numbers"	J. Reynolds, J. Postel	Network Working Group	October 1994	***Status:*** Standard; ***Category:*** Standards Track	Obsoletes RFC 1340, 1060, 1010, 990, 960, 943, 923, 900, 870, 820, 790, 776, 770, 762, 758,755, 750, 739, 604, 503, 433, 349
1723	"RIP Version 2 — Carrying Additional Information"	G. Malkin	Network Working Group	November 1994	***Status:*** Draft Standard; ***Category:*** Standards Track	Obsoletes RFC 1388. Updates RFC 1058
1771	"A Border Gateway Protocol 4 (BGP-4)"	Y. Rekhter, T. Li	Network Working Group	March 1995	***Status:*** Draft Standard; ***Category:*** Standards Track	Obsoletes RFC 1654
1772	"Application of the Border Gateway Protocol in the Internet"	Y. Rekhter, P. Gross	Network Working Group	March 1995	***Status:*** Draft Standard; ***Category:*** Standards Track	Obsoletes RFC 1655

RFC	TITLE	AUTHOR(S)	IETF WORKING GROUP	DATE	STATUS/ CATEGORY	COMMENTS
1918	"Address Allocation for Private Internets"	Y. Rekhter, B. Moskowitz, D. Karrenberg, G. J.de Groot, E. Lear	Network Working Group	February 1996	***Status:*** Best Current Practice***;*** ***Category:*** Best Current Practice	Obsoletes RFC 1627, RFC 1597
1923	"RIPv1 Applicability Statement for Historic Status"	J. Halpern, S. Bradner	Network Working Group	March 1996	***Status:*** Informational***;*** ***Category:*** Informational	
1953	"Ipsilon Flow Management Protocol for IPv4 Version 1.0"	P. Newman, W. Edwards, R. Hinden, E. Hoffman, F. Ching Liaw, T. Lyon, G. Minshall	Network Working Group	May 1996	***Status:*** Informational***;*** ***Category:*** Informational	

(continued)

TABLE A.1 *Request for Comments (continued)*

RFC	TITLE	AUTHOR(S)	IETF WORKING GROUP	DATE	STATUS/ CATEGORY	COMMENTS
1954	"Transmission of Flow Labeled IPv4 on ATM Data Links. Ipsilon Version 1.0"	P. Newman, W. Edwards, R. Hinden, E. Hoffman, F. Ching Liaw, T. Lyon, G. Minshall	Network Working Group	May 1996	***Status:*** Informational; ***Category:*** Informational	
1966	"BGP Route Reflection: An Alternative to Full Mesh IBGP"	T. Bates, R. Chandra-sekeran	Network Working Group.	June 1996	***Status:*** Experimental; ***Category:*** Experimental	
1987	"Ipsilon's General Switch Management Protocol Specification. Version 1.1"	P. Newman, W. Edwards, R. Hinden, E. Hoffman, F. Ching Liaw, T. Lyon, G. Minshall	Network Working Group	August 1996	***Status:*** Informational; ***Category:*** Informational	
2080	"RIPng for IPv6"	G. Malkin, R. Minnear		January 1997	***Status:*** Proposed Standard; ***Category:*** Standards Track	

RFC	TITLE	AUTHOR(S)	IETF WORKING GROUP	DATE	STATUS/ CATEGORY	COMMENTS
2105	"Cisco's Tag Switching Architecture Overview"	Y. Rekhter, B. Davie, D. Katz, E. Rosen, G. Swallow	Network Working Group	February 1997	***Status:*** Informational; ***Category:*** Informational	
2178	"OSPF Version 2"	J. Moy		July 1997	***Status:*** Draft Standard; ***Category:*** Standards Track	Obsoletes RFC 1583

APPENDIX B

Bibliography

This appendix contains references to excellent works on computer networks, TCP/IP, history of the Internet, satellite communications, and other topics that could only be touched on lightly in this book.

Referenced in Text

Comer, Douglas E. *Internetworking with TCP/IP Vol: I.* 3d ed. New York: Prentice Hall, Inc., 1995.

Hafner, Katie and Lyon, Matthew. *Where Wizards Stay Up Late*. New York: Simon and Schuster, 1996.

Randall, Neil. *The Soul of the Internet.* London: International Thomson Computer Press, 1997.

Siyan, Karanjit S. *Internetworking with NetWare TCP/IP.* Indianapolis: New Riders Publishing, 1996.

Tanenbaum, Andrew S. *Computer Networks.* 3d ed. New York: Prentice Hall, Inc., 1996.

Additional Recommended Reading

Black, Uyless. *Frame Relay Networks*. 2d ed. New York: McGraw-Hill, Inc., 1996.

Hecht, Jeff. *Understanding Fiber Optics.* 2d ed. Indianapolis: SAMS Publishing, 1993.

Logsdon, Tom. *Mobile Communications Satellites.* New York: McGraw-Hill, Inc., 1995.

McDysan, David E. and Sophen, Darren L. *ATM Theory and Applications.* New York: McGraw-Hill, Inc., 1995.

APPENDIX C

Acronym and Abbreviation Guide

Table C.1 provides a guide to acronyms and abbreviations used throughout this book. It's not a glossary. Most of the terms are explained in the book, but some are not. Readers should refer to a data-communications glossary for detailed explanations of terms that are not explained in the text of this book. Several glossary references appear at the end of this appendix.

TABLE C.1 *Acronym and Abbreviation Guide*

ABBREVIATION/ ACRONYM	MEANING
AADS	Ameritech Advanced Data Systems
AAL	ATM Adaptation Layer
ABR	Available Bit Rate
ABR	Area Border Router
AGIS	Apex Global Internet Services
AIP	ATM Interface Processor
ANS	Advanced Network and Services
ANSI	American National Standards Institute
AOL	America On Line
API	Application Program Interface
ARIS	Aggregate Route-based IP Switching
ARP	Address Resolution Protocol
ARPA	Advanced Research Project Agency
ARPAnet	Advanced Research Projects Agency network
AS	Autonomous System
ASBR	Autonomous System Border Router
ATM	Asynchronous Transfer Mode
AUI	Attachment Unit Interface
AUP	Acceptable Use Policy
BARRnet	Bay Area Regional Research network
BBN	Bolt, Beranek and Newman
BDR	Backup Designated Router

ABBREVIATION/ ACRONYM	MEANING
BGP	Border Gateway Protocol
BRI	Basic Rate Interface
BSD	Berkeley Software Distribution
BSDI	Berkley Software Design, Inc.
CBR	Constant Bit Rate
CCA	Computer Corporation of America
CIDR	Classless Interdomain Routing
CIR	Committed Information Rate
CIX	Commercial Internet Exchange
CPU	Central Processing Unit
CSnet	Computer Science network
CSU/DSU	Channel Service Unit/Data Service Unit
DAC	Dual Attachment Concentrator
DAS	Dual Attachment Station
DDP	Datagram Delivery Protocol
DIX	Digital Internet Exchange
DLCI	Data Link Connection Identifier
DNJ	Denver Junction
DNS	Domain Name Service
DoD	Department of Defense
DR	Designated Router
DREN	Defense Research and Education Network
DTE/DCE	Data Terminal Equipment/Data Circuit-terminating Equipment
DVMRP	Distance Vector Multicast Routing Protocol
EBGP	External Border Gateway Protocol

(continued)

TABLE C.1 *Acronym and Abbreviation Guide (continued)*

ABBREVIATION/ ACRONYM	MEANING
EGP	Exterior Gateway Protocol
EIA	Electronics Industry Association
EIP	Ethernet Interface Processor
EMI	Electromagnetic Interference
ER	Equipment Room
ESD	Electrostatic Discharge
FCS	Frame Check Sequence
FDDI	Fiber Distributed Data Interface
FFDT	FDDI Full-Duplex Technology
FIB	Forwarding Information Base
FIP	FDDI Interface Processor
FIX	Federal Internet Exchange
FR	Frame Relay
FTP	File Transfer Protocol
GSMP	General Switch Management Protocol
GSR	Gigaswitch Router
GUI	Graphical User Interface
HDLC	High-Level Data Link Control
HIP	HSSI Interface Processor
HIPPI	High-Performance Parallel Interface
HSJ	Houston Junction
HSSI	High-Speed Serial Interface
IANA	Internet Assigned Numbers Authority
IBGP	Internal Border Gateway Protocol
ICMP	Internet Control Message Protocol

ABBREVIATION/ ACRONYM	MEANING
IETF	Internet Engineering Task Force
IFMP	Ipsilon's Flow Management Protocol
IGP	Interior Gateway Protocol
IGRP	Interior Gateway Routing Protocol
IMP	Interface Message Processor
InterNIC	Internet Network Information Center
IOS	Internetworking Operating System
IP	Internet Protocol
IPv4	Internet Protocol version 4
IPv6	Internet Protocol version 6
IPTO	Information Processing Techniques Office
IPX	Internet Packet Exchange
ISDN	Integrated Services Digital Network
ISI	Information Sciences Institute
IS-IS	Intermediate System to Intermediate System
ISP	Internet Service Provider
ITU-T	International Telecommunications Union-Telecommunications
ITU-TSS	International Telecommunications Union-Telecommunications Standardization Sector
JAnet	Joint Academic network
LAN	Local Area Network
LANE	LAN Emulation
LCP	Link Control Protocol
LEC	LAN Emulation Client
LS	Link State
LSA	Link State Advertisement

(continued)

TABLE C.1 *Acronym and Abbreviation Guide (continued)*

ABBREVIATION/ ACRONYM	MEANING
MAC	Medium Access Control
MAE	Metropolitan Area (Exchange or Ethernet)
MED	Multi-Exit-Discriminator
MERIT	Michigan Education and Research Information Triad
MFS	Metropolitan Fiber Systems
MICHNet	Michigan Network
MIT	Massachusetts Institute of Technology
MORENet	Missouri Research and Education Network
MPLS	Multiprotocol Label Switching
MPOA	Multiprotocol Over ATM
MPR	Multiprotocol Router
MPS	MPOA Server
NAP	Network Access Point
NASA	National Aeronautics and Space Administration
NCAR	National Center for Atmospheric Research
NCSA	National Center for Supercomputing Applications
NCP	Network Control Protocol
NCPs	Network Control Protocols
NEC	National Electrical Code
NGI	Next Generation Internet
NHRP	Next Hop Routing Protocol
NIC	Network Interface Card
NII	National Information Infrastructure
NLM	NetWare Loadable Module
NLRI	Network Layer Reachability Information

ABBREVIATION/ ACRONYM	MEANING
NNI	Network-to-Network Interface
NONAG	North American Network Operators Group
NOS	Network Operating System
NPM	Network Processor Module
NSF	National Science Foundation
NSFnet	National Science Foundation network
NSLP	NetWare Link Services Protocol
NSP	National Service Provider
NYSERNet	New York State Education and Research Network
OC-3c	Optical Carrier (level 3 version c)
OC-12c	Optical Carrier (level 12 version c)
OSI	Open Systems Interconnection
OSI RM	Open Systems Interconnection Reference Model
OSPF	Open Shortest Path First
PACI	Partnership for Advanced Computational Infrastructure
PARC	Palo Alto Research Center
PING	Packet Internet Groper
POP	Point of Presence
PPP	Point-to-Point Protocol
PREPnet	Pennsylvania Research and Economic Partnership network
PSINet	Performance Systems International Network
PVC	Permanent Virtual Circuit
QBRT	Quick Branch Routing Technology
QoS	Quality of Service
RAS	Remote Access Services

(continued)

TABLE C.1 *Acronym and Abbreviation Guide (continued)*

ABBREVIATION/ ACRONYM	MEANING
RFP	Request For Proposal
R&E	Research and Education
RAM	Random-Access Memory
RDP	Router Discovery Protocol
RIB	Routing Information Base
RIP	Routing Information Protocol
RIP-1	Routing Information Protocol version 1
RIP-2	Routing Information Protocol version 2
RIPng	Routing Information Protocol new generation
RIPv1	Routing Information Protocol version 1
RIPv2	Routing Information Protocol version 2
RRAS	Routing and Remote-Access Services
RSP	Route Switch Processor
RTMP	Routing Table Maintenance Protocol
SAC	Single Attached Concentrator
SAS	Single Attached Station
SCC	Super Computing Center
SMDS	Switched Multimegabit Data Service
SNA	System Network Architecture
SNAP	Subnetwork Access Protocol
SPAM	Stupid Person's Advertisement
SRI	Stanford Research International
ST	Straight Tip
SURAnet	Southeastern Universities Research Association network
SVC	Switched Virtual Circuit
TC	Telecommunications Closet

ABBREVIATION/ ACRONYM	MEANING
TCP	Transmission Control Protocol
TDP	Tag Distribution Protocol
T-FIB	Tagged FIB
TIA	Telecommunications Industry Association
TIB	Tag Information Base
TOS	Type of Service
TRIP	Token Ring Interface Processor
TTL	Time to Live
TWD	Toxic Waste Dump
UBR	Unspecified Bit Rate
UCLA	University of California in Los Angeles
UCSB	University of California in Santa Barbara
UDP	User Datagram Protocol
UNI	User-to-Network Interface
vAI	vBNS Authorized Institution
vBNS	very high speed Backbone Network Service
vPI	vBNS Partner Institution
VBR	Variable Bit Rate
VCI	Virtual Channel Identifier
VIP	VINES Internet Protocol
VLSM	Variable-Length Subnet Mask
VPI	Virtual Path Identifier
VPN	Virtual Private Network
WAN	Wide-Area Network
XNS	Xerox Network Service

Recommended Glossary References

Shnier, Mitchell. *Dictionary of PC Hardware and Data Communications Terms.* Sebastopol, CA: O'Reilly & Associates, Inc., 1996.

An online version of the *Dictionary of PC Hardware and Data Communications Terms* is available at `http://www.oreilly.com/reference/dictionary/`.

Other good online glossaries include the *Butterfly Glossary* at `http://www.rirr.cnuce.cnr.it/Glossario/glhpage.html` and *The Cook Report Glossary* at `http://cookreport.com/`.

APPENDIX D

Excerpt from the NSF 93-52 Solicitation

This appendix contains an excerpt from the National Science Foundation (NSF) 93-52 solicitation and is provided courtesy of the National Science Foundation.

Title: *NSF 93-52 — Network Access Point Manager, Routing Arbiter, Regional Network Providers, and Very High Speed Backbone Network Services Provider for NSFNET and the NRENSM Program*

Type: Program Guideline

NSF Org: CISE / NCR

Date: May 6, 1993

File: nsf9352

Network Access Point Manager, Routing Arbiter, Regional Network Providers, and Very High Speed Backbone Network Services Provider for NSFNET and the NREN℠ Program

Program Solicitation National Science Foundation

I. Purpose of This Solicitation

NSFNET has supported the data networking needs of the research and education community since 1986. It has become an essential infrastructure for that community and is used daily to facilitate communication among researchers, educators, and students and to provide them with remote access to information and computing resources. The number of users, the number of connected networks, and the amount of network traffic continue to grow rapidly.

NSFNET also supports the goals of the High Performance Computing and Communications (HPCC) Program which was delineated in the President's Fiscal 1992 and 1993 budgets and which became law with the passage of The High Performance Computing Act of 1991 (Public Law 102-194). The National Research and Education Network (NREN/1/) Program, one of the four components of the HPCC Program, calls for gigabit-per-second networking for research and education by the mid-1990s. As steps towards achieving the goals of the NREN Program, "the National Science Foundation shall upgrade the National Science Foundation funded network, assist regional networks to upgrade their capabilities, and provide other Federal departments and agencies the opportunity to connect to the National Science Foundation funded network."/2/ This program solicitation relates directly to these activities.

Since the creation of the NSFNET in 1986, the data networking industry has evolved considerably. New companies have been created and a number of existing companies have shown increasing interest in data networking. These and other evolutionary changes have prompted the need for a new architecture for NSFNET. The expiration of the current Cooperative Agreement for NSFNET Backbone Network Services has prompted the need for a new solicitation for NSFNET services.

To provide for the continued development and growth of NSFNET and to support the goals of the NREN Program, a new architecture has been formulated and is specified here. The implementation of the architecture includes four separate projects for which proposals are herein invited: one or more Network Access Point (NAP) Managers; a Routing Arbiter (RA) organization; a provider organization for very high-speed Backbone Network Services (vBNS); and a set of Regional Networks which connect client/member institutions and which provide for interregional connectivity by connecting to NAPs and/or to Network Service Providers (NSPs) which are connected to NAPs. No solicitation is presented here for NSPs as it is anticipated that costs of operation of the NSPs will be recovered from users of the services that they provide.

The solicitation invites proposals for one or more NAP Manager organizations to arrange for and oversee NAPs (as specified below) where the vBNS, NSPs, and other appropriate networks may interconnect. This component of the architecture will provide access for other networks to the U.S. research and education community and will provide for the interconnection of networks in a NAP environment.

The solicitation also invites proposals for an RA organization to establish and maintain databases and routing services which may be used by attached networks to obtain routing information (such as network topology, policy, and interconnection information) with which to construct routing tables. This component of the architecture will provide for an unbiased routing scheme which will be available (but not mandatory) for all attached networks. The RA will also promote routing stability and manageability, and advance routing technology.

The solicitation also invites proposals for a vBNS Provider to establish and maintain a vBNS that will support applications that require high network bandwidth. In the tradition of NSFNET and as discussed below, the vBNS Provider will demonstrate leadership in the development and deployment of high performance data communications networks. This component of the architecture will: provide for the interconnection of NSF Supercomputing Centers (Cornell Theory Center, National Center for Atmospheric Research, National Center for Supercomputing Applications, Pittsburgh Supercomputing Center, and San Diego Supercomputing Center); connect to all NSF-designated NAPs; provide for the interconnection of other locations which may be subsequently specified by NSF; support the development of a national high performance computing environment (the metacenter/3/); support other high bandwidth applications such as distributed high performance computing and isochronous visualization; and promote the development and deployment of advanced routing technologies. Traffic on the vBNS must be in support of research and education.

Regional Networks have been a part of NSFNET since NSFNET's inception and have been a major force in the drive towards ubiquitous network connectivity for the research and education community. The important role that regional networks have played and will continue to play is recognized in this solicitation. Existing and/or realigned regional networks may seek support to provide for interregional connectivity by connecting to NSPs that are connected to NAPs or by connecting directly to NAPs. Regional Network Providers are also anticipated to: connect regional network client/member organizations; support the general networking needs of clients/members; and provide for the special networking needs of clients/members who have applications which justify high bandwidth. These later functions of regional networks are among the evaluation criteria for Regional Network Provider proposals, but only the interregional connectivity function will be supported under this solicitation.

It is anticipated that this solicitation will result in two or more separate five-year cooperative agreements between NSF and the organizations and/or consortia of organizations chosen as NAP Manager(s), RA, and vBNS Provider. It is also anticipated that this solicitation will result in a number of four-year cooperative agreements with organizations chosen as Regional Network Providers. Combinations of solicited services (such as NAP Manager and vBNS Provider) may be proposed with the exception that the same organization and/or consortium cannot propose to be both the vBNS Provider and the RA. If the same organization or consortium wishes to propose for both the Regional Network Provider Project and for one or more of the other projects, the Regional Network proposal must be submitted separately. Total NSF funding for all awards resulting from this solicitation is expected to be approximately $18,000,000 per year.

This solicitation is issued pursuant to the National Science Foundation Act of 1950, as amended (42 U.S.C. 1861 et seq) and the Federal Cooperative Agreement Act (31 U.S.C. 6305) and is not subject to the Federal Acquisition Regulations.

II. Background

The network of networks known as the Internet includes more than 10,000 IP (Internet Protocol) networks. These networks interconnect more than one million computers and millions of users throughout the world. The domestic portion of the Internet contains a number of NSF supported networks. These include: campus network connections at educational institutions; regional networks; and the NSFNET Backbone Network Services. Broadly speaking, NSFNET consists of all of these networks together with a number of other networks at locations such as government laboratories and private corporations which are connected to regional networks.

The Internet also includes other federally-sponsored networks, such as the NASA Science Internet (NSI), the DOE ESnet, and the DARPA DARTnet and TWBnet. The multi-agency NREN Program includes these networks in addition to the NSFNET. These sponsoring agencies have provided for the interconnection and interoperability of their networks at Federal Information eXchange (FIX) access points.

It is anticipated that networks such as NSI and ESnet will continue to have acceptable use policies which restrict traffic to that which is in support of the missions of their funding agencies. On the other hand, any traffic which is in support of research and education will be permitted on the VBNS.

Because of the breadth of the charter of the NSFNET and because of its wide use by the research and education community, it is projected that the NSFNET user base will continue to grow and that its users will continue to require new levels of connectivity and network services. In addition to the anticipated growth in aggregated traffic, new applications such as distributed high performance computing and isochronous visualization make the provision of increasingly high network performance necessary for the continued success of NSFNET and to achieve the goals of the NREN and the HPCC Programs.

After consulting with many segments of the Internet community, issuing a draft solicitation, and receiving and considering comments on that draft, the National Science Foundation has developed this solicitation for one or more NAP Managers, an RA organization, a vBNS Provider, and Regional Network Providers. In the manner specified below, it is anticipated that NSFNET will:

develop increasingly high performance network services; accommodate the anticipated growth in numbers of users and networks and in network traffic; and transition to a networking infrastructure that is increasingly provided by interconnected network service providers operating in a competitive environment.

III. Network Architecture and Project Requirements

NSF intends to establish a new network architecture for NSFNET in the following manner. A number of NAPs, as specified below, will be established where a vBNS and other appropriate networks will be interconnected. One or more NAP Manager organizations will arrange for and oversee the NAPs. An RA organization will provide routing services such as route servers and route databases for attached networks and will provide and make available certain routing services in support of the Internet community. Finally, regional networks will continue to provide various services for their client/member organizations and to provide for interregional connectivity through NAPs and/or NSPs that are connected to the NAPs. This section gives more details on this architecture and gives specific project requirements.

A. Network Access Points

Network Access Points (NAPs) are to be proposed, subject to the locations and characteristics described below, by organizations responding to the NAP Manager(s) Project. NAPs are described separately in this section because of their relevance to all projects described in this solicitation.

An Internet NAP is defined as a high speed network or switch to which a number of networks can be connected via routers for the purpose of traffic exchange and interoperation./4/ A NAP should have capacity adequate to keep up with the switching requirements of the attached networks. The attached networks are presumed to be part of the connected Internet, but the NAP itself may be of a lower protocol level; e.g., it may be a level two network or switch.

The NAP will be a conceptual evolution of the FIX and the Commercial Information eXchange (CIX). The FIX is currently built around a level two network, a 100 Mbps FDDI ring, with attached Internet networks operating at speeds of up to 45 Mbps. Neither the FIXes nor the CIX currently have dedicated route servers with route databases.

Examples of NAP implementation include but are not limited to: a LAN (like the FIXes); a MAN (Metropolitan Area Network) using a service, such as Switched Multimegabit Data Service (SMDS); and a high speed switch such as an ATM switch.

Traffic on NAPs awarded under this solicitation will not be restricted to that which is in support of research and education. This will, for example, permit two attached networks to exchange traffic without violating the use policies of any other networks interconnected at the NAPs. NSF will utilize announcements in the Federal Register and public discussion with the U.S. research and education community and other interested parties to develop policies on traffic and usage at NSF supported NAPs.

Priority and desirable NAP locations are specified below. NAPs will be established at the priority locations if at all possible. NAPs will be established at one or more of the desirable locations if finances and other circumstances permit. Only general geographic locations are given. Specific locations should be proposed, and NAP attachment policies should promote fair and equitable pricing for and access to NAP attachment.

Priority NAP locations

- California
- Chicago
- New York City

Desirable NAP locations

- Atlanta
- Boston
- Denver
- Texas
- Washington, D.C.

B. NAP Manager(s) Project

One or more NAP Manager organizations will be selected to arrange for and manage NAPs which they have proposed. Prospective NAP Managers may utilize different subawardees for different NAPs where appropriate.

The specific anticipated duties of the NAP Manager organization(s) are as follows:

- Establish, operate, and maintain, possibly with subawardees, all or a subset of the specified NAPs for the purpose of interconnecting the vBNS and other appropriate networks. Traffic on NAPs will not be restricted to that which is in support of research and education;

  NAPs can be proposed to be implemented as LANs or MANs or other innovative approaches. NAPs must operate at speeds commensurate with the speeds of attached networks and must be upgradable as required by demand, usage, and Program goals. NAPs must support the switching of IP (Internet Protocol) and CLNP (ConnectionLess Networking Protocol) packets

- Develop and establish attachment policies (including attachment fee schedules) which would apply to networks that are connected to NAPs
- Propose NAP locations subject to the given general geographic locations. Propose fair and equitable pricing for NAP attachment as discussed above
- Propose and establish procedures to work with personnel from other NAP Managers (if any), the RA, the vBNS Provider, and regional and other attached networks to resolve problems and to support end-to-end connectivity and quality of service for network users
- Specify reliability and security standards for the NAPs and procedures to ensure that these standards are met
- Specify and provide appropriate NAP accounting and statistics gathering and reporting capabilities
- Specify appropriate procedures for access to the NAP premises (if any) for authorized personnel of connecting networks and ensure that these procedures are carried out

C. Routing Arbiter Project

Under the current cooperative agreement, the same consortium which provides the NSFNET Backbone Network Service also acts as routing arbiter. Under the new cooperative agreements described here, the routing arbiter function will be distinct from the vBNS. That is, the same organization and/or consortium cannot propose to be both the vBNS Provider and the RA. The RA will provide for equitable treatment of the various network service providers with regard to routing administration and will provide for a common database of route information to promote stability and manageability of the network.

The RA will provide database management for information such as network topology, policy (routing path preferences), and interconnection information which can be used by attached networks to build routing table configurations. The RA will make this data publicly accessible, but will not mandate its use by attached networks. In addition, this information will be used to configure attached route servers in support of NSPs and other attached networks. Route servers are to support stable routing of the Internet and to provide for simplified routing information to NSPs and other attached networks. It is expected that route servers will use standard routing protocols, such as BGP (Border Gateway Protocol, RFC 1267) and ISO IDRP (Interdomain Routing Protocol, ISO 10747).

The RA organization will also provide certain other services which will facilitate the logical interconnection of the attached networks. For example, it will assist in the development of new routing technologies and the deployment of simplified routing strategies for attached networks. It will also assist in the development of tools which can be used to configure, manage, and operate network routing systems.

The specific anticipated duties of the RA organization are as follows:

- Promote Internet routing stability and manageability
- Establish and maintain network topology and policy databases, possibly at each NAP, by means such as exchanging routing information with and dynamically updating routing information from the attached Autonomous Systems using standard inter-domain routing protocols such as BGP and IDRP. RA activities must support the network service providers which switch IP (Internet Protocol) and CLNP (ConnectionLess Networking Protocol) packets
- Propose and establish procedures to work with personnel from the NAP Manager(s), the vBNS Provider, and regional and other attached networks to resolve problems and to support end-to-end connectivity and quality of service for network users
- Develop advanced routing technologies (such as type of service and precedence routing, multicasting, bandwidth on demand, and bandwidth allocation services) in cooperation with the global Internet community
- Provide for simplified routing strategies, such as default routing, for attached networks
- Promote distributed operation and management of the Internet

D. Very High Speed Backbone Network Services Provider Project

Since its inception, the NSFNET has been a leader in providing for high speed networking services for the research and education community. The vBNS will continue this tradition and will provide for: high speed interconnection of NSF Supercomputing Centers (SCCs); the development of a national high performance computing environment (the metacenter); applications involving distributed high performance computing and isochronous visualization; and connection to the NSF-specified NAPs. The vBNS connections to the NAPs will, for example, facilitate connecting the SCCs to research institutions that have meritorious high bandwidth network applications.

The vBNS must be able to switch both IP and CLNP packets and it must operate initially (at least between SCCs) at speeds of 155 Mbps or higher. Speeds should be achieved directly, not by the provision of multiples of slower speed services. Speeds higher than 155 Mbps are desirable and may be preferred if finances and other circumstances permit. Additionally, the vBNS Provider must participate in the development and deployment of advanced Internet routing technologies such as type of service and precedence routing, multicasting, bandwidth on demand, and bandwidth allocation services.

The vBNS may have connections and customers beyond those specified by NSF provided that the quality and quantity of required services for NSF-specified customers are not affected. In this regard, the vBNS Provider must be able to distinguish between NSF customer traffic and that of other customers and to gather and report traffic statistics (such as throughput and delay) based on these categories. It must also be able to assure proposed service levels for NSF-specified customers.

The specific anticipated duties of the vBNS Provider are as follows:

- Establish and maintain a 155 Mbps or higher transit network service which switches IP and CLNP packets and which interconnects NSF SCCs (Cornell Theory Center, National Center for Atmospheric Research, National Center for Supercomputing Applications, Pittsburgh Supercomputing Center, and San Diego Supercomputing Center) and the NSF-specified NAPs (and possibly other specified locations in the future)
- Propose and establish a set of quality of service (QoS) metrics which will be used to characterize the proposed network services and to ascertain and publicize network performance on an ongoing basis
- Propose and establish a schedule to enhance the speed at which the network operates, quality of service measures, and type of service offerings in line with NSF's broad program goals and consistent with anticipated NSF customer requirements and available funding
- Propose and establish procedures to work with personnel from the NAP Manager(s), the RA, and regional and other attached networks to resolve problems and to support end-to-end connectivity and quality of service for network users
- Participate in the development of advanced routing technologies (such as type of service and precedence routing, multicasting, bandwidth on

demand, and bandwidth allocation services) in cooperation with the RA and with the global Internet community

- Subscribe to the policies of the NAP Manager(s) and the RA; implement procedures based on standard inter-domain routing protocols such as BGP- and IDRP-based to assist in establishing and maintaining the network topology and policy databases

E. Regional Networks Project

Regional Networks have been a part of NSFNET since its inception and have been a major force in the drive towards ubiquitous network connectivity for the research and education community. Regional Network Providers connect an increasingly broad base of client/member organizations, provide for interregional connectivity, and provide other networking services for their clients/members. One such networking service may be the provision of special connections for their client/member institutions that have meritorious high bandwidth network applications.

It is anticipated that regional networks will continue to play these important roles. Existing and/or realigned regional networks are invited to propose how they will meet the interregional connectivity needs of their client/member organizations. Under awards resulting from this solicitation, NSF will support regional networks for the provision of interregional connectivity. They may connect to NSPs which connect to NAPs, or they may connect to NAPs directly. (If they connect to NAPs directly, they may require additional arrangements with one or more NSPs to provide them with inter-NAP connectivity.)

Under awards resulting from unsolicited proposals and/or from proposals submitted in response to existing and anticipated solicitations and program announcements, NSF may support regional networks for activities such as: providing special connections for client/member institutions that have meritorious high bandwidth network applications; providing innovative information services to client/member organizations; and providing connection assistance to new client/member institutions of higher learning.

Regional networks may attach to one (or more) NSPs that are connected to NAPs to obtain interregional connectivity. Regional networks may also attach directly to one (or more) NAPs. Under this second approach, some further arrangement (such as procuring inter-NAP connectivity services from an NSP) would be required to obtain full interregional connectivity.

Under this solicitation regional networks may propose to NSF for support of the fee for either attachment to and use of one NSP or attachment to and use of one NAP. The amount of available funds may limit the number and size of awards that can be made. The amount of each award will in general be related to the number of proposed clients/members which are institutions of higher learning and to the aggregate bandwidth requirements of those clients/members. In each year after the first, NSF support for the NSP fee and/or the NAP fee will decrease and will cease at the end of the regional network cooperative agreement (which shall be no more than four years).

The specific anticipated duties of the regional network providers are listed below. Only the first-listed duty will be supported under awards resulting from proposals submitted in response to this solicitation.

- Provide for interregional connectivity by means such as connecting to NSPs which are connected to NAPs and/or by connecting to NAPs directly and making inter-NAP connectivity arrangements with one or more NSPs
- Provide for innovative network information services for client/member organizations (in cooperation with the InterNIC, the NSFNET Network Information Services Manager)
- Propose and establish procedures to work with personnel from the NAP Manager(s), the RA, the vBNS Provider, and other regional and other attached networks to resolve problems and to support end-to-end connectivity and quality of service for network users
- Provide services which promote broadening the base of network users within the research and education community
- Provide for, possibly in cooperation with an NSP, high bandwidth connections for client/member institutions who have meritorious high bandwidth network applications
- Provide for network connections to client/member organizations

F. Other Architectural and Policy Considerations

It is possible that other NAPs beyond those specified by NSF may be established by members of the networking community. The various network service providers called for in this solicitation may at their own discretion and expense utilize the services provided by such NAPs provided that the quality and quantity of required services for NSF-specified customers are not affected. These providers will be neither required by nor supported by NSF to include such NAPs in their interconnectivity tasks unless specifically designated and/or approved by NSF in advance.

It is anticipated that networks other than the vBNS will connect to the NSF-specified NAPs. Examples of such networks include: NSPs; other federally-sponsored networks; other network service providers (beyond those connecting regional networks); and international networks.

To qualify for NSF support for NSP attachment and/or for the provision of interNAP connectivity, a regional network must attach to an NSP that connects all NSF-specified priority NAPs. Such NSPs must also be able to assist such attachment-supported regional networks to provide special connections to a NAP for client/member institutions which have meritorious high bandwidth network applications. Other qualifying networks can connect to one or more NAPs as requirements dictate.

Attachment to one or more NAPs will require the payment of both an initial and an annual fee (which will depend on parameters such as number of NAP connections and bandwidth of each connection). Fees will be proposed by the NAP Manager(s) and approved by NSF.

To attach to a NAP, a network must implement BGP- and IDRP-based procedures to assist in establishing and maintaining the network topology and policy databases maintained by the RA. Networks attaching to NAPs must operate at speeds of 1.5 Mbps or greater and must be able to switch both IP and CLNP packets. The requirements to switch CLNP packets and to implement IDRP-based procedures may, however, be waived by NSF based on the overall level of service to the R & E community, stimulus to the growth of the network and economies of scale, the government's desire to foster the use of ISO OSI protocols and other considerations of the public interest . . .

Index

B

C

D

I

J

K

L

M

(continued)

S

T

U

V

W